DATE DUE

SIGNALS FROM THE
HEARTLAND

Pen drawing, "Signals from the Heartland," by Sara Fitzpatrick

SIGNALS
FROM THE
HEARTLAND

Tony Fitzpatrick

WALKER AND COMPANY
New York

First published in the United States of America in 1993 by
Walker Publishing Company, Inc.

Published simultaneously in Canada by Thomas Allen & Son
Canada, Limited, Markham, Ontario

Library of Congress Cataloging-in-Publication Data
Fitzpatrick, Tony, 1958–
Signals from the heartland / Tony Fitzpatrick.
    p. cm.
Includes bibliographical references and index.
ISBN 0-8027-1260-6
1. Human ecology—Middle West.   2. Environmentalists—Middle West.
    3. Natural history—Middle West.   I. Title.
        GF504.M53F58   1993
    333.7'2'0978—dc20   92-15732
                CIP

Designed by Ellen S. Levine
PRINTED IN THE UNITED STATES OF AMERICA

2   4   6   8   10   9   7   5   3   1

THIS BOOK IS WRITTEN IN MEMORY OF MY MOTHER,
JAYNE L. FITZPATRICK,
AND IT IS FOR MY FATHER, DAVID P. FITZPATRICK,
SARA, ANN, AND JIM.

C O N T E N T S

ACKNOWLEDGMENTS

There are too many people to thank for their help in this book, and I certainly will overlook some of them inadvertently. So, I thank you all. I cannot thank Dick Coles of Washington University enough. He guided me to many of the people who appear here, and our numerous conversations both fueled my ambition and fed my intellect. Likewise, thanks to all the people in Agricultural Communications at the University of Illinois—especially Ray Woodis, Tina Prow, Doug Peterson, Bob Sampson, and Gary Beaumont—for all their fine support. Janine Adams of the Missouri Botanical Garden juggled many schedules to help out, and it is appreciated. Gerry Everding of Washington University and K. J. Schadt of the Prairie State Authority in Chicago provided valuable technical assistance that is much appreciated. Thanks to my family, Sara, Ann, and Jim, for letting me out of the house so much and also to Sara for her nice contributions. And thanks, also, to all of the wonderful people who appear in the book. I'm very fond of them and appreciate their dedication and committment. The biggest gratitude of all goes to Mary Kennan Herbert of Walker and Company. She gave me the chance, and through her vigilance, confidence, patience, and expertise, this work evolved and came to be. Thanks, Charlie, for making me a "contender."

F O R E W O R D

From the first appearance of Europeans in the New World, there
has been a terrible tension at work in America. On the one hand white
explorers and settlers were overwhelmed with the beauty and majesty
of this place, sufficiently enthralled to imagine that the biblical garden
might lie somewhere in these regions; on the other hand, from the
beginning, they were intent on changing what they had found. And
so it goes on, as it has from the arrival of the first caravels from Spain:
What we have loved we have also undone, unable to resist the
temptation—the need—to remake and "improve."

There is much to admire in the centuries-long work of cultivation
that has taken place on this continent: the achievement of grainbelt
farmers, the endurance of northwoods loggers, the ingenuity of river-
men and railroaders. But a profound nostalgia attends this admiration,
a longing for the world as it was and an enduring need for some
persistent presence of nature undisturbed. This is not to suggest it was
ever possible for us to leave things as they were, ever a possibility of
somehow entering the place without altering it, and even now when
we are so troubled by the consequences of our transforming work, we
would not—even if we could—simply let it be. We are, for good and
for ill, woven into the fabric of the place, changing it simply by being
here, a part of the soul as well as the landscape of America, us and it
mutually defining each other. A part of what makes the place what it
is for us are the limitless possibilities it contains, its capacity to

support the most grandiose of dreams and aspirations. In turn, a fundamental characteristic America evokes in us is a capacity to dream and aspire and then to make those acts of imagination tangible.

Ours is a continuous cycle of creation and loss as we participate in an irresistible process of transformation and change, some of it our work, some of it that of a nature that is as unwilling to leave things alone as we are. So America and Americans exist in a dynamic relationship, each remaking the other, neither able to remain the same. "The land was ours," Robert Frost declared, "before we were the land's," but more likely we become each other's simultaneously, both the possessor and the possessed, place and people equally imprinted on each other. We may regret some of what we have done to the land; we may even regret some of what it has done to us, but we cannot undo the past. At issue for us, knowing what we know from old triumphs and old mistakes, is what we will, together, make of present possibilities.

We must begin with what is for Americans an uneasy admission: We must acknowledge the future is not wholly ours to decide. Our control of this place can never be complete; it remains full of surprises, continues—even now that it is fully mapped and measured—to be capable of both dramatic outbursts and incredible subtlety, can over centuries build grain by grain a vast delta or, in a heartbeat, obliterate a mountain. The best we can manage is a careful truce, a never ending series of negotiations, in which we do the best we can to honor what we depend upon, to conserve as well as cultivate, and, in that process, to be ourselves conserved and cultivated.

The dramatic interaction of people and place will go on, the character of the first expressed on the face of the latter, the nature of the second testing the imagination and the wisdom of the former. This interaction is the story at the heart of the American experience. What follows are chapters in that epic adventure, accounts of individuals who have taken this challenge seriously and who, deliberately, have shaped their own response to the land and water and life at the center of America. These are not prescriptive pieces so much as encouraging ones, full of beauty and joy and reverence, which is how, at our best, we will find ourselves in this place to which we belong.

—Wayne Fields, chair, English Department,
Washington University, St. Louis,
author of *What the River Knows:*
An Angler in Mid-Stream
and *The Past Leads a Life of Its Own*

P R E F A C E

In 1673, when the French Jesuit priest Jacques Marquette and his Canadian companion Louis Jolliet paddled down the Father of Waters in two birchbark canoes, they saw vistas that today can only be matched in a surreal painting: They saw steep, green bluffs along the river, vast expanses of broad prairies, tallgrasses and flowers waving in the breeze, incredible flocks of birds—egrets, cranes, herons, plovers, geese, ducks, turkeys, and eagles along the riverbank. Dozens of different songbirds and exotics, such as parakeets, darted through oak, pecan, hickory, sycamore, and maple trees in the swamps and woods away from the river. Large herds of bison, elk, deer, and antelope grazed the prairies to the shores of the river: Black bear, wolves, coyotes, and panthers preyed on these herds. Otter, mink, muskrat, beaver, and other water mammals abounded on the riverbanks, as did multifarious species of fish in the water itself. The travelers needed only to point a gun to eat.

It was May 1673, a splendid time to tour what was to become this New World's Heartland. Marquette and Jolliet, with five boatmen, passed the future sites of the Quad Cities—Moline, Rock Island, Davenport, East Moline—Hannibal, home of a future riverman, Mark Twain, Quincy, St. Louis, Cairo, and scores of other lesser-known but significant sites. Ostensibly, Marquette was on an evangelical tour; Jolliet had thrown in for kicks, for he loved to explore and map areas. But another motivation was to find, as Columbus himself had sought nearly two centuries before, a "quick" route to the Northwest, and thus, ultimately, a link to the exotic trade of the Far East. Native Americans, near the mouth of the Missouri River north of present-day St. Louis, hinted that the wide body of water that emptied into the Big River upon which the white men traveled would take them a very far distance in that direction. But the two regarded this tip skeptically. On their journey back to Canada, Marquette and Jolliet, probably on the advice of Indians whose word they took this time, crossed into Illinois on the river that now bears that name, traveling all the way back to Lake Michigan. They saw much of the same flora and fauna that they had observed on the much bigger river, but this time they experienced more of the awesome stretches of tall grassland, never before seen by Europeans on such a large scale in the New World.

In 1675, Marquette founded a mission near the mouth of the Fox River where it empties into the Illinois River at present-day Utica, a cautious inauguration of a new order in the Illinois country. Four years later, the flamboyant Rene-Robert Cavelier, Sieur de La Salle, a rouguish sort of Donald Trump of the seventeenth century, began a series of expeditions down the Illinois to its mouth that saw the establishment of the first fort in the territory, Fort Crevecoeur, at the site of Peoria, the marketing benchmark of the United States, where everything from disposable diapers to sexual attitudes are purveyed. Ironically, the attempt at civilization didn't "play in Peoria"; La Salle left a core of men at the fort so he could return to Canada, and in his absence, the men mutinied, destroying what was built and dispersing on their own into the new frontier. In 1683, La Salle commenced building another fort, St. Louis. Bearing no relationship to its famed counterpart, this St. Louis was close to Marquette's earlier mission at the geologically imposing site of what is now known as Starved Rock, a steep, impenetrable promontory overlooking the Illinois River. After this cautious start, numerous French villages popped up along the rivers in the next century.

These events laid the foundation of a new civilization for the nation's Heartland, Gateway to the West, passageway to the Gulf of Mexico and the St. Lawrence Seaway, birthplace and/or home to millions of Americans, living and dead. America's Heartland is dubiously, if not capriciously defined. It is composed of the whole or parts of a dozen states, its eastern border being Ohio—at least western Ohio—its western borders the Dakotas, Nebraska, and Kansas. Again, at least the eastern portions of those states. Some people consider this western border to be indeed the West; others, for convenience, lump the entire states together as midwestern. But a cowboy from the high plains of Kansas or Nebraska has far different sensibilities than those of an Iowa hog farmer, an Illinois grain farmer, or an inner-city dweller in Chicago, St. Louis, or Kansas City. Regionally, they are somewhat related, but spiritually they are all from different worlds within the region.

People who do not live in the Midwest often consider such states as Oklahoma, Kentucky, even West Virginia, as midwestern, but native Heartlanders know these border states as Southern, at least vaguely Southern, anathema to the Midwest despite the border states' proximity and similarities to bona fide midwestern states, whatever those may truly be. Likewise, and with some foundation, "outsiders" often consider Missouri to be a Southern state. So do some of the natives. St. Louis itself is a city so rich in history and cultures that it defies any one definition. It has been said jokingly that St. Louis is the city that combines Southern expediency with Northern hospitality—a confused description, perhaps, but one that suggests the cultural clash that exists in St. Louis. I have found it to be one of the friendliest and most accessible—to art, nature, and entertainment—of all the places I have ever lived or visited.

There were slaves in Missouri through the Civil War. With more than 1,100 battles during that conflict, Missouri soil hosted the third highest number of battles of any state in the war; agriculturally, the southern bootheel of the state, where cotton and tobacco are grown, *is* the South. Then, for that matter, all you have to do is listen to the accents of Missourians, if that is your criterion to judge a region. Southeastern Missourians sound as though they are from the Deep South, as, after all, they very nearly are. The same can be said for many residents of the southern one-fourth of Illinois, settled by Southerners in the first part of the nineteenth century who harbored such Southern sentiment before and during the Civil War that riots broke out in various towns in the region.

Despite the nebulousness of what actually is midwestern, there is little doubt that the glue that holds it together is the bistate region comprising Illinois and Missouri. St. Louis and Chicago were hubs of midwestern and national development, as they continue to be today. The region is driven by agriculture, industry, and transporation.

Which came first, Illinois or Missouri? That distinction goes to Illinois. The first permanent settlement in Illinois was Cahokia, established in 1699, abutting present-day East St. Louis. An early Missouri settlement was established within St. Louis at the mouth of the River Des Peres (say, if you are a St. Louisan, Da Pear, as southside Chicagoans, referring to their beloved Chicago Bears, say Da Bares). But this settlement did not last long, and St. Genevieve, established fifty years later, is considered to be Missouri's first permanent town.

The two states grew rapidly over the next 250 years; the region produced many historical and cultural players, some, like the warriors Black Hawk (who waged war in Illinois and was imprisoned in Jefferson Barracks in St. Louis afterward) and Ulysses S. Grant (who farmed southwest of St. Louis just before he moved to Galena, Illinois, before the outbreak of the Civil War) touched both states. Consider Dred Scott, Scott Joplin, Abraham Lincoln, Daniel Boone, Route 66, Mark Twain (and his literary characters), Ernest Hemingway (who grew up in Oak Park, a Chicago suburb, and whose first three wives were all from St. Louis), Charles "Lucky" Lindbergh, Ike and Tina Turner, Richard Daley, the St. Louis beer barons, Ernie Banks, and Stan Musial. The list goes on.

Missourians in the nineteenth century called Illinoisans "suckers"; the Illini retaliated by calling their brothers "pukes." No such enmity exists today, although St. Louisans call any unheeled person a "hoosier," a term that is pretty much an enigma, bearing no animosity toward Indiana natives whatsoever. The link existing between the two states stretches from before their inceptions through the Civil War to the present Cubs-Cardinals baseball rivalry, a lively, bloodless, entertaining tradition that fills Busch Stadium and Wrigley Field every summer. Fans of both teams reserve true rancor for the New York Mets.

More than 300 years after the early French explorations, it is difficult to imagine a Heartland such as that encountered by the French explorers. Many of the more impressive mammalian species the explorers saw are extinct in the region; the native prairie that spread throughout much of both states amounts to less than one percent of what it was prior to John Deere's development of the steel plow in 1848. The rivers themselves, while recognizable as such from a car window, have become more like transport systems than true ecosystems. Although every decade of development from the Heartland's start to the present has recast the natural character of the region, the half century since the beginning of World War II has perhaps ushered in the most change. The release of power from the atom over Hiroshima and Nagasaki unleashed in Americans a new drive to live better, produce more copiously and efficiently, and to consume ravenously. Technology spawned convenience, novelty. These are seen today in fast-food restaurants, shopping malls, and quick lubes; in suburbs ceaselessly creeping west, and small towns dying, their traditional economic base eroded from an agriculture that has outgrown its own simple past with the post–World War infusion of pesticides (nearly nonexistent in farming before the war), more expedient animal husbandry, improved seed varieties, and specialization. Agriculture continues to be the Midwest's heartbeat, despite losses in prime farmland and fewer farmers. In the 1980s, in Illinois alone, as much as 100,000 acres of prime farmland were lost yearly to the spread of suburbs and economic development.

Loss of habitat for the Heartland's species has occurred almost instantaneously in geologic time, which recognizes the thousands of years it took for the Wisconsin glacier to recede over Illinois as a mere drop in the bucket. Heartland natives have finally taken sight of these changes and, while it is too late to save habitat for some of the species that are lost or declining, or reverse the encroachment of civilization (the word that our buddy Huck Finn so hated), a new attitude is emerging among many midwesterners not content to sigh and shrug the problem away.

That attitude is tinged with the fear that too much has been lost, and is driven by a growing commitment to restore wetlands, streams, prairies, and forests for aesthetic as well as ecological and economical benefits, and to reintroduce endangered species, such as the wolf, into nature once again, where it rightfully belongs.

At the beginning of this decade, on some 2,000 acres of reclaimed coalmined land just west of Peoria, a nonprofit park has been developed by a group called the Forest Park Foundation. The organization has provided lots of hiking paths and has introduced many of the native plants and animals found in the Prairie State on land that might have been neglected or else developed for other purposes. In Missouri, the Nature Conservancy recently bought 80,000 acres of near-wilderness in the heart of the Ozarks from the Kerr-McGee Corporation. The tract is to be sold to the Missouri Department of Conservation over a period of five years. The land adjoins other state and federal lands as well as private forests owned by the legendary University City, Missouri conservationist, Leo Drey. Together, the lands stand as a bulwark against encroaching development from the east. More actions such as these are seen with increasing regularity—in Missouri, Illinois, Iowa, the entire Midwest.

Scapegoats for the Heartland's eco-destruction (which has taken hundreds of years but arguably is every bit as thorough as that which is going on in tropical forests today) are abundant. To blame any single sector such as commerce, agriculture, or industry is simplistic, and in many cases erroneous. To say that everyone somehow is blameworthy is equally pedestrian, but it is closer to the truth.

In the vast, complex world of science, there are many signals—data that help scientists distinguish truth. The following essays about people and the environment in the Midwest represent some signals from the Heartland that tell us what has happened in this part of the country to change its face and what is being done and what will be done in the future to effect a better place to live. These signals are not measured in micrometers, kilobars, or parts per million. Rather, it is hoped that the signals are reflected in the depth of the people themselves and their devotion to their principles and the natural resources that they cherish.

SIGNALS FROM THE
HEARTLAND

THE BIRD WOMAN OF WEBSTER GROVES
Phoebe Snetsinger near the St. Louis Arch. *(Courtesy of Sara Fitzpatrick)*

The Bird Woman of Webster Groves

In 1969, Phoebe Snetsinger, then a thirtyish mother of four, used to climb the carpeted third-floor stairs of her home in Webster Groves, Missouri, to watch in silence and joy the kinetic gathering of migrant songbirds in the lofty oak trees behind her house. The swarms of birds, returning from their winter homes in Latin America, would be convening in her backyard and countless others in the Heartland to regroup as they sought out their familiar wooded breeding grounds throughout the Midwest; Snetsinger, her housecoat wrapped snugly about her, would sit on the flat roof outside her son's attic bedroom and bask in the quiet communion with the birds. At this lambent hour near dawn, while her family slept and the houses on the gentle hills of the neighborhood were still unlit, Snetsinger took mental notes of the species—warblers, vireos, tanagers, orioles, gnat-catchers, thrushes, and others—a practice she had been seriously cultivating for only a couple of years. But mostly she just watched, captivated by the commingling of nature at a precious moment. It was May, her favorite month in the Midwest.

It is January 1991. Phoebe Snetsinger sits in her office, a converted annex behind an immense bedroom on the second floor of her stately home, one story down from her spring roost on the roof. The room is decorated with wildlife posters, bird prints, and maps of exotic areas of the world; snapshots of gulls and shorebirds she and bird-watching friends have taken along the banks of the Mississippi and Missouri rivers adorn ledges of the frosty windows. A globe sits on a coffee table to her right. Now sixty and turning gray, Snetsinger is a vigorous, handsome woman with piercing hazel eyes. She is dressed simply: a navy blue sweatshirt over a red-striped blouse, khaki pants, and running shoes. Everything about her and her environs suggests neatness, orderliness; a microcosm that is controlled. As she talks, in a cultivated though earthy manner, she leans forward, poised for action.

"I've seen the world, but I list sitting on that roof at dawn as among my favorite times," she says. "It was incredible. I could get a good hour of birding in before the kids even woke up. Back then, twenty species of warblers would come through. Watching the treetops now, I don't see any more than a handful of species. Why? I really don't know. And neither does anyone else I know, though habitat loss must surely be a major factor.

"They would come in waves twenty years ago, and many days you could go to Forest Park in the city, or Blackburn Park, in Webster Groves here, and see nearly every kind of songbird coming through. It's a rare day in May these past fifteen years or so when that happens. Birding locally is still good, but it's not nearly as easy or as much fun now. The symphony's gone."

Snetsinger is fond of telling the story of a friend passing through St. Louis from California who called and wanted to see a worm-eating warbler, a migrating songbird that prefers breeding on wooded slopes, a habitat once abundant in the St. Louis region. She remembered regularly seeing the species years earlier in an area near Eureka, then the very outer fringes of suburbia. She drove her friend out there, and at first couldn't find the area.

"There's all these Burger Kings and convenience stores, one subdivision after another. The whole structure of the roads had changed, and I couldn't recognize anything. Finally, I got off on a side road, and I found the spot, a wooded ravine alongside another old broken-down road. I couldn't figure out why it was still there in the middle of all that development. We found a couple of worm-eating warblers, so it was a triumph of sorts. But it's a continual battle to find habitat for birds and birders alike. You have to be amazed at the tenacity of these little fellows holding onto pockets of land both here and in the tropics. Anywhere they go they face cheek-by-jowl development."

Anywhere Snetsinger goes she lists the birds she sees. In bird circles, she is world-class. She has spotted, identified, and listed with the American Birding Association, based in Colorado Springs, 6,700 different species of birds throughout the world, and her count keeps growing. No woman in the world has seen and recorded more birds than Phoebe Snetsinger; only two men have listed more birds than she, and, in the congenial competitiveness of the bird-watching community, she is closing in on them and wants to surpass them. On this steely cold, bleak January afternoon, Snetsinger is between jaunts; a week back from a two-month birding tour of Australia and New Zealand, she is now poised for a month-long tour of southern India, followed by a brief respite, then a journey to Thailand in March. The Bird Woman of Webster Groves is driven to see the avifauna of the world partly because she has malignant melanoma, first diagnosed in 1981, and amazingly contrary to all medical lore, mostly in remission since then. Her ambition for a decade has been to beat time and see as many of the world's birds as possible while the world's "golden moment," as she calls it, still persists.

"Bird-watchers in general feel pretty pessimistic about the future," she says. "There's lots of handwringing, not just on this continent, but everywhere. The world's gone downhill; ecologically, we're losing ground. What with world overpopulation, advanced technology, the rain forests being destroyed, roads being built in existing forests, expanding civilization—everything's moving toward destruction of habitat. You see it in Peru as well as St. Louis. For a naturalist, the world of the future is a grim place. Realistically there's no way to counter the trends. We can save a few things here and there in a kind of holding pattern, but it's a continuing battle. I feel my kids will never see a wild California condor, and that's very sad. The world will be poorer for that.

"On the other hand, international bird-watchers live in what I see as a golden age. Things are not going to get better in the future. But the present is phenomenal. Never before have we been able to see more birds in their natural habitats than we can now. It's still possible to fly for hours over unbroken rain forests in the Amazon, for instance. And there are wonderful areas all over the world where, if you can hop on a plane, you can find marvelous birds in fantastic natural settings. Birding skills are so well developed now that with tape recorders and such, a tour leader can show to a group secretive birds seldom ever seen before in the wild except by natives. This combination of advanced technology and increased skill gives us a situation impossible forty years ago and nonexistent, sadly, forty years from now."

Snetsinger has stood in pockets of extant rain forests of Peru, New Guinea, and Madagascar, spotting birds with her ever-present telescope while literally hearing the woodlands about her fall to developers and squatters trying to eke out a subsistence living on the land. And she has stood in St. Louis's Forest Park, the mammoth park on the city's western edge, in the oak groves behind the art museum, watching thrushes return from their winter homes in May. It is her favorite bird-watching place in the immediate St. Louis vicinity. The thrill in these divergent places is the same for her, the satisfaction complete, the drive curiously similar.

Some people get weak-kneed over the fine qualities of philately, antiques, coins, antebellum homes, pens, or baseball cards. But a bird-watcher, or "birder" is a *rara avis* among all compulsive hobbyists. Webster's dictionary defines the word *bird* as an intransitive verb, "to observe and identify birds in their natural surroundings." Its etymology is traced to 1918. Birding is a sport, a pastime, a need, an obsession for the serious-minded, such as Snetsinger, who visit some of the world's most tucked-away places to fulfill their ambition. Like joggers, people who bird can do so on many different levels. They draw their motivation from aesthetics (Snetsinger calls birds "beautiful little jewels"), the intellectual challenge of being able to identify at a glance an out-of-range species of shorebird feeding along a mud flat with many other similar-looking birds, and the Thoreau-like physical and emotional reward of being one with nature. Then, too, for world-class "listers" like Snetsinger, there is a gentle competitive component to birding, combined with an accountant's compulsive orderliness to record—species, family, plumage—and the journalist's report of conditions, time, and place. Snetsinger has scores of files in closets and on her desk, the index cards written in a textbook-perfect Palmer-method handwriting, detailing the 6,000-plus species she has identified over the past twenty-three years.

No one knows for sure how many people bird-watch. The American Birding Association, which is to birding what the *Sporting News* is to baseball, counts 6,800 American members in its organization, 7,300 worldwide, in 1991. Yet many dedicated American bird-watchers—perhaps two or three thousand—do not belong to ABA, which charges dues and publishes a fine journal with a supplement that includes the list totals of its members on an annual basis. These lists are the official record of the dedicated who follow the progress of their competitors and note where the others are finding birds that they may not have seen and listed. Still thousands of others, from farmers and ranchers to housewives and weekend campers, might go out on bird-watching sorties and technically be considered bird-watchers. The U.S. Fish and Wildlife Service estimates that more than 62 million Americans regularly put out seed in backyard feeders. And experts have estimated that more than 1.2 million tons of birdseed are sold annually in the United States. More than 600,000 bird guides are sold annually in the United States alone.

But the distinction between devotees and dabblers may lie in methods, the urge to list their findings, and the nature of the complusion. The dedicated birder, for instance, wouldn't think of leaving home without a pair of binoculars. Birders come from all walks of life and social strata—a typical group of the Webster Groves Nature Study Society would include a doctor, a housewife, a carpenter, and a humanities professor. Yet birding groups often are dominated by highly technical people. Snetsinger knows many doctors, mathematicians, engineers, "people who have amassed lots of information about things," who are birders, challenged by a need to define and document, often at a moment's notice.

"The birding world is a small one," says Snetsinger. "Anywhere in the world you go you run into someone you know or who knows someone you know. Their common interest transcends all else about them. Birders are very good about staying in grubby hotels in awful places and getting up at three A.M. in the hopes of finding the bird of the day. They're very informal; comfortable old clothes are the norm. And they're very congenial. As a whole, they get along better than any other group I've ever known. Most of my best friends these days are birders."

Snetsinger, by her own account, got a very late start in her quest to see and list the world's birds. She was thirty-five, living in Minnesota with her husband, David, and rearing four small children when she was befriended by a neighbor who was a bird-watcher. The friend convinced her to come along to watch the spring warblers; then she took her to a great blue heron rookery. Immediately, Snetsinger was hooked.

"I thought, 'this is pretty neat.' Here was something that had been happening all my life, and I'd never paid any attention to it. I don't know why. As a kid I was a perfect tomboy. I used to go traipsing with my brothers through the Skokie Lagoons, way up in northeastern Illinois when that area was all country. It's an absolute mystery to me why we didn't pay any attention to birds.

"In Minnesota, the herons, especially, were marvelous. Here were these gangly birds building these incredibly flimsy stick nests way in the tops of trees and somehow managing to produce offspring out of this. I was absolutely fascinated by it. Maybe, psychologically, I needed a diversion from raising so many little children, but it set off a sort of explosion in me. I bought a bird book, started looking on my own, and started keeping track of my sightings."

Snetsinger moved to St. Louis in 1967 when her husband, a poultry scientist, took a job with Ralston Purina Company. They bought a splendid white pillared house in Webster Groves, a southwestern suburb of St. Louis, and Snetsinger immediately contacted the local Audubon Society and became active in Thursday outings with the Webster Groves Nature Study Society. She would hire a babysitter for the children and drive with the group to the Busch Wildlife Preserve, west of the city; Forest Park, the old Alton Lock and Dam north of the city; to marshes and woodlands along the Mississippi, Missouri, and Meramec rivers; to the southwestern Missouri Ozarks and southern Illinois Shawnee National Forest; or just to neighbors' yards to view a screech owl hunkered down in a hole. Mainly, she and the group stayed within a fifty-mile radius of the city—habitat for nearly 350 different species of birds, not all of which she's seen yet. She tried to steer family vacations toward places of avifaunal interest. She took a few foreign trips solely for the birding. Then, in 1981, with only her youngest child, a high school junior, left at home, her life changed drastically.

"My critical turning point came when I found out I had malignant melanoma," she says without a hitch in her voice. "I had had a melanoma on my back that had been removed eight years earlier, but in '81 there was a major recurrence in a lymph node of my armpit. Several doctors told me I had no more than a year to live, with just three more months of reasonable health. I had been healthy all of my life until then, so this was just a staggering blow. I became resigned to the fact that I was going to die. At the time I'd had a trip lined up to Alaska, and I thought, 'well, three more months, my family is almost raised, I'm gonna go. It's time to do what I want to do.' "

She went, returned, and felt fine. She booked another trip to Australia, returned still feeling well, and booked another one. The cancer, to everyone's amazement, is a rare form that acts slowly, totally out of character with typical malignant melanoma. In the ten years since the diagnosis, she's had a minor mass and a recurrent lump removed, but both were isolated occurrences.

"Since I was diagnosed, I've seen two people I know die of malignant melanoma. I've been extremely fortunate. Having the threat of death lets me know how lucky I am to be able to do what I do. You must understand my survival has little to do with my attitude—I took the doctors at their word, I wasn't defiant. I take lots of vitamin C. My friends say maybe it's birding that keeps me going. Or maybe jet lag, or malaria medication that cures melanoma."

Thus began her globe-trotting and the incredible spurt of listing the world's birds that have made Phoebe Snetsinger a birding legend. The daughter of Leo Burnett, who founded the famous Leo Burnett Advertising Agency, Snetsinger has not lacked for funds in her travels, which she mainly confines to countries between the tropics of Cancer and Capricorn; the closer to the equator, the greater the number of birds.

7

Since 1981, she has averaged between five and six trips per year, with her favorite continent being South America, the habitat for at least one-third of the world's birds. Peru, Brazil, and Ecuador are some of her favorite countries there, although Colombia remains an elusive goal because of the hostile drug and anti-American environment. The Andes Mountains provide diverse habitat for varying bird species because of the dramatic altitude changes within the rich tropical zone. In 1990 alone, she toured Israel, China, New Guinea, Peru, Japan, Taiwan, and the New Zealand subarctic, with two tours of Australia, one of her favorite and most comfortable birding havens because, she notes, the natives almost speak English.

Snetsinger's foreign excursions are almost always with groups ("A woman alone is a sitting duck"), and not without incident, humorous and hair-raising. Once in Ecuador she turned to a companion in the forest who literally disappeared in front of her eyes—he'd fallen into an enormous hole and emerged later unscathed. In New Guinea some years ago, she and a male companion were ambushed by natives, abducted, and held captive for a short time, until allowed to escape. Closer to home, she's been followed while birding in Forest Park, only to elude her stalker through paths she knows by memory. The trips mean countless rugged hours of battling inhospitable terrain, leeches, heat or cold, microbes, and local customs, all for a glimpse of a kagu in New Caledonia, the wandering albatross in the Antarctic, or the bizarre monkey-eating eagle of the Philippines, a species that lives up to its name.

The tours are led by a guide who knows the area well, either a local or experienced birder in the region. With the aid of a tape recorder and telescope, the leader helps the eight to fifteen birders find their prizes. While birding standards vary tremendously among individuals, Snetsinger has a rigid listing code that requires her to identify a bird positively by its field marks, sometimes in combination with its song. If the vocalization is distinctive, she doesn't need to rely as heavily on visual features. Some birders, however, rely entirely on their leader's identification, sometimes without ever knowing what features to look for, or actually identifying the bird themselves, a practice she disdains.

"Still, you have to believe people about what they've seen," Snetsinger says. "Birding is not an athletic contest where you're judged objectively. You know practically everyone you're competing with, and it's 'word of honor' on reporting sightings. People who've been with me believe me. The Rosie Ruiz complex—the gal who said she'd won the Boston Marathon when she actually had only run a few miles of it—is very rare in birding."

There are well over 9,000 bird species in the world, and Snetsinger has seen more than 70 percent of them. In Missouri, there are 380 native bird species, and she has seen 327. Some birds remain vexingly elusive for her, and others that she has seen are becoming increasingly hard to find. Gulls and shorebirds are her favorite regional birds, although she has a soft spot for the migrant songbirds. While local birders have seen the mew gull and the Sabine's gull at nearby Carlyle Lake in Illinois, Snetsinger has always been out of town when these birds have appeared.

A photo of her most thrilling local experience rests on a window ledge. The slaty-backed gull, one of the world's forty-five gull species, is an Asian bird that occasionally ranges as far east as Alaska, but had never before been seen in the lower forty-eight states, let alone the Midwest. In late December 1983, a season of record cold, a "mystery" gull was found by an experienced local birder who was simply baffled: The gull didn't fit anything in his considerable past experience. Enter "the experts": Snetsinger and a highly knowledgeable companion, after considerable research and detailed analysis of the mystery gull, primarily the wing pattern, reached their mind-blowing conclusion. The bird was announced with fanfare as a slaty-backed gull, and gratifyingly remained for a month, enabling hundreds of visitors to observe and photograph it.

"Why it was here so ridiculously out of range, goodness only knows," she says. "But it was tremendously exciting and just the sort of discovery that draws one to birding. Not every time out do you see something like that, but I never fail to learn or observe something new on a field trip."

The bistate area, especially near St. Louis, is a rich one to explore, but over the years the rapid development of the region has brought about several baffling, saddening, and contradictory changes. Some of the puzzling changes Snetsinger has noted are the emergence of crows throughout the St. Louis urban and suburban areas in the past several years to the point of nuisance, and the explosion of the house finch population, a western species introduced to Long Island years ago and now converging on the Heartland from both west and east. Exactly why the crow population, modest when she moved to St. Louis in 1967, has burgeoned of late and why the finches are coming is unfathomable. Some wildlife ecologists suggest that crows have increased in urban areas because their preferred habitat, which includes trees, is better found in older urban and suburban areas where trees still stand in comparison to the newer suburbia or the heavily farmed areas of the country. In the immediate area, Snetsinger no longer sees as many vireos or warblers, and there are some birds neither she nor anyone else has seen in the region for years. Often, human misadventure plays a hand in effecting a change. The Henslow's sparrow, for instance, which she used to observe in its breeding habitat at the Natural Prairie Area of the arboretum, a nature preserve southwest of the city near Gray's Summit, disappeared after officials plowed up the prairie plot to reseed with a different mix of "better" prairie seed.

Similarly, shorebird enthusiasts like Snetsinger have lobbied both state departments of conservation to create better habitat for shorebirds, which are partial to mud flats leading to standing water. Such habitat fluctuates each year, varying with the amount of rainfall; it is found naturally in farmers' bottomlands and at many points along the big rivers. The Missouri Department of Conservation attempted to create such a habitat at the Busch Wildlife Preserve and at Marais Temps Clair Preserve, but basically built ponds without the necessary long, gradual expanse of mud. At Horseshoe Lake, an old oxbow of the Mississippi River on the Illinois side, the Department of Conservation maintains the water level to attract a healthy duck population for hunters, but does nothing for shorebirds.

Bachman's sparrow, a doughty, drab little bird Snetsinger saw regularly twenty years ago in southwest Missouri, has all but disappeared from the state; barn owls are almost gone from Illinois and dwindling in Missouri, despite efforts to reintroduce them into different habitats. They are victims of habitat alteration, human persecution, and unbalanced predator populations. Shorebird populations fluctuate. Large numbers of land birds are declining. One, the quaint chuck-will's-widow, whose characteristic call is a plaintive rendition of its name, still can be heard in early summer in rural Missouri but has disappeared from nearby suburban regions overrun by condominiums and duplexes.

In Illinois, where 87 percent of the land—31 million acres—is devoted to agriculture, the bobolink has disappeared at the alarming rate of 19 percent a year in the past decade, according to the U.S. Fish and Wildlife Service. A species of bird that likes to lay its eggs in hay fields, the bobolink has been hurt by the increasingly common crop rotation of corn and soybeans; because farms are larger and less diversified than they were forty years ago, fewer farmers grow hay and those that do make their first cutting earlier in the year to keep pace with production demands. The whirling combine blades in the spring literally rip the bobolink chicks to pieces. Similarly, the service also reports decade-long declines in the yellow-billed cuckoo (8.6 percent), the Acadian flycatcher (7.1 percent), savannah sparrow (6.5 percent), and ruby-throated hummingbird (5 percent). Wood thrushes, migrant spotted birds about the size of robins that live beneath the forest canopy and have long been among the most common birds in the state, may not survive the decade in Illinois. It is estimated that since 1978, as many as 75 percent of all migrant birds have declined in the whole of eastern North America. In Missouri 60 percent of neotropical migrant birds have declined over the same timespan.

Population ecologists, a perplexed lot, spent the 1980s debating whether the diminished rain forests or dwindling North American habitat is the chief culprit behind reduced bird numbers. Recently they have reached a tentative consensus about why populations in urban and suburban areas like St. Louis and Chicago are declining so rapidly. It has to do with geometry. While it would seem logical that songbirds could still thrive in fragmented woodlands as opposed to large parcels, the smaller woodland has more edge per unit area than the larger woodland. By nature species that prefer deep interior forests, many songbirds must contend with bird residents that have adapted to the forest edge, such as the ubiquitous crows, blue jays, and grackles. Skunks, possums, and raccoons, even household Fidos and Garfields find nests, eggs, and chicks fair game. Many migratory birds make vulnerable nests that are cup shaped, inviting predation; some that are declining drastically, like ovenbirds and worm-eating warblers, nest on the ground.

Bird fascinate us because of their color, their song, their aesthetics, their intincts, but perhaps most of all because of the special thing they do that humans cannot: They fly, evoking in us an enviable sense of freedom. Each spring the migratory songbirds trek thousands of miles from the tropics in vast flocks, returning northward to breeding sites to which they are drawn by an enigmatic, God-given instinct that some ornithologists have speculated is related to electromagnetism. Their journey is bold and treacherous; they fight wind patterns, tropical storms, and the twentieth century. It is estimated that as many as 976 million birds of all species are killed each year because of their fatal attraction to lights and windows: They literally fly into their reflections. In a reaction some think is related to their electromagnetic instincts, they also smash into radio and TV towers; their carcasses litter the ground each spring. No one knows what percentage of this incredible number of "civilization" deaths comprises migratory songbirds.

Once in North America, they fly to their breeding sites and, remaining no more than four to six months, raise their broods. Those that survive the journey turn back in August and September, facing much the same plight, on a more rapidly expanding scale, that they face in the north. A songbird that is healthy and lucky might live to eight years.

If bird-watching brings such great joy, what does it teach us?

Snetsinger pauses momentarily and spins the globe that she is holding. "It teaches you to notice your environment. It's impossible to deal with birds in isolation. If you are a birder, you have to have a feel for ecology. Birders are inevitably asked, 'so what if we lose a species or two, they're not as important as humans.' And the response is also invariable, the metaphor of the miner's canary that nineteenth-century miners used to detect poisonous underground gas. If the bird survived, so would humans. On a larger scale, the whole bird scene is indicative of that—if your birds are diappearing for some reason or another, you'd better start worrying, because eventually it's not just birds in trouble, but trees, the food supply, and ultimately you.

"On a smaller, but just as important, scale, it teaches you that something miraculous and totally unexpected can happen at any moment. Life is like that, too. Do you want to see one of my favorite birding places?"

We pass through the expansive bedroom, larger than most living rooms, up the third-floor stairs to a landing. On the left a neat bedroom has been carved out of what had been an attic; straight ahead are windows that lead to the roof. Beyond the long, flat roof are nude tall oaks, their branches coated with ice, the effect almost unnatural, like paraffin on candles. The neighboring houses are nestled comfortably in the gentle hills, white smoke rising from chimneys into a gray blanket of a sky.

"Coming out here has become a ritual with me in the spring," she said. "It's very peaceful out here in May, but each spring it's quieter. When you're in the presence of so many birds, the feeling is almost a palpable one. When you can't find many birds anymore you feel something that's like a personal loss.

"You know, recently I went back to the Lake Zurich area where I'd grown up to see the farm, now drastically changed, that my dad bought and where we lived from the time I was eleven years old. I had the same trouble finding the old sites as I did finding the habitat for the worm-eating warbler. All the landmarks are gone. So much of the area is unrecognizable.

"It occurred to me that if migratory birds had the faculty of being intellectually baffled, then that's exactly how they'd feel when they can't find their breeding sites in the spring anymore."

In January 1992, Phoebe Snetsinger listed her seven thousandth bird, a Ceylon Frogmouse, in Sri Lanka. She is the first American and the first woman to view that many birds. She is expected to surpass the number one bird-watcher, a man from Switzerland, soon.

THE SIX SWAMPS OF ROBERT MOHLENBROCK
Robert Mohlenbrock in the field near Southern Illinois University.
(Courtesy of Beverly Mohlenbrock)

CHAPTER 2

The Six Swamps of
Robert Mohlenbrock

Picture a summer traveler leaving St. Louis on a Sunday afternoon and heading eastward into the great Prairie State. He passes Busch Stadium and the Arch, familiar symbols of the Gateway City, crossing the Mississippi along the battered, bumpy confluence of three interstate highways, and chooses I-64. On either side of the interstate, wetlands, now filled with factories and smokestacks sending up curling white plumes, still foster a habitat for shorebirds and egrets, swooping down to feed against a futuristic horizon. The traveler passes a burned-out, abandoned, and decayed section of East St. Louis, struggling for decades to right itself, a city where garbage sat uncollected in streets and alleyways throughout all of 1990 and where Little League umpires are shot by disgruntled coaches. He hurtles southeastward into broad expanses of *Illinoisia*—soybeans, corn, wheat, and grain elevators, small towns hedged by classic country churches, venerable pin-neat red-brick schools, gas stations that serve as corner stores, IGAs, Dairy Queens, and farmer banks.

On a whim, the traveler departs the interstate at the Illinois 127 exit and encounters a peaceful old state highway that, compared with I-64, provides a magnified view of Middle America. In Nashville, Illinois, the seat of Washington County, he drives through quiet tree-shaded streets, past Methodist and Baptist churches, calm after late-morning services. This is not the capital of country music in Tennessee, an afternoon's drive further south. No, this particular Nashville definitely has an Illinois flavor. Teenagers in pickups, tanned from fieldwork, hang out downtown in an empty parking lot, teasing and flirting, gearing up for the county fair, next weekend's party, and the upcoming football season. The scene is common throughout rural Illinois, in scores of small towns like Nashville fastened, as author William H. Gass has written in *In the Heart of the Heart of the Country*, to the edge of a cornfield, a safe, sound, somnambulent, at times soporific, existence.

Outside Nashville, he notices a change almost immediately. The flavor changes from Illinois to southern Illinois, a different scenario entirely. The wide vista of Illinois crop staples has disappeared and with it the super farms and grand farmhouses. Scale has suddenly been reduced, the landscape broken into smaller farms, remnant woods, ponds, mobile homes. Instead of a sea of corn, there are more and more trees, earth that is rolling, soil of clay rather than the famous Illinois silt loam. Signs along the highway point to God, peaches, apples, rodeos, and coal companies.

On the outskirts of Pinckneyville, he passes a rusted forties-era Allis Chalmers tractor for sale in front of a weedy, burned-out service station. He approaches the town square, the most dangerous zone to be found in a small town, the road shooting him like a pinball through an arcade southward to Murphysboro, Carbondale, Marion, Herrin, Johnston City, Harrisburg, Shawneetown, Vienna. He has left the Illinois of tourist brochures far behind.

It is known as Egypt. There are the towns—Cairo (pronounced Care-o) and Karnak—and legends to explain the name, but its moniker is curious, as are the land, its people, its customs, and ecosystems. Much of this part of Illinois is coal country, not exclusively prairie lands like so much of the rest of the state. The soils are derived from the forests that spread throughout the region, surviving today in the lush Shawnee National Forest that blankets the southernmost six counties. Illinois, surprisingly, is the nation's third leading producer of soft bituminous coal. Deposits rest as close as fifteen feet from the topsoil of two-thirds of the state. The towns of Herrin, Marion, Carterville, and Johnston City in Williamson County, Benton, West Frankfort, Zeigler, Christopher, and Sesser in Franklin County, and DuQuoin and Pinckneyville in neighboring Perry County have been company coal towns for decades, scenes of bloody strife between union workers and scabs in the 1920s, and sites of coal-mining tragedies since the nineteenth century.

Then there are its people, who do not resemble the solid farmfolk symbolic of the Prairie State further north. The settlers of southern Illinois came from Kentucky, Tennessee, all the way eastward to Virginia and the Carolinas. As a result, the flavor and accent of the region are distinctively southern. And although southern Illinois gave more than its quota of volunteers to the Union cause, during the Civil War, the area harbored many Southern sympathizers, and dozens of local men joined the Confederate Army. In part because of these sentiments, Cairo, at its strategically important locus at the confluence of the Ohio and Mississippi rivers, was, along with St. Louis, one of the first areas in the western frontier that the Union sought to control in the first several months of hostilities during the Civil War. The town became a major supply base for Ulysses S. Grant's early campaigns in Missouri, and for his famous "unconditional surrender" victory at forts Henry and Donelson in Tennessee.

As a kid growing up in northern Illinois, exposed to the classically flat accents of midwestern broadcasters on Chicago TV and radio, I was always conscious of the different accents found throughout the state. My cousins in Beardstown, for instance, in west-central Illinois—not in the Deep South, yet far closer to St. Louis than to Chicago—sounded downright Southern to me—they drawled. Regional accents within a state, of course, often are influenced by the ethnic mixes that settled the area, and the isolation of the people from other backgrounds; the lack of a melting pot. Natives of southern Illinois, especially the smaller towns away from the university-influenced Carbondale, are most likely to sound like cousins of Ernest P. Worrell, minus the exaggeration. Cowboy boots, straw hats, and pickup trucks are the norm.

Southern Illinois has always had its mystique. Northern Illinois natives grow up with the concept of "downstate Illinois." To a Chicagoan, downstate refers to any area outside of Chicago and its immediate suburbs, including Rockford, the second largest city in the state and a good deal north of Chicago. To a resident of northern Illinois, the line of demarcation is not so distinct and the criteria that define it vary among individuals. Accents, one criterion, change noticeably in Illinois somewhere south of Bloomington in McLean County. Baseball loyalties, an important criterion to many, are mixed between devotion to the Chicago Cubs or the St. Louis Cardinals all throughout central Illinois, a mystery to Cubs fans who have never been able to fathom why natives of one state would root against a team that is based in their state. This paradox is easily explained by the proximity of a community to either of the major cities, and the quality of the airwaves from St. Louis's KMOX or Chicago's WGN, plus family tradition.

To most Illinoisans, southern Illinois is a place where the bizarre, violent, and offbeat occur. In the late summer of 1963, residents of Fairfield in Wayne County, slightly northeast of Mt. Vernon, reported seeing flying saucers for a short period. There were jokes that the people down there were probably dipping into the moonshine again, with the explanation that the region had a history of rum-running that rivaled any region in the South. Years later I read both Paul Angle's *Bloody Williamson* and Donald Bain's *War in Illinois* and was enthralled with tales of bloodshed between union and scab coal workers and the battles over the local distilled spirits trade between the Shelton brothers and Charlie Birger gangs. In operations that were centered in and near Herrin, extending northwest all the way to St. Louis, Birger and the Sheltons battled each other in cold-blooded murders arranged by hitmen and in pitched battles along roadways featuring machine-gun-outfitted custom tanks!

The region even has the distinction of being the first place in the continental United States ever to have been the recipient of a bombing raid when Charlie Birger's farmhouse was bombed from the air by a pilot in a biplane. The war ended with Birger's execution by hanging, in 1928, and his regionally famous chipper last words on the gallows in Benton in front of a huge, festive crowd: "It *is* a beautiful life," he said. And down he dropped. His was the last such execution in Illinois and it marked the end of an era where the roughnecks of southern Illinois had made Al Capone and his mob look like pikers in comparison. The Ku Klux Klan, too—usually associated only with atrocities in the Deep South—was very active throughout the Heartland then, involved in the liquor dispute as the largest vigilante group on the continent, archenemies of the rum-runners and "foreign types," such as the immigrant Italian and Polish coal miners who came, with blacks from the South, seeking work prior to the Depression.

Southern Illinois University at Carbondale, tucked away from major population centers in the forests, hills, and lakes of the region, is highly respected in a number of academic areas, among them environmental studies, biology, and medicine. The university has done extensive, cross-disciplinary research to ameliorate poor economic conditions in Little Egypt. Among state schools, SIU has long had a reputation for its easygoing, laid-back manner, its party environment, and back-to-nature feel.

The traditional Halloween party downtown, a staple since the 1950s, became the prototypical "wild scene" upon which other schools, including the University of Illinois, patterned their own festivities and to which they sent participants. It grew so rowdy and violent it has since been banned.

Added to the rich gumbo that is southern Illinois is its biogeography, which makes it unique not only among Illinois regions but among all areas of the United States. Southern Illinois was molded by the last of three Pleistocene era glaciers between 12,000 and 15,000 years ago, which scientists believe pushed down with them a number of plants from the north that survived after the glaciers receded; among them, the American harebell, a member of the bellwort family, normally found only in Wisconsin, Michigan, and Minnesota, is found in cliff crevasses and undisturbed sandstone areas in the rocky hills of the Shawnee National Forest, the quarter-million-acre tract of woodlands that drapes the topography of five southern Illinois counties south of Carbondale.

Four hundred million years ago, the Atlantic Ocean extended across the lower Heartland as far as southern Indiana, Illinois, and Missouri.

The sea came up almost to where the glacier ended. As a result, millions of years before county lines were drawn up and Illinois was granted statehood in 1818, the southernmost five counties of Illinois, Pulaski, Alexander, Pope, Hardin, and Johnson, were completely inundated by the sea, which, after retreating, left behind the same kind of habitat that we now associate with the coastal plains hundreds of miles away. The soggy habitat is marked by very low terrain with deep impressions—we know them as swamps—where trees such as the bald cypress and tupelo gum, some of them nearly a thousand years old, grow. In fact, the deep southern Illinois wetlands is the farthest north these two species grow. It is difficult to imagine coastal swamps smack dab in the heart of the Heartland, in the Prairie State herself, but that is part of the southern Illinois beauty, charm, and legend.

If a visitor continues past Pinckneyville toward Carbondale on this jaunt, he or she may have the good fortune, as I did one warm June day, to meet Robert Mohlenbrock, Ph.D., emeritus professor of botany at Southern Illinois University. Mohlenbrock, with his wife Beverly, is now head of his own biological consulting firm, Biotic Consultants. He retains an office at SIU, but his time these days is almost entirely devoted to his consulting, which puts him and Beverly on the road throughout the nation nearly every other week to teach short courses on plant identification, and to his writing, a "hobby" that has resulted in his authorship of 38 books and almost 400 articles. To the devoted half million readers of *Natural History*, Mohlenbrock is author of the highly popular "This Land" column in each issue, which presents the biologist with but one of his endless writing deadlines each month, and allows him to describe the biotic history of all the nation's national forests.

A native of southern Illinois, born and reared in Murphysboro, just seven miles from Carbondale, Mohlenbrock has spent his whole professional career in his native region and knows more about it than any other natural historian. He received both his bachelor's and master's degrees from SIU, leaving only for the three years it took him to attain his Ph.D. from Washington University in St. Louis, where he worked at the famed Missouri Botanical Garden. Despite his proximity to home, Mohlenbrock does not suffer from provincialism—

he has traveled and studied the world over and is among the world's most highly regarded, and, needless to say, most prolific biologists.

A large, gentle bear of a man, Mohlenbrock is avuncular, warm, brown haired, and serene. There is a quality to his voice that is at once sincere and knowledgeable, confident yet comforting. Gatsby described Daisy Buchanan's voice as "full of money." Mohlenbrock's voice is full of nature.

He met me at my hotel lobby and I followed him along Route 13 into the SIU campus, passing old storefronts and the clacketing Illinois-Central Gulf Railroad tracks going through the heart of town, past boardinghouses, Greek-pillared sorority and fraternity houses, the yards abloom with crepe myrtle and magnolias, to Dr. Mohlenbrock's hangout at the plant biology lab.

"So you're interested in the swamps," he began. "I've drawn up a little itinerary for you." But first he told me about the history of the region.

The people who settled the area in the early nineteenth century, Mohlenbrock explained, brought with them one basic skill—farming. When they settled in the southern Illinois area, seeing hardly anything but the tall, bald cypress swamps, all they could figure out to do with it was to cultivate it. So they drained the swamps by digging patchworks of ditches and dikes and diverting the water toward streams such as the Cache, which in turn drains into the Ohio River. Then they cut down the trees. Taming the swamps for agricultural purposes meant eventually destroying the diversity of fauna and flora. When the settlers came in the early 1800s, bear, wolves, coyote, cougar, deer, elk, buffalo, beaver, otter, and mink abounded. The gradual settlement of the land drove the species out, either from loss of habitat or overhunting.

"Ninety-five percent of the original habitat is gone," Mohlenbrock said. "We're truly fortunate to have any left at all. What *is* left are the areas that probably were too deep with water to drain. But what we have is just marvelous. Ironically, two old lumbermen near the Kentucky border are the people most responsible for the preservation of most of our swamps."

In the early 1970s, then chairman of the SIU botany department,

Mohlenbrock and other conservationists at the university spearheaded a drive to survey the natural areas of the region and develop a conservation program. They found that all of the bald cypress swamps with the exception of Horseshoe Lake, a Canada goose refuge near Cairo, were privately owned. Most of them were owned by a lumber company, Main Brothers, located in Karnak, Illinois, population 646. The task force, which besides Mohlenbrock and his university group, also included representatives from the state and Shawnee National Forest, asked Main Brothers if they would be willing to sell their lands for preservation. They agreed to, at the right price, but the state of Illinois could not afford the price at that time. The Nature Conservancy, as many times in the past, then stepped in and arranged to buy the land from Main Brothers for the state, with an arrangement that the state would gradually pay the Conservancy back.

The Main brothers, now retired and living in Karnak, had indeed left these lands because the waters had been too deep to drain. Their legacy of wetlands to the state is of great value; the remaining wetlands are symbolic of another mainstay in Egypt's natural history, logging, an industry that still thrives and is the source of a typically tumultuous southern Illinois controversy.

For years the U.S. Forest Service has set aside timber lots in the Shawnee National Forest that they would offer to private lumber companies for harvesting. While more than 90 percent of the state's 4.2 million acres of forests are in private ownership, the practice of selling off small parcels of public lands still continues, and it has fervent opponents on both sides of the primary issue, which is clear-cutting. A core of preservationists, in the tradition of turbulent Egypt disputes, have gone to desperate measures to prevent clear-cutting, including sabotaging lumber companies and driving iron stakes into trees sold to the companies—the stakes do little damage to the trees, but prevent the companies from cutting them down. There also have been mass arrests of preservationists in the Shawnee who chain themselves to trees to prevent their cutting. Many in favor of harvesting the Shawnee argue that cutting a little woodland back here and there does no real environmental harm. And the proponents are battling to maintain a livelihood that in itself, they say, is threatened by the preservationists' attitude. The preservationists counter that the Shawnee should continue to be a vast protected tract with as little fragmentation of habitat as possible, to protect especially the populations of neotropical migrant birds that breed there in the spring and summer. Clear-cutting, they contend, increases "edge" habitat species and reduces the populations of plants and animals that are native to the forest. Clear-cutting, logging proponents say, is part of wise management of old forest lands—it's actually beneficial to the forests to extract "dead wood."

"There's a great tension that's very real here between the militant preservationists and the prologging faction, and I fear it can turn violent," Mohlenbrock told me. "Then there are always the guys who see no reason to save anything at the expense of the local economy. Some of the timber men have a hard time getting by, you have to realize. And there is not a wide economic base in southern Illinois.

"I can't be considered anything but a preservationist myself. But I'm not totally against building lakes or ponds as long as the process is not killing off species. I honestly think there's room to harvest some of the areas that are getting old and don't harbor any particularly endangered species. And there's no reason why we can't preserve the areas that do foster endangered habitat. The U.S. Forest Service is much more aware of the public than it has been in the past. I think they are seeing the value of compromise, and as far as forest lands and swamps are concerned, I hope that attitude will prevail."

An admirer of all of the natural areas that bejewel southern Illinois, Mohlenbrock is particularly enamoured with Egypt's swamps and is encouraged by efforts to preserve them. Recently, for instance, a consortium of government and private groups, including the Nature Conservancy, the Illinois Department of Conservation, Ducks Unlimited, and the U.S. Fish and Wildlife Service gathered their forces to protect approximately 60,000 acres of wetlands around the Cache River near Ullin, just northwest of Cairo. Most of the lands are farmer owned, a good portion on the periphery of swamps that were drained as recently as the 1970s for planting soybeans, especially, in the booming era of high agricultural prices. The Fish and Wildlife Service, the driving force of the consortium, has delivered some 35,000 acres of the land and dubbed it the Cypress Creek National Wildlife Refuge. About 12,000 acres of that parcel is farmland that the service plans to buy—but only from willing sellers. The intent is to reforest the farmland and let the swamps extend naturally. The swamps in that area are home to more than 170 species of birds, including osprey, bald eagles, and great blue herons. Several cypress trees have been recorded there that are more than 1,000 years old.

"When the swamplands were drained, few species were lost altogether, although undeniably the numbers of those species subsided," Mohlenbrock said. "Of the swamp plant species, almost every one can be traced back to eastern species, plants that are commonly found in the Georgia/north Florida area."

Trees found in the swamps of Egypt include the bald cypress, tupelo gum, swamp cottonwood, water elm, and water locust; beneath these there are shrubs such as the Virginia willow and swamp rose atop a foundation of incredible wildflowers, such as two species of the pink Saint-John's-wort found only in bald cypress swamps, three species of the indigenous beggar's tickseed, and the sponge plant, a spongy plant with air pockets in its leaves that buoy the leaves to the surface of the water.

"Altogether, there are probably close to fifty plant species that are found only in bald cypress swamps, and right here in southern Illinois is the very northernmost edge of this habitat," Mohlenbrock said. "In addition, cottonmouths, or water moccasins, are common. The green water snake, a southern species, occurs in these swamps, the only habitat in Illinois where it can be found. A number of indigenous fish, the pygmy sunfish and the Ozark blind cave fish are both found here and nowhere else in Illinois. The swamps are also the northernmost habitat for the rice rat. The eastern wood rat, a rock-loving species that lives on the cliffs above the swamp, is found here and in southern Missouri. Almost every one of these animals is on the state's endangered species list."

Robert Mohlenbrock was trained at Washington University and the

Missouri Botanical Garden as a legume taxonomist—a "plant identification man," as he calls himself. He came to SIU-Carbondale (there's another branch of the university at Edwardsville, just east of St. Louis) after receiving his Ph.D. in 1957 to replace a faculty member for just one quarter. The professor who took the expected short leave never came back, thus launching the uninterrupted career of one of the nation's most respected naturalists. Mohlenbrock didn't want to spend his whole career limited to working on one particular group of plants. While he does not profess a preference for any particular kind of plant over another, he considers endangered plant species his specialty.

"The things I'm most concerned with are the few endangered plant species in Illinois that are down to the last handful," he said. "Mead's milkweed is one I'm concentrating on now."

This plant, a perennial herb with a fragrant cluster of greenish purple flowers at the tip of its stem, has been forced out by intensive cropping and other development throughout Illinois. It occurs in only four areas of the state, three of them in southern Illinois, and in two out of those three the plants don't flower and set seed. The Turk's-cap lily is found in just four places in southern Illinois, and it blooms in only one of those four places. Another plant, found only along the Illinois and Mississippi rivers, the false aster, recently added to the Federal Endangered List, is known to occur in only five places, one in Missouri and the rest in Illinois along the Illinois River from Alton extending up to Beardstown. The plant used to grow in areas that flooded frequently, in bottomlands and adjacent lowlands; in the past fifty years, the U.S. Army Corps of Engineers built a series of levees along the Illinois and Mississippi to control flooding. Now the false aster is being overrun by species not adapted to periodic flooding. The well-intended action to control floods is an obvious boon to agriculture, but it is another consequential illustration of ecologically robbing Peter to pay Paul.

In addition to surveying Mead's milkweed with hopes of locating additional plants in Little Egypt, Mohlenbrock was cataloging endangered species in the Mark Twain National Forest in Missouri, and as part of his biotic consulting company, he works with a group called the Wetlands Training Institute, headed by two of his former students, which helps educate people throughout the United States in ways to preserve wetlands and observe their ecosystems. Mohlenbrock teaches week-long seminars on how to identify wetlands plants, a discipline he finds challenging because it forces him to bone up on plant species outside his native region—species that can be found in such divergent places at Florida, Colorado, Arizona, and Maryland.

And there are the books, always the books. He has written thirty-eight of them, including a field guide to wildflowers, one about the United States national forests, and the widely heralded *Where Have All the Wildflowers Gone?*

Mohlenbrock traces his interest in the natural world to his childhood, when he would go for walks throughout the woods near Murphysboro and along the banks of the Big Muddy, taking mental notes of the diverse flora and fauna he found. His greatest influence was his high school biology teacher, Esther Smith, who was, he said, "a dedicated soul, a serious scientist who would provide for those who were serious." Ms. Smith devised projects for her budding scientists such as Mohlenbrock, and gave them every opportunity to see their projects through to fruition. Mohlenbrock's project was a catalog of the trees of southern Illinois. That high school assignment, he told me, chuckling, was the first in a series that continues to this day. Ms. Smith would take Mohlenbrock and others who wanted to go to one natural area or another and sponsored trips with students groups to the Great Smoky Mountains, one of which included the young Mohlenbrock. Mohlenbrock and six other young men so came under the sway of the Esther Smith influence that they all went on to major universities and attained doctorates in biology. To a man, they claimed her as their special spark. They tried to get her an honorary degree from SIU, but the notion sputtered in bureaucratic red tape, and Ms. Smith died before the honor could ever be bestowed upon her.

"She called us her boys," Mohlenbrock said, fondly. "She introduced us to all the great natural treasures that are around us."

Mohlenbrock is concerned about the politics of endangered species in the coming years and often warns against powerful lobbies in the nation's capital and their clout with decision makers. He offered the example of a drive in Texas to build another large water reservoir in an area of the state that fostered the only habitat for an extremely rare snake, the concho water snake. Although environmentalists stated their cause eloquently, the plans still were carried out, the only concession being that the size of the reservoir was cut back supposedly to make room for the snake.

"These kinds of issues are the ones ahead of us," he said. "The bureaucrats in D.C. are doing their best to weaken the Endangered Species Act. Species and their defenders will be going head-to-head with developers in confrontations over the land. There's nothing so novel about that, but the gravity of the situation has become much more severe than ever before. People say, 'So what, we lose another snake. We've got plenty of snakes.' My feeling is that it's a living creature, and it's a shame to see a living creature go extinct. We can surely make a little room for everything.

"Despite the hurdles, though, I'm guardedly optimistic. I really believe compromise is the answer," he reiterated. "There's a new groundswell of awareness about the environment, and I think more people than ever before are conscious that we owe it to ourselves to preserve our species."

Mohlenbrock pulled a piece of paper from his breast pocket and two maps from his hip pocket. The piece of paper, printed off a word processor, was titled "Notes on Swamps in Southern Illinois," with a subtitle, "Six Best Swamps in Southern Illinois." He laid open the maps on the long table between us. One map was a tourist's guide to the Shawnee National Forest, the other a recent road map of southern Illinois. With these three documents at hand, Mohlenbrock gave me a quick preview of the areas he had highlighted for me on this trip.

The paper read, in this order: Heron Pond, a State of Illinois Nature Preserve; Little Black Slough, a State of Illinois Nature Preserve; Buttonland Swamp, now a part of the new Cypress Creek National Wildlife Refuge; Grantsburg Swamp, a Research Natural Area in the Shawnee National Forest; Horseshoe Lake Conservation Area, a State of Illinois Conservation Area.

In his own writing, he had added a sixth: "Mermet Conservation Area, a newly opened preserve established by the state." Located alongside Mermet Lake, the Mermet Swamp is just minutes from the Ohio River, a few miles northwest of Metropolis, Illinois. All of the swamps were located within no more than an hour's drive from each other. Mohlenbrock had provided the names of naturalists in the area, SIU scientists or state specialists, all veterans in matters of southern Illinois natural history. I would need a guide at Grantsburg ("a very snaky area, you go past rocky slopes full of copperheads, and then in the swamp itself there are lots of cottonmouths. I strongly suggest you don't go in there without a guide"), and at Little Black Slough because it was closed to the public. He praised all of these locations, but spoke so warmly of the merits of Heron Pond that this particular place beckoned to me, almost a siren song.

"Heron Pond is the most accessible of the swamps from here. It's a short drive, really, and it's very representative of what the area probably looked like thousands of years ago. There's a dock you can walk out on and be smack-dab in the middle of the swamp. With the mist rising above the water, you'll think you're in the Okefenokee. It's *un*believable."

Mohlenbrock, needing to sit in on a Ph.D. dissertation presentation, shook my hand and invited me back. I departed the biology building, leaving magnolia-flushed Carbondale behind, and zoomed off to explore a swamp.

Past lush woods and shimmering Crab Orchard Lake, just outside Carbondale, past Carterville and Herrin to the north, escorted by the ghosts of Charlie Birger, the Klan, and the Sheltons speeding along in their Model Ts, bullets whistling through the brush, to Marion, the unofficial capital of Egypt. Down 57, just outside of Marion, the oak, hickory, maple, and cedar woods on either side of the interstate gradually fill in the landscape until, departing 57 for 24, you are in an almost steady monoculture of woods—the great, green resource of the Shawnee National Forest. About three hundred feet above a jutting limestone rise in the road, two soaring turkey vultures patrol the region like nature's policemen overseeing the vast tract of woodlands, home hundreds of years ago to the Shawnee Indians and bastion today of an Illinois about which few have any inkling.

Vienna (Vy-anna) is a tiny burg couched in old hills. I passed quiet streets lined with stately, Greek-pillared houses and long wraparound porches in the Southern style, hound dogs, rocking chairs and porch swings still in vogue with nary a backyard deck to be seen anywhere. Vienna is the Johnson County seat; the courthouse is situated on a hill on the square broodingly overlooking the southern end of the village of 1,400.

Vienna was the home of the late Paul Powell, Illinois Secretary of State in the sixties, a legendary, crafty, crusty politico known statewide as the Vienna Fox. The citizens of Illinois knew his nasal, twangy voice from countless radio commercials urging the people to renew their driver's licenses and make out their checks "to me, Paul Powell, Secretary of State." In a bizarre twist so characteristic of Egypt, upon Powell's sudden death in 1970, shortly after the public accolades and requiems poured in honoring him, investigators found $800,000 in cash stuffed into shoe boxes at his Springfield residence. No one knows for sure how he amassed the fortune, but there were insinuations— and jokes—about writing "checks to me, Paul Powell," that persist in Illinois today. The story rings of a real-life denouement in a Faulknerian short story, and it is the only shadow to lurk over the quaint village.

Past Vienna on Route 45 on the southern branch of the Lincoln Heritage Trail, the three-state journey following Lincoln's ascent from the Heartland to the presidency, through a long, cool stretch of forest canopy along the highway, I followed the signs for Heron Pond and Wildcat Bluff, an adjoining area of limestone glades, bluffs, and sections of native prairie. Heron Pond, Wildcat Bluff, and the adjacent Little Black Slough are part of the 8,214 acres the state has set aside and designated as the Cache River Natural Area. Comprising approximately 900 acres, Heron Pond is the smallest of the natural areas, but its size in no way is indicative of its clout. No less an expert than Mohlenbrock has called it "pristine," an extremely rare distinction for any place in this part of the Heartland.

The area, owned until 1973 primarily by the Main brothers, is host to an incredibly diverse wildlife, including the great blue heron, green heron, and the yellow-crowned night heron, which all nest along the Cache River as well as near the swamps; a plethora of songbirds, vultures, hawks, occasional eagles, ducks, and geese; fox, mink, muskrat, beaver and coyote, and the endangered Indiana bat; such southern fish species as the grass pickerel, slough darter, bowfin, channel catfish, and the pygmy sunfish. Copperheads, cottonmouths, and timber rattlesnakes are plentiful and poisonous, though there have been few reports of people getting bitten. Mohlenbrock had mentioned two of the weirdest creatures to come out of Heron Pond—a young alligator (it had been dumped) and a very mature (200 pounds!) snapping turtle that was a resident.

Route 45 emerges out of the woods to pleasant, broad, hilly pastures, feeder cattle grazing the grasses, green hills to the west, incredibly quiet, peaceful country. The gravel road that leads to Heron Pond is covered by a dark, twisted canopy of trees, their roots sticking out like swirling demons discouraging intruders, a signal that what lies ahead is a different existence. I pulled into the parking lot at road's end, big enough to handle maybe thirty vehicles, but containing only two. As I dosed up with DEET and changed into my hiking boots, a retired couple from Ohio passed and exchanged pleasantries. They were on their way back from a trip and had heard about the swamps in this area and were mighty glad they'd stopped to see this one. "It's just like Georgia, but it's Illinois." the man said with a chuckle. "Unbelievable."

After about a tenth of a mile on the trail, I passed the suspension bridge over the Cache River and stopped there to take in the Irish-coffee-colored water gurgling over a minifall, a darting bluebird lighting upon a bony cottonwood, and the eerie, primeval calls from the swamp just yonder. Something—a heron, perhaps—made a wailing, mournful cry like a child bawling. The Cache is a hypnotic, contemplative river, its banks eroded over thousands of years by the ebb and flow of water. Tree trunks, having fallen from countless storms, are strewn in a naturally haphazard manner, creating swirls and eddies and habitat for beaver, mink, and muskrat. Never very wide, the river at this stretch is no farther across than fifty feet, no deeper than two or three feet, yet it is wild enough looking to qualify as a nature experience of the first order all by its murky lonesomeness. When the state song "Illinois," with its haunting opening line, "By her waters gently flowing, Illinois, Illinois," was being penned, its author probably didn't have in mind the Cache with its rugged, sluggish charm. I could have stayed on the bridge for a half hour, but there was the lure of the swamp behind me with its ancient trappings and sounds.

The trail is well marked, easy to follow, and it offers scenic glimpses of the Cache to the right. Often in a swamp you can hear more than you can see, and that was the case this day, as frogs and toads leaped from the underbrush across my path and through the tangle; snakes, which make a distinctively heavier rustle in the greenery, slithered by unseen. The trail is dark, moist, and cool, pitted with circular holes for the burrowing reptiles, and at points where rivulets converge and spill down the bluffs and into the banks of the Cache, covered with rocks to ease a traveler's passage. Poised along these rocks was a wolf spider, the biggest spider I had ever seen in my life, in this part of Illinois. Bigger than a man's fist, its thorax was the size of a Reese's Peanut Butter Cup, its legs long and menacing.

At another of these rocky junctures, two people were halted and I made a tentative approach. A young, honey-blond woman in jeans and a halter top pointed nervously toward the rocks just to the left of the trail and mouthed some whispered, indecipherable words. I got closer to her companion, a young man with a zoom lens on a camera strapped around his neck. He was creeping toward something atop the rocks. The woman pointed again, "A cottonmouth," she whispered. "I'm afraid he'll get too close."

There, gliding along the rocks toward some underbrush was indeed a cottonmouth more than three feet long which suddenly stopped on its slow journey, turned, and darted its tongue at the unfazed photographer. "He'd go right in there and pick him up," she whispered. "Anything for a picture. Jeff, get on back. I think he's getting nervous around you."

The cottonmouth found its sanctuary and Jeff reluctantly gave up the hunt, not without a few shots to his credit. The three of us chatted quietly along the trail; Jeff West was from Springfield, Nancy Wheeler from Marion. She had a charming Southern accent; his was midwestern. This was his second trip to Heron Pond, her first. She had grown up in Egypt and had never known that Heron Pond had existed. He had made his first trip without a camera a few weeks back and now was hooked. He'd never seen anything to compare with this anywhere else in Illinois and wanted to make sure he got good pictures on this trip. He sold photographs as a free-lancer and was certain he'd have a market for Illinois swamp shots. "The cypress and tupelo," he said with awe. "Some of them are nearly a thousand years old."

The trail finally came to a point where the swamp encroached upon it, and we could hear what we took to be honking geese flapping across the water. At a bend along the trail, the boardwalk became visible and with it the true green beauty of the Heron Pond swamp.

The boardwalk, extending perhaps one hundred yards into the swamp, sways with each step you take. We passed a green fence lizard, about three inches long, that seemed to be playing with us as it rattled along wooden posts, and we maneuvered for a better gander at the tupelos and the tall bald cypresses, mossy green, lean, and reaching toward the sun. Frogs heaved their rhythmic, bassoonlike notes, myriad bird calls and chirping insects added to the chorus. Yet amidst all the noise, the creatures of the swamp are often in hiding. I saw the beady eyes of water snakes, but most often saw only the little ribbon trails in the duckweed film on the surface of the water, the equivalent to the jet's contrail. The bald cypress "knees," knobby, gnarly roots surrounding the bald cypress, looked like monster fists protruding from the water. The swamp rose, a bushy plant with bright pink and lavender flowers, draped the knees like a bracelet. I heard a splash in the waters behind me. But whatever creature—beaver, muskrat, otter, turtle, mink—made the noise was submerged or hiding when I turned toward the sound. The splashes continued with unabated regularity; each time I looked the most I saw was a circle in the duckweed. Goosebumps raced down my flesh at a most god-awful noise coming from behind the swamp toward the river, a roaring, snarling sound that might have been a bobcat. But it was never repeated.

Stroll the boardwalk and ponder the post-Pleistocene at Heron Pond; be thankful for the Main brothers and Robert Mohlenbrocks of this world. Stare out at the green haze rising from the pond, losing yourself in the mist, lost in time, lost in Illinois.

KEEPERS OF THE GARDEN
Peter Raven, director of the Missouri Botanical Garden; Don Falk, director of the Center for Plant Conservation; and Lucile McCook, Missouri Botanical Garden botanist, at the garden's Climatron. (*Courtesy of Sara Fitzpatrick*)

Keepers of the Garden

At 7:30 on a damp March morning in the Midwest, the folks are gathering in the Lopata Hall Gallery on the Washington University campus in St. Louis. This is the monthly breakfast meeting of the School of Engineering's Century Club, an august body of alumni that includes many of the area's premier builders, designers, and developers. Milling about the basement floor of the modern edifice, eagerly seeking coffee, danish, juice, and conversation, are engineers and executives from McDonnell Douglas Corporation, Arthur Andersen, Ethyl Corporation, IBM, Anheuser Busch, AT&T, Southwestern Bell, McCarthy Construction, and at least a dozen more companies, about 250 people in all. The air is charged with a certain tension, the din of conversation rising with each passing minute. Dean James McKelvey, white haired and benevolent, in the last of twenty-seven years administering the School of Engineering, smiles warmly from the speaker's podium as he surveys the crowd. It's one of the biggest he's ever seen for a Century Club breakfast, and he's delighted to see old and new friends alike flocking together like expectant birds. McKelvey's guest speaker for this month apparently has the power to pack 'em in—an excellent choice for breakfast appeal.

Yet today's guest lecturer, strictly speaking, is not really one of their own. Peter Raven is director of the world-renowned Missouri Botanical Garden. Unlike most of the guests of the Century Club breakfasts, he holds a Ph.D. in botany from UCLA, and not an engineering degree. He has an appointment with Washington University as Engelmann Professor of Botany, and he also has adjunct posts with the University of Missouri at St. Louis, and St. Louis University. Without reservation he is one of the premier biologists of his time and a prophet of global ecological holocaust. In every sense of the word, he is a St. Louis institution, a Stan Musial of botany.

The crowd fills every available seat as Dr. McKelvey introduces his remarkable guest. The litany of Dr. Raven's achievements is impressive: Author of 400 papers and 16 books; coauthor, with Washington University professor George Johnson, of the one of the most popular textbooks on biology ever written; home secretary of the National Academy of Sciences; an appointee of President Bush to the National Science Board; honored as Person of the Week by Peter Jennings of ABC in 1988; and named the St. Louis Man of the Year in 1989, the top banana of all local awards.

Raven rises to the podium to a hearty reception. Dressed in a blue blazer and gray slacks, he is a pleasant-looking man, about six feet tall, vigorous in movement, intent in expression. He betrays no evidence of the lingering jet lag he bears from his recent return from Taiwan where he met with Chinese and international botanists to implement a paragovernmental organization that would catalog the entire Taiwanese biodiversity on computer and develop it for use in making helpful chemicals and drugs. The week before that, he spoke to a similar-sized group as the Century Club in a standing-room-only conference room at the American Association for the Advancement of Science annual convention in Washington, D.C.

In the next thirty minutes, Raven highlights forty-five years of the world's eco-destruction, beginning with the post–World War II fog in London that ruined women's nylons and poisoned the Thames River, and concluding with a plea to save the rain forests and end global hunger. Interspersed are explanations of the greenhouse effect, the depletion of the ozone layer, the dreadful loss of species in the tropics and subtropics, an explanation of inflation, and Third World debt.

The crowd, hushed with anticipation but responding with an occasional snicker or chortle at Raven's sarcastic asides, can't get enough. It is as if they are a congregation awakened from the usual soporific sermon to that rare occurrence where the minister or rabbi finds himself giving the sermon of his life. Raven, though, gives his particular sermon at least every other week to audiences from 50 to 500, in all the four corners of the world. Yet he delivers his message with the sincerity of one who is speaking for the first time. And the guilt-ridden audience, literally sitting on the edge of their seats as Raven reveals one alarming statistic, graph, or shocking slide of a starving infant or denuded forest after another, loves it.

When Raven speaks, he begins fast and simply goes faster. Stiff-necked, he twists from side to side as he makes a point, surveying the room like an auctioneer looking for bids. Listening to him, you can't help detecting a faintly mocking quality in his voice, and if you close your eyes and listen harder you realize it's ever so slightly reminiscent of the actor Jack Nicholson. The mocking tone is not directed toward his audience. It is native to his voice but might be enhanced by the truly unpleasant facts he presents in his speeches and even his private discussions, and perhaps by an inner knowledge that no matter how many people he is talking to and no matter what their commitment to setting the world straight, the word still has not reached enough people, and it may be too late to preserve all that must be saved.

He presents the facts in a riveting staccato style that mesmerizes an audience and nullifies any reporter's attempt to record his words, unless the reporter knows shorthand. His most fervent topic: the loss of species.

"There are 1.4 million species of life that have been named in the world, including 750,000 kinds of insects, 42,000 vertebrates, and 250,000 plants. About 90 percent of the plants and vertebrates are characterized. Of course, lots of them we know only superficially. Various kinds of sampling exercises show, though, that there are actually between 10 million and 100 *million* different organisms in the world, really. We've named *no more than 15 percent.* So, of these millions of unnamed species the best estimate is that we'll lose 20 percent in the next thirty years if deforestation continues at the same pace as it has in the past decade, which averages to a deforested area about the size of Illinois every year. *Think* of that.

"Now, that's 20 percent of the plants and vertebrates—and not only the nameless insects. We're losing them very rapidly, and that's very serious because we base everything we do on our ability to use species in one way or another. Nearly one out of four medical prescriptions for drugs in the United States is based on plant or microbial products or from synthetic derivatives of them. The anticancer drug vincristine, for example, is derived from the Madagascar periwinkle; ivermectin, which destroys intestinal worms, and cyclosporine, an immunosuppressant, are derived from a Norwegian fungus. Even aspirin, the most common of all drugs, came originally from willow bark. Less than 5 *percent* of the world's population ever thinks of that. Every time we lose a plant it's like the loss of 40,000 genes to the world—genes that may give us a new medicine, drug, or chemicals to improve and save lives.

"In the tropics, about 500,000 species have been named, but we can safely assume that there are at the very least 3 million, possibly more, yet to be discovered. About 50 percent of the world's plant species occur only in forests that are rapidly being uprooted. That means roughly 120,000 of the estimated total 165,000 tropical plant species will not survive at this rate. We are living in an age of extinction unlike any other in the history of the earth. It took the dinosaurs millions of years to become extinct, and in the past forty-five years untold *thousands* of species have disappeared, all in the name of progress, development, and growth, three words of ambiguity here in this century.

"Since 1950, the number of people in industrialized nations has dropped from 33 percent of the world's population to only 23 percent now. By 2020, those of us in the developed world will represent only one-sixth of the population. This segment owns 85 percent of the world's wealth. Three-fourths of the world's people have the remaining 15 percent. One point two billion people in the world are in absolute poverty. Five hundred million receive less than 80 percent of the minimum caloric intake per day. Fourteen million under the age of four die of starvation each year.

"Yet how does a nation like Brazil, with half its population living in poverty, try to resurrect itself? They overexploit their natural resources to pay off their $120 billion debt—the soybeans, lumber, and natural resources exported to the United States and other industrial countries rather than used at home to help their own population. If the world population were frozen at its present state, we would still destroy the world completely in time if we maintain our modes of operation—the overreliance on fossil fuels, destruction of habitats, the spilling of chemicals into streams, and so forth. Poverty is what must change. The global population will stabilize in one hundred years at two to three times its present size, whereas nothing will happen to the poverty situation unless we address it adequately, and there is no sign that we are."

At the end of this peppery assault, the audience stifles a natural impulse to rise to their feet in applause, and Raven, smiling his warm but somewhat guarded smile, takes questions for another half hour from a score of hangers-on. Although the Century Club breakfast is an invitation-only event, several people with notebooks and tape recorders are getting as much of this down as they can. That happens everywhere Peter Raven speaks.

At the entrance to Busch Stadium, downtown home of the St. Louis Cardinals, stands a statue of Stan "The Man" Musial, who, even more than Lucky Lindbergh, may be the most symbolic St. Louisan of them all. Part of the legend beneath his name reads, "Here stands baseball's greatest warrior." The effect is enough to run a chill down your spine, even if you're a Chicago Cubs fan.

As director of the botanical garden, Peter Raven is to the city's environmental conscience what Musial is to its civic pride. The Missouri Botanical Garden in St. Louis—as prestigious as Kew Gardens in London and the New York Botanical Garden in the Bronx, the elite botanical gardens of the world—is like Busch Stadium to the city's populace. Both places, the garden and the stadium alike, are a sort of spiritual haven. It would be fitting if a statue of Peter Raven were erected in front of the Missouri Botanical Garden, which someday may become a reality. But for now St. Louis must make do with a statue of Henry Shaw on his deathbed, a dubious memorial in an otherwise bucolic oasis in the Gateway to the West.

The statue of Shaw reclining on his bed with an outreached hand stretched toward his stately home is in the heart of the Missouri

Botanical Garden inside a mausoleum he had had constructed shortly before his death in 1889. Less than fifty yards to the west is a similar mausoleum, for all intents and purposes as soundly constructed as the one in which he is buried, yet bereft of any monument or purpose. Shaw, it seemed, didn't like the one to the west and had ordered another one built. As I looked at the site on a raw March afternoon, with a surprise coating of snow covering the grass and hedges of the garden, I realized the truth in the old saw, "There's no accounting for taste." However, the mausoleum is a reflection of common practices of Shaw's time. And the man made an enormous impact. The garden is still popularly known as "Shaw's Garden."

The rest of the garden is a marvel in design, function, and beauty, a panoply of flora, water, architecture, and theme; the air, richly redolent of humus in the greenhouses and exhibits, is sweeter inside the garden than in its cold surround, the southside streets of the city. Directly south of Shaw's mausoleum is his house, built in 1849; it was his summer residence. When you drive through the grids of brick apartment buildings, duplexes, and corner convenience stores leading to the garden, many in somber disrepair, the omnipresent drone of traffic on I-44 in the background, the thought that this was once country is an alien notion.

Shaw, an English native, came to St. Louis in 1819, just shortly after the War of 1812 and thirteen years before the region's next conflict, the Black Hawk Indian War of 1832. He was a wealthy businessman who amassed his fortune in real estate after establishing a cutlery and hardware business upon his arrival. At the time, St. Louis was a bigger hub of commerce than Chicago, Cincinnati, or Louisville. Inspired in part by the Royal Botanic Gardens at Kew, Shaw sought to return some of the land he had acquired to the citizens who had made him wealthy, and years before his death, planned to turn his own experiment in nature into a public institution that would assuage people's souls and educate them in the ways of science. He willed his garden and much of his estate to a trust with explicit plans to keep the place a well-maintained public treasure. His scheme has endured, not without faltering moments. In the 1920s the city skies were black from soot and sulfur, by-products of coal burning. The garden then sold orchids as a sideline, but the plants were being ruined by the pollution. The orchids were transferred from the garden to the arboretum, a large parcel of land some forty miles west of the city off I-44 near Gray's Summit, which flourishes today with reintroduced prairie, woods, hiking trails, and other attractions. By the 1950s, the greenhouses and other buildings were badly maintained; funding the institution had become difficult and public concern had dwindled. A drive led by St. Louis lawyer John Lehmann reinvigorated the garden and by 1960, with the opening of the Climatron—the vast, geodesic-domed greenhouse that now contains over 1,200 species of tropical plants—a new era of pride and beauty began. Closed for repairs for two years, the Climatron reopened in 1990, ushering in yet another phase of long-range planning for the garden.

Like the metropolitan area itself, the garden is filling up, an outgrowth, in large part, of Raven's direction and vision. Unlike the city, though, the plan for the garden's seventy-nine acres is fixed, the structures and contours refined. That gray afternoon I walked much of the grounds, visiting the oldest greenhouse in the garden, a brick building filled with aromatic camellias and hanging baskets, and the Climatron with its waterfall, aquarium, banana, citrus, mango, and dozens of other plant species sprawled throughout, feeling soothed and refreshed by the simulated tropical dankness. Another older building housed the biblical garden flowing with cacti, crown of thorns, palms, the spiny devil's backbone, and hedgehog plants.

Beyond the central area of the garden lie Raven's additions and flourishes brought on since 1971, the year he came to the garden. Among them are the quaint English Woodland Garden, the lush Japanese Garden, laid out on a gentle hill and adjoining a five-acre lake, and deep in the southern corner of the garden, the nearly finished Center for Home Gardening, an 8.5-acre spread that will contain more than twenty individual gardens and clusters of one-story, wooden buildings, which, under the direction of plant pathologist Steven Cline, will soon display exhibits and sponsor classes for urban amateur botanists. Scattered throughout the grounds are scientific displays—on tropical deforestation, acid rain, and other science lessons—all reflecting the Raven touch.

The garden under Raven's direction has made extraordinary strides; since arriving in 1971, Raven has built the science staff from three full-time botanists to fifty who are on assignments throughout the world. Then, 200,000 people visited the garden; 850,000 toured it in 1990. The herbarium, an outgrowth of Henry Shaw's passion for plants, has doubled in size and now houses a collection of more than 4 million specimens; the library contains more than 110,000 volumes on the world's flora.

Before assuming the position of director, Raven already had distinguished himself as a highly eminent, if not legendary, biologist. A native of the San Francisco area, he was eight when he entered the student section of the California Academy of Sciences and benefited greatly from the tutelage of John Thomas Howell, an inspiring botanist. When he was fourteen, Peter Raven published his first scientific paper, reflecting his experiences on a Sierra Club outing. After receiving his Ph.D. from UCLA, Raven held several different academic posts, including a full-time faculty position at Stanford. There, Raven became famous for developing, with colleague Paul Ehrlich, the word and concept of coevolution, a stepwise evolutionary race between plants, insects, and animals, whereby one would advance somewhat and then in the course of evolution another would advance and use the original species as a resource so that both would change to their mutual advantage. The relationship of a plant with its pollinator is a prime example, although the younger Raven was especially impressed with the evolution of plant chemicals, particularly ones used in medicines, which evolved as an evolutionary strategy of the plant to avoid being eaten by its various parasites.

Raven's reputation, locally and globally, is so robust that meeting him can be a daunting experience. As I sat at the circular conference table in his pristine office in the Lehmann Building, named after the lawyer who helped resuscitate the garden, I realized that here is a man who has characterized thousands of species of plants, and, looking at his eyes, which at times don't twinkle when a smile waves across his face, I sensed he was scrutinizing me as he would a plant specimen he had found in some woods. Somewhere in the reaches of his vast cataloging mind, I thought, he must be working on another problem or digesting what species of person he had before him, or, perhaps, envisioning the felling of trees in Brazil, Madagascar, or the Congo.

"Our overall goal is to increase the awareness and information about plants at a valuable time, here and now in an age of extinction," he told me. "To effect this goal, we have to make certain we—and I'm talking about botanists throughout the world—find new species and preserve all species. To keep track of what we have left in the world, we're building large-scale data bases both here and at other institutions in the world to make sure that information is available to all people of all countries." Whew! Then he speeds on: "We have to make sure the data bases are interconnected. In conjunction with building data bases, we want to build a strong network of dedicated conservationists in the Third World, countries in Latin America and Africa, where so many species are being lost, show them how this is done, and make sure they continue to see the importance of preservation. To give you an example, there may be as many as 50,000 different kinds of plants in just three countries, Columbia, Peru and Ecuador, in Latin America. That's three times as many plants found in the United States and Canada combined. These plants are poorly characterized, yet from them could be developed uses for food, medicines, oils, fats, waxes, and other purposes, but the work has scarcely even begun."

The Missouri Botanical Garden is the largest program in the world that works with tropical plants. Yet its outreach, under Raven's guidance, includes programs to preserve the flora of China, Australia, the Soviet Union, North America, and countries in Latin America and Africa. One of Raven's many global appointments is the American chairman of a joint committee with the Chinese government to revise and publish in English a whopping library of 125 volumes about Chinese plants and then turn the tome into a modern data base that someday will be shared throughout the world. The Chinese connection is a vital one. Of the 125 volumes, 85 of them have been written since 1950, available only in Chinese and sequestered from the rest of the world until now.

"The work with the Chinese is particularly important," he said, "because China's population has grown from 350 million in 1949 to 1.2 billion at the present time. Much of their natural resources and ecosystems have been destroyed or drastically altered. There's little left of the 30,000 kinds of plants that exist in China. Six thousand of these plants are used as sources for medicines; they are economically the most valuable set of plants found in the world. They also have wild relatives of soybeans, for instance, that can be used here and in other parts of the world to cross with existing varieties to maybe develop insect- or disease-resistant plants. Another reason we're interested in Chinese plants is because they have the relics of plants that were much more widespread around the whole Northern Hemisphere before the coming of the Ice Ages millions of years ago that spread extinction throughout Europe and North America."

He showed a fossil from eastern Oregon of a dawn redwood leaf embedded in stone. The dawn redwood is extinct in North America, but about 1,200 remain in China in the wild. In the absence of major glaciers, the dawn redwood and other plants survived in China, so despite its land size being about the same as that of the United States, its 30,000 native plants are nearly twice the number found in the United States and Canada, with 17,000 plants, and nearly three times that of Europe's 10,500 plants.

"Plants can be multiplied and replicated from seed much easier than breeding of endangered animal species," he noted. "There are probably a million dawn redwoods left in the world. They're a special relative of bald cypress and redwoods. Were it not for the relatively mild climate of China, the dawn redwood would be completely gone from the world, and with it our link to similar plants millions of years old. So, there are many reasons the plants of China are of interest."

Raven is famous for his quest to save the world's plant species, but he hasn't overlooked his own country nor his adopted region, the Heartland, as his many contributions to the Missouri Botanical Garden and midwestern research projects suggest. Recently, in the fall of 1990, he spearheaded another charge to save plants that, in the babble of concern about tropical species, few people ever hear about. He was instrumental in bringing the Center for Plant Conservation to the botanical garden. Headed by Donald A. Falk, the center had been operating for six years in Jamaica Plain, Massachusetts, near Boston. Its focus is to save the nation's approximately 3,000 endangered plant species from extinction by establishing them in some twenty plant "banks" throughout the country, including the botanical garden, raising a viable seed stock and ultimately reintroducing the plants into natural areas. The center switched from the East Coast to the Heartland because of the already powerful connections the Missouri Botanical Garden has throughout the country and Raven's experience with data bases. Also, the center's physical location at the garden will more easily facilitate integrating its efforts with the Flora of North America Project, another operation centered at the garden, which seeks to draw together the first thorough catalog of all the plants growing in both the United States and Canada.

"Because we have joined forces with the Center for Plant Conservation, we are for the first time close to halting in one corner of the world—the United States—the continual extinction of plant species," he said, his entire face lighting up. "I'm excited about the things we're planning here with the center."

The center has 400 of the nation's 3,000 endangered plant species growing in the numerous plant banks around the country. It also has seed stock and specimens of the approximately twenty endangered plants in the St. Louis region—eastern Missouri, southern Illinois, eastern Kentucky, and eastern Tennessee. Half of these are located in the botanical garden; they include various strains of clover, grasses, and goldenrod, and other plants that once thrived in areas polluted or cleared during the twentieth century.

The plants declined for a combination of reasons—water and air pollution, the conversion of lands from wetlands and woods into agricultural lands, farmers' growing reliance on pesticides after World War II, the spread of cities, more recently, acid rain, and, in some cases, simple harvesting. Ginseng, for example, a native of Missouri, is increasingly rare because of a constant demand for it as a health food.

While it is difficult to document how many plants have been wiped out specifically by air pollution, University of Illinois Extension plant pathologist Malcolm B. Shurtleff in the 1980s determined that the damage to food and fiber crops, trees, turf grasses, and ornamental plants amounts to nearly $250 million each year. The damage comes primarily from ozone and nitrous oxide emissions, the bane of the Industrial Age. Produced when sunlight reacts with nitrogen oxides and hydrocarbons from automobile exhaust and other sources, ozone damage is the biggest problem and is most severe in city areas, where it can drift along for hundreds of miles into the country. Nitrogen oxides are produced by power plants that burn coke, soft coal, or high-sulfur oil, don't drift quite as far—maybe fifty miles—but their effects are deadly. Affected plants are stunted or defoliated; white and yellow blotches and streaks mar the blades and leaves. For years, farmers and gardeners suspected blight, viruses, bacteria, or insect damage when all along the problem was traceable to fuels and commerce. While the air is cleaner than even twenty years ago, the great industrial surge and developmental sprawl of the first seventy years of the century took an undeniably heavy toll on the nation's plants.

In the Heartland, Missouri hosts about 2,200 different plant species, Illinois slightly more, perhaps because of its richer soils and broader expanse of prairie. Missouri is an intriguing state for plants because of its diversity: The northern half was glaciated, similar to Iowa and Illinois, the southern half is composed of ancient mountains. The glaciers that spread thousands of years ago from the north left most of Illinois flat and fertile, with only the southern tip and northwestern corner resembling anything like hill country.

Whereas Missouri has lots of distinct habitats for plants, no more than several of those native to the state are endemic only to Missouri, Raven said. A more typical, curious occurrence is where a plant is rare in Missouri but common elsewhere. Raven mentioned that a particular kind of bellflower, in abundance in the Arctic, along the coast of Maine, in the Oregon Cascades, northern Canada, and Alaska, is found in one place in south-central Missouri, along limestone cliffs overhanging the Jack's Fork River, a clear remnant of the Ice Ages.

"You have to remember," he said, "that 18,000 years ago Missouri was a spruce-fir forest, a lot like Canada, complete with moose, caribou, and that whole ecological accoutrement. There's nothing left here now like that. But the bellflower was around then and it has survived in this one spot because it has never faced competition from other species. You'd think it would be too dry a habitat, but it gets by because it feeds off the rivulets that flow through the limestone."

Similarly, in Illinois, a rare flower, *Illiamna remota*, a long-stemmed plant with white petals like a daisy fanning out from yellow-centered flowers, is found only on an island in the Kankakee River, in northeastern Illinois, although populations, strangely enough, are documented in both Indiana and Virginia. There is no explanation for this bizarre distribution, but its discovery has fed the imagination of many a botanist wondering if there may be similar finds in other areas.

From the window of his office, Dr. Raven can see his home, a fine old building about fifty yards ahead. He can also see the barely visible rows of streets beyond that lead all the way up from the banks of the Mississippi to the botanical garden, which, in addition to being his work headquarters, also has been his home for the past twenty years. Like the six full-time directors of the botanical garden before him, a house on the grounds is part of his employment package. He also has a farm in the Missouri Ozarks near DeSoto where he spends as much time in the woods and fields with wife, Tamra, and children, Katie and Francis, as he can. It's clear he has set deep roots here.

"The people of St. Louis love the garden, and so do I," he told me. "From time to time I think of what this area was like before its settlement. There's a saying that 250 years ago a squirrel could go from the Atlantic seaboard to Kansas without ever touching the ground. That was how rich the forestlands were then. But here, this was all prairie, the Grand Prairie, stretching from the banks of the river and beyond, all divided neatly into these long French fields by the early settlers. Then, of course, St. Louis developed, as it still is today, but if you analyze the soil in this part of the city you'll see it's all prairie soil.

"People have been using the world very intensely. Since 1950, 20 percent of the world's topsoil has just vanished. In forty years, it's depleted, and there's no replacing it. Yet you still hear farm agents talking about 'allowable losses' of topsoil, as if it were replaceable. People have begun to get a sort of hold on environmental problems, but there's still that kind of dynamic—the struggle between looking out for ourselves and still caring for the earth that nurtures us—that we have to settle." He's thinking about prairie soil, and the world, here in St. Louis.

His colleague Don Falk as a kid became fascinated with two things that seemingly were diametrically opposed to each other—nature and industry. The setting to observe this interaction was made to order: Pittsburgh, a brawling, gritty city, fueled by coal and steel, populated by immigrants pouring into a mecca of opportunity, a classic industrial success story. Situated at the western edge of the Appalachian Mountains and on two thriving rivers, the city was also near some beautiful natural settings. The rivers, Falk realized early, were natural entities, brimming with fish and aquatic life, even though threatened by pollution. Yet they also were essential industrial elements of the economic systems that supported Pittsburgh. You could fish them; you could float a barge down them.

Since the age of four, Falk spent summer vacations with his family in the mountains, mainly in New England. On these trips he learned at an early age to observe nature closely, to treasure it, and learn from it. He saw early in his life that the boundary between society and natural systems constantly was becoming more blurred. The way society and nature interact is "the most extraordinary and fascinating interface for my money to be found anywhere on earth," he's fond of saying. For the past decade, he has devoted his life to mending the ills of that interface.

Pondering this relationship in his undergraduate years at Oberlin College in Ohio and his graduate study at Tufts University near Boston, where he received a master's degree in environmental policy, he hatched the idea to start the Center for Plant Conservation, now housed at the Missouri Botanical Garden. The center manages the world's largest conservation collection of endangered plants. A conservation collection, rather than having one or two specimen plants of a species, captures the genetic diversity within a species by maintaining a large, diverse collection of related plants, which helps preserve the plants' evolutionary potential. The heart of the organization is the network of botanical gardens and arboreta throughout the country forged by Falk's hustle and determination to "set an example to the rest of the world that the United States is serious about saving her own plants and not just telling the rest of the world to save theirs," he has said. "I also began to realize that, depending how you cut it, we have something on the order of 20 percent of our natural flora in danger of extinction. Nearly 1,000 genera have endangered species within them. This is a very serious threat to the evolutionary diversity of the continent. If we lose one out of five plants, we lose the raw material for continued evolution and adaptation to climatic change."

Falk, and Lucile McCook, Ph.D., a botanist recently hired to work at the center, are two of the people most responsible for preserving and propagating our country's 360 endangered plant species. They met me at the garden behind a greenhouse in the midst of cold frames that foster twenty endangered plants in the lower midwestern region. Conversing lightly, they browsed among the plants, peering at them like shoppers at a flea market. They are an unlikely pair, Falk and McCook, drawn to the Missouri Botanical Garden by a mutually fervent desire to save the nation's endangered plants.

Falk, in his forties, is lean, lithe, and boyishly handsome. A sharp dresser, he carried a dark, pinstriped suit jacket over his shoulder as the warm April sun beat down during another visit to the garden. He is quick to grin and crack a joke, but underlying his relaxed demeanor, he is deadly serious about saving the nation's plants. McCook, on the other hand, is a woman of the earth. Affable and attractive, she is sturdily built, thirtyish, blond, and slightly smudged with good Missouri soil; dressed in blue jeans and a tee shirt, she carries a potting trowel the way a baseball coach constantly totes a fungo bat—as if it were attached. She speaks rapidly and excitedly in a Southern accent that has Texas written all over it, though she's actually from nearby Shreveport, Louisiana. She came to the botanical garden from the Smithsonian Institution, where she worked on a fellowship for two years; before that she earned her doctorate in taxonomy at Cornell University. She's done some very highly admired work with rare orchids of South America, related to our native lady slippers, plants that are among the rarest in the world.

On this particular visit, the topic was not orchids, but clover. Falk and McCook took me on a tour of the center's midwestern species. McCook pointed to a plant that looked remarkably similar to clover sown in thousands of farmers pastures, only this particular clover had been thought to be extinct until just a few years ago. "This is *Trifolium stoloniferum*," she announced. "There's lots of hope for this plant. I feel that it's going to be an overwhelming success story."

"Did you bring your cow?" Falk asked, with a grin. "This plant is related to *Trifolium repens*, which is a common clover of European origin. When the buffalo roamed at will across the prairie, this was one of their favorite meals."

One of the wonders of plant preservation in an era of diminishing habitat is that scientists in perhaps the most developed nation in the world still are able to find species never before recorded and, from the extant written record and whatever anthropological clues there are, piece together a profile of the plant. *Tri. repens*, for instance, known more informally as running buffalo clover, was first rediscovered in woodland edges in Kentucky, southern Ohio, and West Virginia. From written records and herbarium specimens, botanists surmise that the plant once was native to the entire lower Midwest. It grows in moist, fertile soil, often near streams or ponds, and prefers the shade found in woodland edges. The scant historical record indicates that running buffalo clover—or else plants very similar to it—was often found along bison trails, and that it actually depended on the disturbed habitat created by the trampling of bison hooves to reduce competition from other plants. There are also indications that it grew in areas disturbed by fire—either fires that the Indians set deliberately or else the great prairie fires sparked from lightning that were so common before the nation's settling by Europeans. The Indians, dependent on bison as a food source, knew the ecological value of fire in building a mosaic of plants along the prairie so that certain species didn't crowd out the others. In setting fires, they tried to ensure that they would always have a population of bison to hunt in their area by keeping a healthy supply of the animals' favorite foods on hand. Natural fires, while still occurring today, do little to foster species diversity because the habitat is so fragmented.

"Two hundred years ago in a one hundred-square-mile area of tallgrass prairie a fire spreading downwind in the right season would cover an enormous area," Falk observed. "Today, if one breaks out, they call in the fire department."

One of the reasons McCook holds high hopes for running buffalo clover is that the plant reproduces vegetatively instead of by seed—its spreading runners put down roots that can take over an area. If it can be reintroduced into an area where deer predation is minimal, it propagates itself rapidly and efficiently. In a prime example of what Falk calls integrated conservation, he and McCook are working not only to save running buffalo clover at the botanical garden, but also are coordinating efforts between a Missouri state botanist who is studying where the proper habitat might be for reintroduction, and the state and federal officials to get permission to reintroduce it. The chain of integrated conservation organizations that includes the Center for Plant Conservation consists of networks of botanical gardens and arboreta throughout the country that, through the center, might work with U.S. Fish and Wildlife specialists who reintroduce species on appropriate sites.

The crux of the problem of plant preservation lies at the very beginning of life: the seed itself. McCook is quick to point out that she and other plant conservationists too often work in a vacuum when it comes to their knowledge of endangered plants. Because no one before them ever wanted to cultivate many of the plants, there is great mystery about how to save and store the seeds.

"It's a real guessing game at times," she said. "We have some of the best horticulturists in the Midwest working with us, but nobody has ever cultivated some of these plants before so we often have to immediately hedge our bets by growing as much seed as possible in the hopes that we lose as little of the population as possible. At the Missouri Botanical Garden, we make a big effort to work with the most endangered plants first. Doing so, we find we're really grabbing at the tip of the iceberg. We want to get them growing now because in ten years it might be too late."

There are several examples of these rare plant that were growing in the cold frames. One, *Lesquerella filiformis*, is a diminutive annual native to Missouri's limestone glades, the grassy, thin-soiled spaces with limestone rock emerging from the surface. If the glades are not burned regularly, trees, predominately cedars, and other plants tend to take over the limited habitat. Our endangered *Lesquerella* species, also called bladderpods because of their hollow, spherical fruits, grow in scattered sites in Kentucky and Tennessee.

The Missouri bladderpod, in full bloom in April, is a plant with seed that germinates in the fall—most plant seed in the area germinates in the spring. A thin-rooted, spindly annual, it looks like a wildflower in the best sense of the word. McCook works closely with a plant ecologist at Northeast Missouri State University in Kirksville, Michael Kelrick, who keeps her supplied with seed that she gamely tries to store. At the botanical garden's Woodland Garden, she is building an artificial miniglade to grow plants like the bladderpods so she can study how the plants grow and self-seed.

Successful storing of seeds varies among plant species. Rare oak seed, for instance, doesn't thrive well stored in refrigerators or on dry shelves like seed of most other plants; it prefers being snuggled in moist soils. McCook dries many seeds with a dessicant to get enough moisture out so the seeds won't rot. Often, she will divide seed populations, dry-storing some and cold-storing others. Sometimes she sends seeds to a USDA seed storage facility where they put them in ultra-low-temperature storage facilities. One such place in Denver, Colorado, will store seed and hold them for years so there are always banks of populations.

Browsing among the cold frames, we peered not only at one rare specimen after another, but at a floral history of the region. *Apios priceana*, or Price's groundnut, is a vine legume that grows underground from a large tuberous root. After overwintering, it shoots up beautiful long vines with pink and lavender flowers. Very few populations of the plant now exist in the wild, located in five southern and midwestern states. One of these populations exists on a deeply eroded hillside in Mississippi, nestled between a bustling highway and a new house in suburbia. University of Mississippi biologists are studying the tubers of Price's groundnut, a member of the bean family, to see if they could be developed into a commercial form of starch.

The researchers, McCook said, may have borrowed this idea from the Indians. There is evidence that Native Americans encouraged the plants to grow throughout the midwestern and midsouthern region because they dug the tubers and ate them with the same gusto as the Irish consumed potatoes. These clues, derived from observing where the remnant populations exist, are surprising anthropological insights into Indian culture—most Indians in the region mainly have been typified as hunter-gatherers, but the existence of the few remaining populations of Price's groundnuts indicates they had agricultural leanings as well.

Falk pointed out *Plantago cordata*, the heart-leaved plantain, and remarked about its peculiar necessities for survival: Found typically along clear-running, gravel-bottomed streams, this plantain's seeds have a sticky coating that serves as a sort of float, carrying them after the fall from the plant's fruits downstream to the nearest gravel bar where they stick to the gravel and germinate right where they land. The plant needs clear water and undisturbed streams, not too common commodities in the Midwest any longer, although there are populations in Illinois and Missouri, including a few on the outskirts of St. Louis. Disturbed habitat and water pollution have contributed to the plant's poor seed germination, leading to its dramatic decline.

"It's really problematic how a plant like this one will survive in the short term," Falk said. "Water pollution has really done a number on it. We do know that where it grows, it does fine. We'd love to see it expand, but there are so many other variables involved in its life cycle—keeping its habitat and then making sure the habitat stays clean—that we can't be overly optimistic about it. Protecting, managing, and ultimately maintaining habitat is the cornerstone of conservation work."

We walked past the plants up a slight incline that faced a crusty stone building, a tall smokestack running up its side, the old coal-fired powerhouse for Henry Shaw's greenhouses. The new heating system is a hot-water boiler pumped through pipes from the powerhouse to the greenhouses. There are plans to remove the obsolete smokestack.

"When I knew I was coming here, I kind of balked," McCook said of her relocation to St. Louis. "I thought, 'the Midwest, there's nothing there but cornfields.' But I was wrong. "There's a remarkably rich flora here, and I can't wait to explore it."

OF DUCKS AND LINCOLN'S VALLEY

Steve Havera, director of the Forbes Biological Field Station, Havana, Illinois, banding a wood duck for a population study on the nesting area near the Lake Chautauqua National Wildlife Refuge. *(Courtesy of Max Schnorpf, State of Illinois Comptroller's Office)*

Of Ducks and Lincoln's Valley

Havana, Illinois, lounges on the Illinois River about two-thirds downstream from the river's source southwest of Chicago. A picturesque town of 4,000, Havana is a "Little Easy" of the Heartland. Like her big sister New Orleans, Havana has seen grander times but still retains a congenial flavor of the past. There are several ways to approach the town, all of them scenic, none of them interstates. Perhaps the most compelling is Route 97 out of Springfield, a trek through history and tradition, quietly blending myth and memories of three state giants, Lincoln, Masters, and Sandburg, and revealing a beguiling natural landscape.

On the way to Havana, a dozen or so miles out of Springfield on 97, you pass the site of New Salem. A re-creation of the village where Lincoln tended Denton Offut's general store, New Salem is where Honest Abe first ran for public office, fell in love with Ann Rutledge, paced the forest understory in his famed dark depression after her death, joined the militia to fight Chief Black Hawk, studied law, honed his reputation as rail splitter and master wrestler, and finally left to enter politics and practice law in Springfield. The road drops into a wooded valley at New Salem, log houses, ox-drawn carts, and a water-powered mill on the Sangamon all visible from the windshield. Lincoln's presence along the road is palpable. Carl Sandburg's craggy touch is ubiquitous, too, in the rolling, sandy hills along the riverbanks. Although Galesburg, some sixty miles to the northwest, was

Sandburg's home, his description in his famed Lincoln biography is so evocative the feeling a reader has in passing through is one of déjà vu.

Beardstown, a sister city of Havana some thirty miles downstream, is my own birthplace. Every time I pass through this valley, I feel my past, and a link to Lincoln, with whom many native Illinoisans feel an ethereal, haunting kinship. In Beardstown's city hall on the town square, still in place as it had been in the 1850s, is the trial room where Lincoln defended Duff Armstrong, the son of old friends, in a murder charge. There he proved in a famous defense, known as the Almanac Trial, that Duff's accuser, who said he witnessed Duff killing a man by the light of the moon, could not possibly have seen anything that night because the almanac showed that there was no moon visible that evening. If you should ever see the city hall, walk its wooden floors, and view the tiny jury box and witness stand, you can very nearly see Lincoln again, too.

To get to Havana, you go over the Sangamon River, at this juncture a surprisingly wide, dashing stream, making its journey to empty into the Illinois north of Beardstown. Lincoln poled flat boats of goods down this stream, and then floated down the Illinois to the Mississippi near present-day Grafton, and then all the way down to New Orleans, where he first saw slaves being sold at a market. The sight of that auction touched him so profoundly, it has been said, that it indelibly imprinted his antislavery attitude. Today, most of the Sangamon is so narrow and silted that it seems impossible ever to have sailed on it at all. But Lincoln did, and the experience helped mold the character of one who advanced from the quiet valley all the way to the White House.

This stretch of Illinois is a remarkable bottomland, seemingly formed out of three rivers, the Sangamon, the Spoon, and the Illinois, but it actually is a geologic remnant of a time when the Mississippi River, nearly 21,000 years ago, carved the Illinois River floodplain from the St. Louis area all the way north of Peoria to the little town of Henry. The last of the three big glaciers, the Wisconsin, moved the Mississippi west to its present location. The glacier melted, its waters forming the Illinois River in a basin that is 327 miles long. All along the basin, more than 300 lakes and sloughs were found, most of them formed from the natural settling of the Illinois River.

The soil in Mason County and on the east side of the river where the glacier stopped—Cass and Tazewell counties—is sandy. Irrigation rigs stroll through the fields of corn and soybeans to bolster porous soils ideal for growing melons. Fruit and vegetable stands abound every few miles along the road, ranging from tiny ma-and-pa operations to long, permanent buildings that sell tomatoes, gourds, and pumpkins beyond the melon season. The melons are regionally famous. Beardstown cantaloupes, the first of the season in the region, are highly valued and sold in markets from the historically famous Soulard Market in downtown St. Louis, to grocery stores in Peoria, Chillicothe, and all the way north to Morris.

Before reaching Havana on Route 97, you come to Petersburg, Illinois, a stately old town, the home of Edgar Lee Masters, whose *Spoon River Anthology* anticipated Sandberg's literary imprint on the valley. The Masters home is preserved in the village, replete with atmosphere and antique shops. The occasionally isolated, lonely lives of the people that Masters evoked in his poems are belied by the present cheery face of Petersburg.

Ten miles north lies Havana, a town today, as in the past, that is awash with ducks. The school athletic teams are called the Ducks. A local blues singer and his band, Pork and the Havana Ducks, a gargantuan fellow and his gang of good ol' boys, played all the towns in the bistate area during their heyday in the seventies. Much of the bric-a-brac for sale in downtown Havana, in one form or another, reflects the duck motif. That the town should identify with ducks is only natural: The Havana area is an integral part of the Mississippi valley flyway, the corridor for thousands of migrating ducks, geese, even eagles and osprey that pass through each fall. There is water aplenty in the Havana area. The Spoon River empties into the Illinois at Havana, the Sangamon about thirty miles downstream north of Beardstown, yet the area's remaining bottomland lakes from Peoria to Meredosia, southwest of Beardstown, have long been the bread and butter of waterfowl habitat in the Illinois River valley.

Three highways, 97, 136, and 78, converge at Havana. You can find anything in the town from the Wareco Station, a bustling marvel of entrepreneurship where attendants in white uniforms and red caps will service your car in the honored tradition of full oil and water checks, a complete window wash, and a check of the air pressure in your tires. Everything from a loaf of bread to shotgun shells can be bought in the store inside, and people scoot in and out all day long to chat, shop, or simply to use the restrooms outside. Just west of the Wareco Station, over a rise that may have been a riverbank thousands of years ago, rests downtown Havana, Mason County seat. The courthouse here is new by Heartland standards, built maybe just fifty years ago in contrast to the ubiquitous Civil War monument to the soldiers of the valley who gave their lives in the great fraternal conflict.

Downtown Havana is a mishmash of old brick storefronts and renovated buildings with shingled faces. Many of the old stores are going out of business or are for sale. On a fair October morning a few weeks before duck-hunting season opened, I strolled downtown Havana, passing Del's Men's and Women's Apparel, which offered merchandise along the sidewalk at up to 50 percent off, and Moehring's Hardware, which topped Del's with 70 percent reductions, but had so little inventory left it could not sport a sidewalk sale. Park's Family Shoes already had beaten the other businesses to the barn door, as had two boarded-up bars off the main drag. Though far from dead, Havana is a very different entity than it was in the 1940s when it, Beardstown, and Peoria were what the old-timers call "wide-open" towns, where gambling, booze, jazz, and anything else were centerpieces of midwestern popular culture. In the waning years of this century, Havana still thrives, though more as a bedroom community for Peoria and Springfield—nearly equidistant—than as its own force.

Nowadays, at first blush, nothing much of consequence appears to be happening in Havana and the timeless Illinois River valley. However, Dr. Steve Havera, director of the Forbes Biological Field Station just north of town, will tell you differently. He knows the placid valley conceals some dark secrets. He'll tell you that the Illinois River, its bottomland lakes, and feeder streams, are filling up with sediment, topsoil displaced from careless decades of intensive row-crop farming, intensified after World War II and continuing today, combined with wasteful deep moldboard plowing. The clogging of these ecosystems has changed the habitat for the waterfowl migrating through the valley, diminishing their supply of moist-soil plants and increasing the toxins such as ammonia, mercury, lead, and PCBs gathered in the sediment, and decreasing the number of benthic organisms available for diving duck species, which have disappeared throughout the valley. The Illinois River valley faces biological extinction from sedimentation; such bottomland lakes as Chautauqua and Peoria could be dead bodies in less than twenty years. The legacy of duck hunting over the decades, lead shot, has been killing waterfowl and will do so for years to come because of the persistence of the element in the soil. Ducks and geese, detecting the hard, seedlike shot intended to kill them, ingest it mistaking it for legitimate food, the toxic lead destroying the birds despite the hunters' errant shots. The alterations in habitat, the filling in of the Illinois River valley with sediment, like the settling in of houses and urban sprawl on Illinois farmlands and the Missouri Ozark hills south and west of St. Louis, have made a seemingly pastoral environment a quietly mordant one.

The Forbes Biological Field Station, named after Stephen A. Forbes, the state biologist who established the site in 1894, was the first inland aquatic biological station in the United States to be equipped for ongoing investigation and the first in the world to seriously study a river's ecosystem. Because of the abundance of records housed there and the nearly one hundred years of continual study, the Illinois River is considered to be the most studied river system in the world. Its history is checkered at best, and Havera, as director of the station and a successor of Forbes himself, knows it as well as anyone alive.

"It's estimated that the Illinois River would naturally fill up with sediment within the next 1,000 to 2,000 years, but here we've almost done it—in only forty years," said Steve Havera, with a disapproving shake of his head. "When you fly over the greater Mississippi valley all you see up to the rivers is farmland, when those areas used to be marshes, wetlands, and bottomland forests. Rivers per se are a figment of the imagination. We have allowed the best topsoil in the world to ruin some of the best wetlands in the world. That's not very wise public policy, is it?"

Steve Havera is a tall, rangy man, dark haired and youthful in bearing. He has a pleasant, angular face. There is often a smile on it, despite his strong convictions and indignation about ecological wrongs to the Illinois River valley. When you meet Steve Havera, you have the rare opportunity to encounter someone who loves what he's doing and, furthermore, is aware of that fact. His job he has desired since he was a very young man, the way a high school athlete dreams of making the pros. Some of those he has admired the most, such as Forbes and Frank A. Bellrose, have held the position he now has. And he has realized his professional dream without leaving the Illinois River valley, which is his home.

Like so many conservationists, he exudes the outdoors even when he is captive inside a building. We were sitting in what had been the garage of the old Illinois Natural History Survey Biological Station outside Havana. It is now a comfortable conference room, surrounded by pictures and drawings of Illinois River valley fauna. The new addition to the old building, which was built in 1940, is courtesy of a National Science Foundation grant of $50,000 matched by State of Illinois funds that were awarded in 1986. There is a panoramic view of central Illinois wheat and cornfields out the east window, and woods out the west window, the trees decorated with nesting boxes for wood ducks.

Dr. Havera and an aquatic ecologist colleague, Richard E. Sparks, wrote the grant proposal for the new addition, which houses computer rooms, a library, studies, and laboratory space, making it a minireplica of the grand old Natural History Survey Building on the University of Illinois campus. Writing is one of the many fortes of this Heartland Renaissance man, who also owns a 180-acre farm and conducts myriad science experiments relating to much of the valley's wildlife. He has written scores of articles published by the *Illinois Natural History Survey* and other journals, works that have been distributed worldwide. He is presently working on a book, *The Waterfowl of Illinois*, a definitive study of its kind. An ideal week, he told me, would be one in which he is writing at least half of the time, with the rest devoted to research and educational outreach programs to schools in the area.

Born and raised in Peoria, Steve Havera fell in love with the river as a young boy, fishing, hunting, and exploring the river and its bottomland lakes. He completed undergraduate school, majoring in biology, at Bradley University in Peoria, then enrolled at the University of Illinois. He briefly toyed with the idea of farming with an uncle outside of Pana in east-central Illinois. In his early days of graduate school at Illinois, he was drafted into the army during the Vietnam conflict, and served in the military police for two years. He returned to the University of Illinois and received his M.S. in 1973, and his Ph.D. in January 1978. He worked at the Urbana headquarters until June 1978 when he transferred to the Havana station, fulfilling his boyhood dreams. In 1982, he became director of the then Havana field station.

As we traded stories about our past, it became obvious that we had followed similar trails, had encountered many of the same people: the valley, Lincoln's valley, was part of both of us; we had attended the same university, both of us working for the state and with the same state scientists, though this was our first meeting. Perhaps out of this familiarity, I felt between us what can only be described as a sort of *aficion*, as defined by Hemingway in *The Sun Also Rises*. We spoke of things in the valley, knowing of them the way others might not perceive them. Thus, when Steve Havera registers sadness or disgust— which he does with a disdainful curl of his lips, or a shake of the head—I felt or "knew" the emotion instantly.

"The Illinois River has seen lots of trouble in this century, and when you want to talk of the natural history of Illinois, you begin with the river," he said. "Before the turn of the century, it was an ecological marvel. But in roughly ninety years, we've lost approximately twenty-five out of forty-nine species of mussels out of the Illinois, and 67 percent of all fish species that were present before settlement are now extinct, or else their numbers are highly depressed. That leaves only about forty truly viable fish species in the river. Aquatic plants such as pond weeds have drastically declined, and that in turn affects fish populations that use the plants for spawning sites and protection for fry. The loss of the plants means reduced numbers of waterfowl that feed on them or their seeds. Invertebrates and zooplankton need them for habitat, so there's yet another decline. The same with moist-soil plants, which grow on mud flats and are excellent food for waterfowl. They are often inundated with water at a critical growth time because of more rapid water runoff to the river and the inability of the silted-in bottomland lakes to hold water. Sedimentation, pollution, and disturbance of the river have played the major roles in these developments, and they can all be traced to human activities."

Sedimentation, Havera explained, hurts aquatic plant communities because it generates turbidity in the river, which in turn eliminates the sunlight needed for photosynthesis. It leaves the river bottom too soft for the plants to get the firm hold in the bottoms they need in order to stand up to wave action caused by fish and commercial and recreation boats.

Missionary zeal first brought Europeans to the valley in the late 1600s when Marquette and Jolliet first sailed upstream, followed by La Salle a few years later and hosts of Jesuits seeking to convert the Native Americans. In the 1700s, beaver was the draw, as the valley was seemingly rich in that commodity so highly valued in the East, Canada, and the Old World. But the fur trade, it was found, was even richer west of the Mississippi River, and white intrusion spilled over westward for the next 150 years. Meanwhile, pioneers, noting the rich, fertile prairie, set about clearing the woods and draining the prairies, putting plows to the soil and settling in communities along the river and its tributaries. The hostilities of the Black Hawk War of 1832, though confined mainly to northern Illinois and southern Wisconsin, brought violence to the valley in incidents near Ottawa, Peoria, and far upstream near Hennepin. At war's end, all of the Indians were placed west of the Mississippi River in Iowa and Kansas, leaving the valley open to the thriving era of the Industrial Revolution.

The series of human assaults against the Illinois River and its accompanying ecosystems did not intensify until around the turn of the century when drainage began. Then, in 1900, the Sanitary and Ship Canal was opened at Chicago, diverting Lake Michigan water bearing enormous loads of raw sewage and industrial wastes down the Illinois River. Chicago then, as now, was the burgeoning hub of Illinois: Its drinking water was drawn from Lake Michigan, but its beaches were becoming unsightly with the washed-up detritus of civilization. So they sent it all downstream, severely polluting the upper Illinois River.

"By 1927, the amount of water coming into the valley was estimated at 10,000 cubic feet per second," Havera said. "That raised the water levels here about three feet, flooding the area often but most importantly killing off pin oaks and pecans, excellent wildlife food sources that are absent to this day."

In the 1930s, the Lake Michigan diversion was changed to 3,200 cubic feet per second, where it stands today despite recurrent rumors of its increase, such as happened in the drought of 1988 when state officials considered upping the flow to offset low water conditions throughout the valley. But the upper Great Lakes states and Canada firmly refused because every inch of water taken out of the St. Lawrence Seaway makes a big impact on the economies of shipping and generating hydroelectric power along the seaway.

Although the Illinois River still receives diverted Lake Michigan water, its quality has much improved over the decades due to the installation of sewage-treatment plants in Chicago and other municipalities and stringent water pollution laws.

The second major disturbance to the river involved the development of thirty-eight drainage and levee districts and three private levees for agriculture between 1880 and 1926. These structures removed 200,000 acres of an existing 400,000-acre area of floodplain, draining natural habitat for waterfowl and animal species from La Salle in north-central Illinois to the river's mouth near Grafton, close to St. Louis. Levees were constructed that were twenty-five feet tall, drainage ditches dug so water could continually be pumped out, protecting the newly created farmland from the caprice of the river.

"With the development of the levee and drainage districts, we lost natural lakes and other habitat," Dr. Havera told me. "Because half of the river's floodplain had been levied, the river couldn't spread out anymore. This, in effect, raised the flood height. Engineers estimated in the 1940s that if the same amount of water came down the Illinois River valley as in 1904 before most of the levees were built, the flood heights would be ten feet higher; that is, the river cannot handle the same amount of water without causing the flooding of unprotected land. In recent years, we've had more floods along the Illinois. The remaining lakes are filled with sediment. The lakes now receive all of the silt load instead of half of it as they would if the river could spread out on its own."

Later, in the 1930s, six major dams were constructed along the Illinois River to change what had been a river into a channel roughly seven feet deep and flowing, or rather oozing, at the incredibly sluggish pace of less than a mile per hour. The dams created enormous restraining pools that governed the river's already slow speed.

What happened over the course of these changes was the destruction of a river and its affiliated ecosystems. In the first decade of this century, Havera pointed out, there were 2,500 commercial fishermen on the Illinois and slightly more musselers. The river was considered to be one of the best sport and commercial streams in the nation, and perhaps the best mussel river in the country. Today, commercial fishermen still exist on the Illinois, in numbers too insignificant to count, and mussels are still taken from the river, the market being the Japanese, who value them for the pearl-making process. Most of the fish trade is for carp and catfish, although a few stretches are good sportfishing. Water quality of the river has actually improved since the early part of the century, although it suffered grievously in the sixties and seventies. Today, trace amounts of chlordane and PCBs can be found in the water. In 1991, the EPA imposed restrictions on eating certain fish taken north of Peoria because of high PCB levels found in fish samples. The levels of these chemicals found in the river are not generally high enough to warrant alarm, according to the EPA, yet they are an ever-present signal that many of the wrong things are still reaching the waters of the Illinois.

Over a dozen species of ducks regularly visit the Illinois River valley near Havana each year on their migration from the north to wintering areas principally in Arkansas and Louisiana. Canada and snow geese accompany them. Steve Havera and I strolled through the halls of Forbes Biological Field Station past glass-enclosed cases that held mounted ducks and geese of the valley, handsome creatures, especially the robust-looking geese. Some major duck species include blue-winged and green-winged teal, American wigeon, the northern pin-tail, mallard, black duck, wood duck, ring-necked duck, canvasback, and hooded and common merganser. Among the races of Canada geese are Richardson's and the Giant Canada goose. Each bird presented a story in itself, but Havera was most interested in success stories, particularly the wood duck and Canada goose, both now abundant in the valley.

"The wood duck was nearly harvested to extinction in Illinois early in the twentieth century because there had been no restrictions on shooting them in the early spring when they returned from overwin-tering," he said as we walked up the stairs. "But they're now the most abundant duck in Illinois because of approximately forty years of hunting restrictions. The Giant Canada goose was thought to have been extinct, but Dr. Harold Hansen of the survey rediscovered a few in 1962 and the Illinois Department of Conservation began a reintro-duction program in 1969. Today, the Giant Canada Goose represents 16 percent of all harvested geese in the Mississippi flyway. Between 1985 and 1990, the Giant Canada goose nesting sites in Illinois increased from a handful of counties to all 102 counties. I have a pair of Giant Canada geese on my farm pond. They hatched seven goslings this spring. It's a thrill to see their comeback right on your own property."

One and one-half million Canada geese were gearing up now to pass through the Mississippi valley flyway, Havera pointed out, compared with just about 300,000 ten years ago. Why, he asked rhetorically, are Canada geese doing better than certain duck species such as the familiar mallard and pintail, both of which have depressed popula-tions? One reason might be that the Canada geese nest farther north than the duck species—on the western James Bay and southern shore of the Hudson Bay in Ontario—in remote areas not nearly as exploited by humans as are the nesting habitats of the duck species. Many ducks nest in the Dakota and Canadian prairies, which have been beleaguered by drought in recent years. A good number of potholes favored by ducks dried up and were tilled for crops, ruining the breeding habitat. Once the drought subsides, Dr. Havera believes, the mallard and pintails should do better.

At the top of the stairs, Steve Havera introduced two of his assistants, Katie Roat and Michelle Georgi. A tall woman with a bit of gray in her hair, Katie Roat manages inventory, the library, day-to-day activities, and exhibits of the Forbes Biological Station. She has coauthored publications with Havera, including one on the history of the station. A long-time citizen of the valley, Roat has nearly the same grasp of the valley's biological history as Havera. Young, blond and athletic looking, Michelle Georgi, like Havera, is tinged with the outdoors. She conducts weekly censuses of ducks and geese in Illinois by accompanying a licensed pilot on flights throughout the state and counts the number of ducks and geese she finds in various habitats. While the numbers are not 100 percent accurate, the method provides a reliable index and is much more expedient than the old method—censuses by ground observations.

"I can census the major wetlands in the whole state in two days this way," Michelle Georgi explained to me. "A ground count would take weeks."

But this kind of duck counting is not for the fainthearted. She has the pilot swoop down to a few hundred feet above land during the census flights; the pilot is accustomed to the rapid descents during the growing season, but Georgi is not a barnstormer by temperament. She only does this about half the year, during fall and spring migration. Yet, she emphasized, she loves it.

"She's quite talented," Havera said admiringly, after Georgi returned to her office. "Among her other qualities is a strong stomach. Most folks lose their lunch on flights like that."

The census data are invaluable to the study of waterfowl, he added. The aerial census in Illinois was started in 1948 by then director Frank Bellrose. Figures have been kept every year since. For instance, Havera pointed out, in 1948 there was a census high of 1.5 million mallards counted in the Illinois River valley. The peak count in 1990 was 300,000. During the interim, the numbers have fluctuated, but the trend clearly shows a disturbing decline and the main reason for it, again, Havera emphasized, is sedimentation and degradation of habitat.

"Mallards make up 80 percent of the duck species passing through the Illinois River valley," he explained. "They've become much more dependent on waste grain in adjacent farm fields than on their natural habitat, aquatic plants, which disappeared because of sedimentation. Even waste grain is less abundant than in the past because harvesting equipment is much more efficient these days and fall tillage more prevalent.

"Our records show in 1940 seeds and parts of aquatic plants comprised 15 percent of a mallard's diet. In 1980, the number was zero. Mallards primarily fed on corn and moist-soil plants—plants that grow on mud flats—in recent years, plus other plants such as Japanese millet and buckwheat, planted by duck clubs and staff at public hunting areas. Now, this is an important fact because if the habitat is there for the ducks they'll stay for a couple of weeks to stock up and replenish themselves for their migration. If it's not there, they'll leave in a day or two to find more suitable food sources elsewhere. Undoubtedly, one reason there are not as many mallards as before is the loss of food source."

A dead duck's gizzard reveals a lot about the creature and its environment. Katie Roat took me into a bright, clean room lined with wooden shelves and sliding drawers. She slid out one drawer loaded with small glass jars containing seeds removed from mallard and other duck species' gizzards. There were duckweed, seeds of wild rice, pondweeds, sorghum, bulrush, smartweed, coontail, water and pond lilies, corn, soybean, and at least a dozen others. She also showed mussel shells and buttons made from Illinois River species and a jar of fingernail clams in solution, cute, dark, curling tiny creatures that, living up to their names, look like clipped fingernails of infants. Fingernail clams, a prime food source for diving ducks, are now very scarce in the Illinois River, as are diving ducks themselves, which now stop during migration mainly along the Mississippi River.

"A disturbing trend is showing up now on the Mississippi River," Havera said, joining us. "We're seeing fewer diving ducks along the Mississippi than in the past, another indication that it is filling in with sediment like the Illinois."

Approximately 300 species of plants have been found in the gizzards of mallard ducks over the years as well as 65 species of animals, primarily aquatic invertebrates such as the fingernail clams, snails, and aquatic worms, reflecting an incredibly diverse diet. Between 1979 and 1982, Illinois Natural History Survey scientists analyzed the gizzards of 9,600 mallard ducks and found evidence of this smorgasbord, plus a few surprises.

"We also saw that they were eating seeds of some plants that you would think are pretty unattractive to them," Havera said. "We've found multiflora rose, poison ivy, and osage orange, or hedge, seeds, all pretty tough on the digestive track. We've even found marijuana seeds. That was one happy duck. He stayed around a while, I bet."

Havera laughed and went downstairs to find his camouflage coat and hat. He wanted to show me some of the wildlife refuge behind the station. A low blanket of clouds was moving in, bringing a misty rain and chilly temperatures, a signal that the ducks would be flying soon, followed shortly thereafter by the geese, blanketing the valley in just a few days. We crossed Quiver Creek—a roiling stream here, dammed a few hundred yards to the north—on a suspension bridge strung with fifty-year-old cable from the University of Illinois at Urbana. The bridge, about twenty-five feet above the creek, swayed with our quick, light steps. Havera explained that the creek was named by early settlers who thought the peatlike ground along the creek and lake seemed to shake or quiver. Across the bridge, Havera turned right, heading north along the gravel road on top of the levee that runs around the Lake Chautauqua Refuge, government land owned and operated by the U.S. Fish and Wildlife Service. He moved over to the sandy banks of the levee that holds back Lake Chautauqua and scooped up some sand.

"Talk of what you can find in a duck's gizzard," he said, sifting the sand. "Well, throughout this soil and in areas elsewhere throughout the valley you can find expended lead shot. It's been here for years and has been a negative factor on duck populations. This is the first year a total ban on lead shot has gone into effect, and we hope we'll soon start seeing results from it."

Our society has long been concerned with the lead found in houses, gasoline, and in industrial waste, but it took over a century, Havera explained, to bring a total ban on the use of lead shot to hunt ducks.

The battle to halt the use of lead shot has been a long, tough one, fought by some of the Illinois Natural History Survey luminaries such as Havera's predecessor Frank Bellrose, and former head of the Center of Wildlife Ecology Glen Sanderson. The manner of death for waterfowl ingesting lead is gruesome, but the public has long been indifferent, and skeptical hunters have fought the change for fear that a shift to steel shot would tend to be more crippling to waterfowl instead of killing them cleanly, as they claim lead shot does, and out of concern that steel shot would damage shotguns. Also, waterfowl hunters long claimed that steel shot is not as effective at long range as lead shot. However, conservationists conducted many studies over the past two decades to dispel the myth of the messy kill. And modifications in steel shot were encouraged to develop better shot shells. Conservationists presented a plethora of convincing data to sway hunters gradually, and this fall would be the first when lead shot would truly be banned throughout the country.

Typically, waterfowl that are exposed to lead shot might only ingest one or two pellets. The effect sometimes is not instantaneous, as it would be with cyanide, for instance. Their bodies waste away over several weeks' time, losing as much as 50 percent of their original weight. A poisoned waterfowl is one sick, pathetic bird. It often cannot fly, and eventually cannot walk because of progressive paralysis in its wing and leg muscles. There is often a rattling in the throat and occasionally a yellow slime dribbles from the throat of an infected bird. Death by lead poisoning threatens many species of ducks and geese including mallards, black ducks, mottled ducks, redheads, ring-necked ducks, and canvasbacks, some of the most important game species found in the United States, comprising 43 percent of all game species. While the tables are turning in the right direction, the legacy of old practices—spent shot riddled throughout the wetlands of the valley—will take its toll on ducks and geese for years to come. Two to three million birds die annually from lead toxicosis in the United States. The number will gradually decrease with the ban on lead shot, but lead's toxic half-life is very potent and durable: The spent lead will stay lurking in the soil for many years.

"A recent study of ours on the Mississippi River showed some duck species with 30 to 60 percent elevated levels of lead in their blood," Havera said. "But we have been conducting these hunter compliance surveys, and examining the carcasses of harvested waterfowl at public hunting areas and places called commercial pickers, where they clean the carcasses after the kill. We use a modified metal detector that can tell what kind of pellets are in the fowl. Two years ago, we got 15 percent noncompliance with the new law. Last year, it was down to 3 percent. It takes time to adapt to a change. This is the first shooting change for waterfowl hunting since 1935, when they did away with live decoys and the use of bait to lure birds, as well as limiting the number of shells to be legally carried in a shotgun from five to three."

We passed the dam and took off down the road on a quiet walk through oak, sycamore, sumac, and maple trees, flush with moist fall colors, the mist in the air becoming now a gentle rain. Havera pointed to the somnolent backwaters of Quiver Creek. We were now in the Lake Chautauqua National Wildlife Refuge. Other wetlands along the Quiver are owned and maintained by private duck-hunting clubs, he pointed out.

"The clubs too often get a bad rap," he said. "Many people erroneously view hunters as somehow despoiling nature, maybe simply because they are shooting ducks and geese, but waterfowl hunters are the ones maintaining and preserving these wetlands for habitat. They pay their way. Nature in the long scheme of things would be poorer without them. Take Ducks Unlimited, for instance. They're probably the waterfowl group with the highest profile. Recently, their emphasis has shifted from habitat in the north to areas farther south. They're trying to improve habitat."

There was a clatter in an oak tree, a raccoon whose routine we had disturbed taking refuge up the tree, pausing behind a branch to glare at us in a punitive, contentious way, then scurrying higher up, finally turning away from us indifferently.

Steve Havera reversed his course and headed back toward Forbes Station. The area immediately around us has been through more facelifts than the legendary Mae West. In the 1920s, just north of here, Havera told me, there was a big natural impoundment, Thompson Lake, that was claimed, drained, and farmed. It vanished from nature in its true form in the familiar tradition of nearly all the 8.3 million acres of wetlands that existed in Illinois before settlement. Today, Thompson Lake is the Thompson Lake Drainage and Levee District, part of a network of drainage districts throughout the lower Illinois valley. Today, there are only 400,000 acres of natural wetlands remaining in Illinois. If reservoirs and farm ponds are added to that number there are a total of about 1.5 million acres, with an estimated three-quarters of a million acres artificial. What wetlands are left, Havera stressed, are not nearly the same quality of what existed before.

"There's not a more productive system anywhere than a wetland," he said. "They restore the water table, purify the water we drink by breaking down the pollutants that wash into them, they trap the sediment and keep it from reaching the rivers and big lakes, and of course they're home to waterfowl and other wildlife. Unfortunately, we've abused them terribly, especially in the past one hundred years or so. More people are becoming aware of their value, but we need to get a handle on their real dollar value so we can compare the economics of an acre of wetlands with an acre of corn. We have long-entrenched government policies to pay farmers not to produce on some of their acres, yet over the century they've gotten the go-ahead to drain wetlands so they can make a buck. What's the result? Progress has always been linked with taming the environment. But can we really say that what has happened in the name of progress is real progress? I don't think so."

We passed the bridge and walked up the bluffs. Havera pointed at the tall, barren cottonwoods about us, a roosting spot for dozens of bald eagles that often winter in this part of the Heartland. During the cold months, Havera will sit at his desk on the second floor of the Forbes Station and pause for inspiration to gaze at the eagles, whose numbers have grown in the valley and throughout the Mississippi flyway in the past two decades. They would be returning here in a few weeks. Lake Chautauqua is the most used area in the lower Illinois River valley for bald eagles. The last census showed 1,500 eagles winter in Illinois alone, compared to as few as just 63 in 1960. The magnificent bird, the only sea or fishing eagle that lives in North America and, as every schoolchild knows, the symbol of our country, is among the largest of fowl on the continent, as long as forty-three inches with a wingspan typically of six to seven feet and a surprisingly light weight of between eight and fourteen pounds. While they primarily nest farther north in the continent, using Illinois and Missouri as a wintering site, nesting habitat has been observed in the Illinois River valley for the first time in 1986 and 1987, although the eagles later abandoned the sites. Nests have been confirmed in southern and far northern Illinois, and a confirmed sixteen eaglets were hatched in the state between 1978 and 1987.

Between 300 and 400 bald eagles winter along the Illinois River; the bulk of their number use the Mississippi. In a mild winter, more will spend the winter along the Illinois; they prefer the Mississippi in colder winters because of the profusion of dams, and thus easier fishing, along the Father of Waters. The eagle's comeback has resulted from its protected status, designated in 1940, which made it a federal offense to shoot, possess, or trade one. Also several pesticides, notably the infamous DDT, were banned. These chemicals had interferred with the reproductive success of eagles and other fish-eating species such as the peregrine falcon and double-breasted cormorant, through the process of bioaccumulation, a cycle which starts with fish consuming pesticides in the water, the eagle eating the tainted fish, the toxic concentration accumulating to the point that when the eagle hen lays her eggs, the shells are so thin the egg cracks, preventing the birth of eaglets. A summary of death causes to 1,429 bald eagles nationwide between 1963 and 1984, performed by the National Wildlife Laboratory, showed 23 percent, or 329, died from gunshot wounds, which was the highest cause of death. Various other traumas were next at 21.1 percent, followed by electrocution at 9.1 percent, accounting for 130 deaths. Lead poisoning caused 5.8 percent, or 83 deaths, and other poisonings, including pesticides, accounted for slightly less than 5.2 percent, or 75 deaths.

"They're a delight to watch," Havera said, peeling apart some tall grass. "They might even be taken off the endangered list in Illinois. It gives a fellow some hope."

Wood ducks skidded along the broad, mirrorlike waters of Lake Chautauqua, a body of water that nearly seemed to surround us as we stood in the October rain. They were taking off and landing with the frequency of traffic at a small municipal airport, their calls filling the moist air. Lake Chautauqua is a 4,500-acre wildlife refuge. A levee extends for fifteen miles all the way around the lake to keep the Illinois River from spilling into it. It is not always successful. A 1943 flood washed out the levee, and it is still weak, the river filtering in at various spots. While there is water everywhere here, one almost needs a scorecard to keep track of what was as opposed to what is. Havera mentioned two aerial photographs that showed this part of the valley in 1931 and 1978. The older picture shows both Quiver Lake to the south and Lake Chautauqua to the north, both of them two big healthy bodies of water. The 1978 photo showed wide swaths of Quiver Lake filled in with sedimentation and mud flats on Lake Chautauqua.

"It's beautiful," I said, nodding toward the lake.

"Looks ten feet deep out there, doesn't it?" Havera posed, his dark eyes looking across the water. "It's only about three feet deep. In the summer, it gets down to only about a foot sometimes. Some of the best topsoil in the world is in there now, spilled over from the Illinois River.

"If you came here in mid-November, the lake would be filled with ducks and geese, about 50,000, but in the forties there were over a *million* ducks alone that came through here. The lake was eight feet deep, loaded with aquatic vegetation. There were two boat marinas on the lake. People came from all over the country to fish and hunt here."

He stopped, shook his head as only Steve Havera can do, transferring his sense of loss to me. Then he smiled tenuously. "With all of the technology and expertise we have shown in taking out the wetlands, we should be able to reinvigorate the few oases that are left and create even more. It's not cost-efficient to dredge the lake—it's 3,500 acres, and at $20 per cubic foot, that's a lot of money for a body of water that will fill in again in another five years if we don't keep the soil where it's supposed to be, in our agricultural fields. Some of the drainage and levee district should turn the pumps off and let the water seek its own level. We can put these bottomland areas into natural time capsules, restore quailty water and aquatic habitat. We can bring them back if we show people what a great value they are. If we need to farm the area again in another seventy or eighty years, turn the pumps back on."

We crossed Quiver Creek across the tremulous bridge and shook hands at my car. There I thanked him and asked him if he thought there was an upswing in people turning to nature.

"I think we live in a society that has become too high-pressured, too high tech, and more people are seeing that nature can provide a very nice, peaceful escape from that," he said. "Why, we just finished up with the Spoon River Scenic Drive Fall Festival, and those tours brought in nearly 150,000 people from all over. I think people are hungering for nature. That's good to see. It's what we need to do, to live with it, not beat it to submission, not tame it. We used to think that we inherited our nature, but for the last couple of generations we've been borrowing it from our children. We can't have that any longer." He slapped me on the back and returned to the Forbes Biological Field Station.

Katie Roat had mentioned an oddity in the valley that I had missed on my trip out. She had described two small hills visible along Quiver Beach Road that are Indian burial mounds. The rain was picking up, but I wanted to see the mounds, so I retraced my journey through the wooded trail of the Forbes Station, scaring up plump red foxtail squirrels darting among the spiky osage oranges, and got back on the road. About a mile away I noticed the white picket fence that enclosed two elevated areas that for all the world looked like anonymous hills overlooking Quiver Lake. I stopped and pondered them. Trees had grown about the green mounds, but the site had been left intact for hundreds of years.

In the 1920s, archaeologists had dug up remains slightly northwest of Havana, southeast of Lewistown, home of the Dickson Mounds State Museum. Artifacts and skeletal remains of Mississippian Indians are on display there, to some a gruesome sight, to others a fascinating panorama of what had been in the valley. Depending on one's perspective, the museum represents a valuable history lesson or a crass, heartless, ignoble eyesore. Under pressure from Native American groups and others the state of Illinois has finally agreed to close the museum. But there has been no such tampering with these mounds at

Havana, despite great pressure to see what's in there. It is thought, Katie Roat told me, that because of the dual nature of the mounds, prehistoric royalty are buried there. In all of Lincoln's valley, these unobtrusive burial mounds might bespeak even more than the monuments, displays, and recreations of Lincoln lore that abound. The mounds remain either to be despoiled or, maybe, with the luck of the eagles, to be treasured.

Missouri Dreamscape

Richard Coles, director of the Washington University Tyson Research Center, shows members of a field trip the remnants of a mouse that a shrike impaled on a locust-tree thorn at the Tyson Research Center, Eureka, Missouri. *(Courtesy of David Kilper, Washington University Photographic Services)*

C H A P T E R 5

Missouri Dreamscape

O nce you're past the bridge spanning the legendary Father of Waters, it's less than 30 miles from the signature St. Louis Arch to the Tyson Research Center in southwestern St. Louis County. Though it is a brief journey, it takes a traveler through two centuries of development in the nation's Heartland and deposits him in a natural dreamscape.

Interstate 44 is the trail you follow, a bustling six-laner that shoots past the grimy shells of factories, stacks of forlorn brick apartment buildings, some of them a century old; the sprawl of the St. Louis University Medical School complex, a part of the oldest educational institution in a city that has hoisted three flags in its existence; neat, venerable city neighborhoods like the Hill, a patch of brick shotgun houses settled a century ago by Italian immigrants, the city's most distinctive ethnic neighborhood that spawned Yogi Berra and Joe Garagiola and features a restaurant on every corner of its Old Town. And then, abruptly, the suburbs—Maplewood, Rock Hill, Webster Groves, Glendale, Kirkwood, Crestwood, Sunset Hills, each successive place name trendier than the last, the architecture of the houses yielding from the ubiquitous brick, with which St. Louis was built, to wood taken from Missouri and Arkansas timberlands. Blocks of limestone carved out of the hills to make way for the interstate flank the highway.

Crossing the Meramec River, you reach Fenton, a corporate town built around the massive Chrysler plant to your right, and the vista widens to encompass a flat valley, the floodplain of the Meramec, dotted with the golden arches, Hardees, 7-11s, minimalls, drive-up banking stations with names like Centerre, Mercantile, by now one of the area's few, vague reminders of its French heritage, dating back to the eighteenth century. The few open stretches of earth are littered with construction tractors gouging the land, port-o-potties, lumber scraps, and tumbling fast-food wrappers, essentials for the building of the next shopping mall or housing development. Suddenly, the land— rolling hills from just beyond the river—gradually rises and you get the distinct feeling you're not in St. Louis anymore. The hills are larger, the landscape more vast, and to either side of the highway forests of oak, hickory, cottonwood, sassafrass, and eastern red cedar have replaced the buildings, noise, plumes, and pall of St. Louis. At the crest of one hill you see a panorama, relatively free of people, the undulating carpet of trees that is the northernmost edge of the Ozark uplift. Realizing you've fled the industrial giant of 2.5 million to the east, your spirits rise, then drop as you see the highway signs urging you to slow for construction and a half acre of trees bulldozed to your right—it's apparent the state crews are widening the highway to accommodate the increasing stream of traffic from the west to St. Louis.

Nothing alerts the traveler to the existence of the Tyson Research Center. The forewarned know to look for exit 269, Antire and Beaumont, to make a quick right and follow the exit ramp to the top near a bridge that's one hundred yards south of the center. You make the right and see a dirt road, flanked by construction trailers and pickups, leading to a gate and house with rough-cut cedar siding to the right of the gate. Recently harvested logs are stacked neatly along the fence that is the perimeter of Tyson. Your eyes sweep to the left at the hill rising steeply above the checkpoint and see, obscured by trees, a billboard identifying the Tyson Research Center. A large cautionary yellow sign at the gate reads This Is Not Lone Elk Park, an important distinction because Lone Elk, which borders Tyson, is a county park, and Tyson is a private research and education center owned and operated by Washington University in St. Louis.

As you listen to the myriad calls of birds and take in the mystery of the road ahead of you that disappears seductively behind a stand of hardwood trees, you're hard put to think you've left St. Louis twenty miles behind and that just eight miles down I-44 is Six Flags Over Mid-America; three miles to the southwest is Times Beach, the dioxin-tainted ghost town that dominated much of the environmental news of the early eighties.

On a brilliant, leaf-splashed October afternoon, I followed this trail to keep an appointment with Richard Warren Coles, Ph.D., professor of biology at Washington University and director of the Tyson Research Center. Coles had invited me out for what he promised to be a thorough tour of the 2,000-acre living biological laboratory, where hundreds of species of higher life, in some function or another, are studied, and endangered and ailing species are bred and mended. The center houses the Wolf Sanctuary and the World Bird Sanctuary, formerly the Raptor Rehabilitation and Propagation Project, two privately owned groups that pay a modest rent to the Tyson Research Center but, apart from Coles's readily available consultation, are otherwise unaffiliated with the university. Although I had known Coles for nearly four years, I had never had the chance to fully tour Tyson. And lately, aside from interstate trips to relatives and airplane surveys of the continental United States. I had been far removed from nature and was feeling its autumnal, nostalgic pull. Coles had promised me lots of fresh air and glimpses of some of the nearly 1,000 species that exist in the Tyson domain.

Coles is a man healthfully obsessed with nature wherever he may find it, and he is fearful of the world's lost appreciation of it. A charismatic man who has studied a vast number of species, he can and will tell you how one species relates to a dozen others. Of all his projects, he is perhaps most troubled by the dwindling numbers of migrating songbirds, many of which winter in Central and South America and return to the United States and Canada to breed.

I pulled my car past the gate, stopped, and was met by an elderly, spry fellow dressed in Levi's blue. He told me to pull my car over to the side and come in to register. I stopped behind the checkpoint station alongside a hand-lettered ad for birdseed and got out of the car.

"Name's Cook, Ralph Cook," the man said, extending a hand. "Who you with?"

He shook hands with the surprisingly gentle, warm touch of a countryman, and I told him I was here to see Coles for a tour.

"That'll be a treat," he said. "Dick knows this place better'n anyone. Follow me. I'll give him a call."

I followed Ralph into the gatehouse, a cheery, oak-paneled building with the air of lost decades and another purpose to it, its approximately 1,000 square feet dominated by a warm, charcoal-colored, potbellied stove in the middle. Ralph signed me up on a visitor's sheet and got on the phone. I looked out a window as a pair of tiny birds I could not identify swooped past and darted to the woods, a refreshing sight after the ubiquitous crows that somehow dominate the St. Louis urban and suburban areas.

"Dick'll be out in a few minutes," Ralph said walking toward me. "He's got a call he's waiting on. Quite a place, isn't it? You probably know the army built this as an ammunition depot when the war broke out. There's about fifty-two bunkers scattered around these 2,000 acres. They'd store the ammo there and test weapons. I used to work not far from here. At night, you could hear the sound of guns in the hills when they'd be testing tracers and taking target practice. They used it for the Korean War, too, then passed it onto the university in 1963. I been retired now for eight years, but then I started helping out here. The next thing you know, I'm working again, but I couldn't have a better job. Ten days on, twenty days off. And Dick's a great boss. And what a birder. My gosh, I don't think I've ever met a better birder."

Another car pulled up and Ralph went out to greet a man who wanted to know if he could buy mealworms at the gatehouse. I overheard Ralph saying he was awaiting a shipment of mealworms from the university; a biologist named Suga, who studies bats, ships out his excess mealworms, a staple in the laboratory bats' diets, to Tyson, often via Coles, who should be arriving any minute, maybe with some worms. The two men chatted on the stoop and in the span of ten minutes two vans and several cars pulled in, the cars containing Tyson volunteers, the vans students and instructors from the University of Missouri at St. Louis (popularly referred to in St. Louis as UM-SUL) and St. Louis University. Researchers at these universities and others in the area conduct studies at Tyson at no cost, Coles had told me, and professors often schedule field trips to the preserve. Coles welcomes these visits because the investigations reveal even more about things happening at Tyson, to the advantage of everyone.

Coles, carrying a folder with some papers in it, got out from a Toyota pickup and walked toward the building. He wore blue jeans, running shoes, and a pullover sweater. He is a sturdy, vigorous six-footer with a long, heavy stride very much suited to the outdoors, almost a plowman's gait. He sports a snow-white Hemingwayesque full beard and his thinning hair, combed back, is as pale as the beard. There is great vitality in his face, a placid robustness that makes you think, somehow, of a Shakespearean actor. The eyes are blue, clear, and expressive, constantly vigilant. The face is a happy one.

He greeted me and then the visitor, whom he knew from previous visits, and apologized for not having the mealworms, though he would bring them out tomorrow and Ralph could refill the feeders.

"The mealworms draw the most incredible array of birds, especially bluebirds," he explained, and as we got into Coles's truck and headed toward the blacktop that leads to his office, we drove into the surreal blend of nature and history that is the Tyson Research Center. If you ignore the telephone lines to the left and the fact that you're driving on a blacktop, you feel that the environment around you the first quarter of a mile is as unspoiled as when the Shawnee and Osage roamed the woods.

Down a path on the right a grassy mound rises against a hill; from the distance, it looks as if the mound could be a burial ground, but Coles dispelled this notion. "I want to show you one of the bunkers, and what we've tried to do with them for research."

Coles brought the truck down the path and halted it in front of the bunker, which has a short set of steps leading to a small loading platform. He pulled open a steel door and I followed him into the cavernous maw of the bunker. It was cold, dark, and empty, a tiny cathedral that could have housed a small pioneer congregation, the altar in front, the choir where we stood.

Pointing a flashlight to the left, Coles revealed a ridged area fortified with cement and a black hose that led to it. "Some time ago," he began in his lilting cadence that echoed in the cavern, "there was a proposal to build a large dam upriver along the Meramec River, which at one point nearly abuts Tyson. Well, this project created controversy. Some people were bitterly opposed to the idea; others saw it as an improvement for the river. Caves were a focal point of the controversy because they harbor colonies of bats that use them as their winter habitat.

"One of my pipedreams is to develop a bunker as a refuge for hibernating bats. Two species, the Indiana and grey bat, are officially endangered because of loss of or disturbance to their habitat. I thought the bunkers were well suited for this purpose, and it could give us a chance to study them, especially during hibernation. But a problem with the bunker is humidity. You can feel it is cool in here, but not as moist as a natural cave. Bats need a habitat of at least 85 percent humidity to successfully complete hibernation. So we built this curb to the left and piped in water from a nearby spring. The resulting 'pond' elevates the humidity. Armed with appropriate permits, we brought in two dozen nonendangered (little brown) bats that fall. They hibernated promptly and spent the winter losing no more weight than the bats that we left undisturbed in their cave up the Meramec. Bats lose a bit of weight normally during hibernation. It was decided not to build the dam after all. So the bat project lost its urgency, but I still think it's a worthy enterprise. Someday, in addition to using a bunker as a bat hibernaculum, we might try to establish a breeding group here as well."

I noticed a box to my right and asked about it.

"Oh, that," he said, chuckling. "We were going to use this bunker as an example of what you could do to build a cavelike habitat for bats and other cave dwellers, when we realized we didn't have bats in here. So we brought a nuisance bat we had recently captured, just for authenticity. Here he is." Coles opened the box and revealed the quaint black geometry of the slumbrous creature, a big brown bat, tiny and inert.

"They're much smaller than people tend to believe they are, usually harmless, and are helpful as insect catchers. Someone has to care about them. They need a place to live as we all do," he said, closing the box and stepping out of the bunker.

"Hopefully, the members of a breeding group would return to the bunker as they would any natural cave," he said, walking down the steps. "I've also thought of enclosing the area outside the door with a big net, leaving the door open so bats in the group could move back and forth between the 'cave' and the external world."

We were on the road again, passing bunkers on either side identified by green signs that said Igloo 19, Igloo 22, army nomenclature untouched in fifty years. We saw box traps for deer dotting the landscape, an enclosed area with weather study equipment, and inviting draws and gulleys. I mentioned to Coles the bizarre, yet congruent, effect of the bunkers.

"Yes, and ironic, too," he said. "They're a literal revelation of the biblical saying, 'and their swords shall be beaten into plowshares.' One of the reasons they almost blend in naturally is they are meant to be camouflaged. In an enemy air raid fifty years back, pilots would have had difficulty distinguishing these mounds from the usual hills of the Ozark uplift."

We reached an opening to the right and Coles pulled his truck into a gravel pathway that led to a ranchlike setting, with a one-story frame building dominating the middle with trailers and sheds scattered to the sides.

"The building in the center there houses maintenance and garage space, my office, a classroom, and volunteer headquarters," Coles explained. "The rest of the buildings in view are used by the Bird Sanctuary and Wolf Sanctuary. The bird folks are getting the grounds ready for an open house next week."

The World Bird Sanctuary harbors over a hundred birds of several dozen species of raptors—hawks, vultures, falcons, owls, among others. Some of these are endangered, like the midwestern populations of the barn owl. Others are less rare but are at the project for rehabiitation from injury or for rearing as orphans. In addition to propagating and caring for raptors, the project expanded its husbandry to parrots a few years ago. The world's parrots include a number of endangered forms. By attempting to heal parrots, Coles said, the project was able to lend its expertise to an area of active environmental concern—the ruination of the tropical rain forests.

He took me through his office—The Black Hole, a sign on the door read—a hodgepodge of paper and memorabilia so purposefully slap-dash that it resembled a bird's nest in the wild: through a paneled seminar room where he and other Tyson colleagues conduct workshops; and he showed me an aerial photograph of Tyson, outlining the rest of the journey we'd be taking soon. The photo showed Tyson insulated from what is referred to locally as West County suburban sprawl by Lone Elk County Park on its eastern front and West Tyson Park, also a county park, on its western flank. To the north lies another buffer, Castlewood State Park. The exposed south beyond the interstate, he told me ruefully, is being mined for limestone, but doesn't appear to be ready for real estate development just yet. Recently, the Missouri Department of Conservation acquired and protected a 980-acre parcel between Tyson and the Beaumont Scout Reservation on the Tyson south flank, effectively guarding the Tyson perimeter.

"One more stop before we go," Coles said as I trailed him down a hallway and through some French doors to the right. In the room, which appeared to be a converted kitchen, three women chatted as amiably as sisters preparing Thanksgiving dinner, only the fare was not turkey, dressing, and the trimmings, but rather raccoon, hawk, and owl.

Coles introduced me to the women, volunteers at Tyson, who were restructuring road-killed or otherwise dead-but-found wildlife salvaged and donated to the center for instructional purposes. I went around the long table and met Jane, who was sewing up a longitudinal-cut raccoon; Bobbi, who was putting the finishing touches on the talons of a red-tailed hawk, and D'Aun, who talked of her upcoming scuba-diving trip to Belize as she worked deftly on a barred owl's wing.

As the women worked, Coles opened drawers pungent with mothballs and showed me one remarkably restructured bird—from wrens to falcons—after another, all collected from Missouri landscapes and brought to Tyson for the nimble-fingered amateur Tyson taxidermists. "Perfect models for our students to study," Coles said.

At the garage, we switched trucks, from Coles's two-wheel drive to a biology department four-wheel drive Dodge pickup that had spent the morning getting its battery recharged, and from there embarked on a chilly, dreamy tour that invoked distinct eras of civilization. Coles took the truck along a rutted road that ringed the western edge of Tyson and, with the glee of a child, spotted dozens of species of flora and fauna, quarries where Indians hundreds of years ago dug for chert, rock nodules once enclosed in aged limestone. The Native Americans used the chert to make arrows, blades, hoes, and other tools. Along the bumpy road, Coles articulated several pipe dreams similar to the one involving the bunker and bats.

"Now, there, to your left," he said, pointing down a steep gully with deep draws and jagged limestone outcropping, "in the valley was a settlement called Mincke Village. It was a company town that existed between 1877 to 1927, a pretty thriving little community at the beginning, built up around the limestone quarry, which was active over the same interval. When we get toward the bottom of the valley, you'll see remains of log and stone houses, a school, the company store, and limestone processing structures. Once the quarry was pretty well mined out, the community just dwindled to next to nothing and was finally abandoned. The Mincke family owned the land and elected not to renew or extend the original fifty-year lease with mineral extraction rights, and other quarries elsewhere satisfied local needs for rock, gravel, and slaked lime."

As the truck lurched over huge ruts, Coles pointed out the three distinct layers of forest growth: The canopy above, with older trees such as the oaks, hickory, maples and walnut, elm and ash; the understory, occupied by redbud, dogwood, hawthorns, Carolina buckthorn, pawpaw; and then the ground vegetation, the wildflowers, grasses, moss, lichens, mushrooms, and others. It was a very typical and viable eastern deciduous forest.

"What a habitat," I observed.

"Of course," Coles pointed out, "while the center provides habitat for many species of wildlife, and in the case of amphibians man-made ponds which provide an almost exact replica of a natural habitat, it's not a perfectly undisturbed virgin forest as such, especially for the birds here. Even the building of a rough road like the one we are on changes things a bit for wildlife."

Coles explained that species such as songbirds need unfragmented woodlands in parcels of at least 80 to 100 acres, with some deep-forest songbird species requiring as much as 500 acres of unfragmented habitat, without interference from predators and parasites that move along the boundaries of woodlands. Raccoons, skunks, possums, crows, blue jays, and grackles exploit these edges and raid songbird nests for eggs and the chicks. Parasites, most notably the brown-headed cowbird, lay their eggs in songbird nests allowing the songbird foster parents to hatch the cowbird young and rear them. The larger, stronger cowbird young grab most of the food, often starving out most or all of the songbird brood.

Coles cited agricultural practices, such as fencerow-to-fencerow grain farming; suburban sprawl as evidenced by shopping centers, subdivisions, and athletic fields at the edge of communities; and the building of roads, power lines, and railways as prime, recognizable gestures causing habitat fragmentation. Also, climatic factors such as drought and competition with other more flexible species such as chickadees, blue jays, and crows make a yearly impact.

A species of bird that was once common only in midwestern prairies—centuries ago they were "camp followers" of bison herds—the cowbird now thrives throughout the eastern United States where forests have been cleared to create farmland. Birds breeding in those forest fragments that do remain in the east are vulnerable to cowbird penetrations in the woods from the omnipresent edge or interface with the cleared land nearby. The cowbird will enter the forest thirty or forty yards from the edge in its search for host species' nests where the cowbird hen will lay her eggs.

"The odds are stacked against the songbirds in a scenario like this," he said. "There are fewer unfragmented forest habitats of adequate size for these species in the continental United States. There are some still in southern Missouri and southern Illinois. We hear so much of what tropical deforestation is doing to nature—and it *is* substantial—but that often has been cited as the primary cause for songbird decline. Well, the Latin American Manifest Destiny is little more than déjà vu of our own drive in this century to tame the continent. The birds can't breed here as they used to because their whole habitat has been drastically altered. Every time you see communities expanding in the name of progress, you're seeing altered habitat. What we see in west St. Louis County is happening all over the country."

We were at the floor of the valley, and as Coles talked I'd been watching the dolorous remnants of Mincke Village, the foundations of concrete and stone plainly visible. To the right, blasted out of a one hundred-foot cliff, was the last vestige of the quarry, a gaping cavern that deer use to cool off on hot summer days and bats inhabit during fall migration and for hibernation in winter. Coles pointed to the grassy area outside the cavern.

"We invite inner-city children to tour the center and we sometimes have picnics there," he said. "Many of them have never been out of the city, and they're absolutely convinced they'll be eaten by tigers or pythons. Still, our Field Science Project once arranged an overnight camping experience for about fifty kids. They had a ball! They slept out in the quarry-cavern. Some of them were almost in tears when it was time to leave—they just didn't want to go back."

We drove up the steep hill that would take us above the quarry and soon headed northwest, lurching along the road that paralleled the Missouri-Pacific Railroad tracks behind an eight-foot cyclone fence to the left. Abruptly, Coles jerked the wheel to the left, putting us perilously close to the shoulder of the already tenuous road, and pointed out the window at some small birds about the size of chickadees in a poplar stand.

"I don't believe it!" he said in awe. "I *don't* believe it. Kinglets! Look, there are both kinds. See the small patch of feathers on their crowns—they're fluffed. They do that when they're excited. The yellow-orange ones are the golden crowned species; the red are the ruby crowned. They're a lot like the tits, very common in Europe, but the tits are not found here."

He stared a long moment at the rollicking group, less than a dozen in all. "I haven't seen kinglets this cooperative in their display for at least seven years," he said finally. "Wait till I tell everybody. This just makes my day."

Coles, still abuzz about the kinglets, stopped at a hill's crest and pointed out the green ribbon of the Meramec River below the bluffs to the left as it meanders through Castlewood State Park. The view was tranquil, stunningly quiet. At the next turn in the road, we startled a group of deer, my heart, like Coles's at the sight of the kinglets, leaping with the ancient soar of sudden discovery. Four deer bounded across the road from a grazing site, their tails flashing in the evolutionary decoy developed for their self-protection, then calmly paused and lowered their "flags," thus blending into the woods to our right.

Within minutes, Coles punched my arm and pointed straight ahead at a flock of large, sleek birds flying across the road and into the woods to our right. "Wild turkey!"

I mentioned that they look smaller and less ruffled in the wild, and Coles said that there have been a few myths built around the bird.

"The turkey in the wild is a wily bird," he said. "You hear all these stories about them herding together and smothering each other in a stupid stampede. Well, that may be true of the farm birds, but not the turkey in the wild. He's a well-adapted fellow. Funny thing is, I never saw a turkey in the wild until about fifteen years ago. There just weren't any in my part of Pennsylvania, and their numbers were low, nationally, until about twenty years ago. Now after some protection and a reintroduction program by the Missouri Department of Conservation, they're being hunted again. I saw my first one here in 1974. They weren't breeding at Tyson at the time, but a few birds wandered by from a nearby release site, and now we have a very healthy population."

Between bounces, I asked Coles how he became director of the Tyson Research Center and where he developed his incessant curiosity about all things natural. He recounted a tale of growing up in Swarthmore, Pennsylvania, coming under the influence of a neighborhood shaman, C. Brooke Worth, a renowned naturalist who nurtured young Coles's insatiable drive to learn about nature and took him on countless field trips to forests, swamps, and the beaches and salt marshes of the New Jersey shore. After toying with the idea of becoming a chemical engineer, he declared biology his major at Swarthmore and graduated first in his class. He received a teaching fellowship and his Ph.D. from Harvard. He landed at the Claremont Colleges in California, where he and his wife, Mary, gradually became disenchanted with the Los Angeles basin. Through a tip from a friend on the Washington University biology faculty, he learned of the need to fill a directorship of a research center. The combination of teaching and directing—with less emphasis on the traditional academic pursuit of publishing—was a natural draw. And when he got the chance to tour the Tyson Center with Washington University wildlife ecologist Owen Sexton, it was instant love. That was 1970, and Coles has never felt disgruntled yet: "A little frazzled at times, but never disgruntled," he told me.

He stopped the truck at a fenced-in area, and I knew immediately this was the Wolf Sanctuary. We got out of the truck into the gray, chilly air and walked toward a padlocked gate that Coles opened. I had been yearning all day for a glimpse of the wolves. We climbed steel stairs onto a concrete loading dock, remnant of the depot years, now obviously an observatory. The small pastures before us—about an acre apiece—were enclosed and seemingly devoid of wolves.

Suddenly, to our left, a cream-colored canid trotted a well-worn path toward the fence, looked our way, and trotted off. It retraced its steps, and soon paraded by us again, this time leading a half dozen others who followed in the ritualized, syncopated trot that, like a pendulum holding back stored energy, allows this animal its splendid bursts of speed. Coles called to the lead wolf, who stopped momentarily and stared at us, its wide-set eyes friendly but fraught with unfathomable centuries of wildness. It then took off to join its mates in the worn circular romp inside the fence.

"It's unfortunate that wolves have to have this captive sort of atmosphere for their survival," Cole said. "It makes you yearn all the more for the day when the fence can be forgotten. That day is drawing nearer, we hope."

Tyson's Wolf Sanctuary, which fosters anywhere from fifteen to thirty wolves every year, has played a key role in rehabilitating and reintroducing into the wild a pack of red wolves in North Carolina, and it has the world's largest breeding stock of the endangered Mexican wolf.

In front of us a big gray wolf had come up for a drink of water and stared, no malice seemingly intended. He was a beautiful animal with a heavy coat, his glare almost inviting. Feeling secure by the bulwark of the fence, I tested the theory about eye contact by staring straight into the icy fire of his eyes with no consequence. The wolf drank and trotted off.

We passed the research ponds, New Pond, Railroad, and Salamander, and deep in the woods reflected on the beauty of the view at the highest point at Tyson, 810 feet, according to Coles; then drove slowly along a ridge near the southwest corner of the center.

"The tour's about done," he said. "But I've got to show you the area where we do the migrating songbird surveys."

Coles pulled the truck off the road to the left, and we crept down a steep cleared path that took us gradually down a hill with sloping drops on either side. Just as I felt the hill getting disturbingly steep and was about to comment how far away from the road we were getting, he stopped, put on the emergency brake, and got out of the truck. I followed.

A stake had been driven into the earth on either side of the road with a tennis ball numbered 11 atop it. This was to demarcate the last subdivision of a narrow, twenty-acre swath surveyed in the woods. Coles and volunteers conduct the census twice a year, making ten successive visits in January and again in June to track the relative numbers of wintering and breeding birds that are present in Tyson each year. In the cold of winter and dampness of spring, Coles and his assistants will stand patiently for three mintues at each of twenty-two observation posts in the woods with a survey map and pen in hand to record the locations and numbers of various species they hear and see. Coles calls the January effort the winter bird population *survey* and the spring one the breeding bird *census*. Both counts include birds that are permanent residents in the oak-hickory forest. The winter surveys may include such northern visitors as the purple finch, pine siskin, dark-eyed junco, evening grosbeak, and various sparrows that winter in the central United States. The spring census is based on sight and sound—the characteristic song of male birds who advertise their territorial holdings to other members of their own species. The spring census involves such migrant species as vireos, warblers, orioles, flycatchers, cuckoos, tanagers, and gnatcatchers. These species winter in Central and South America and return in the spring to breed in Missouri and elsewhere in North America, returning south again in late summer.

It is this latter group of songbirds that concerns Coles and many other ornithologists. Since 1980, the numbers of migrating birds in Tyson's counts are dramatically down from the early years of the survey. One of the more common songbird categories, the migrating warblers, have dropped off more than 30 percent at Tyson. Gnatcatchers, orioles, cuckoos, and others show similar disturbing declines over the past decade.

"The spring numbers are very troublesome," said Coles. "There is something happening, but it's still not completely clear that just one factor—for instance, tropical deforestation—is the major culprit."

Coles looked off wistfully down the sharp slope over the hills to Interstate 44, its steady hum now audible in Tyson woods. Beyond the interstate and the white mounds of limestone, mining equipment and trucks were active in removing the rock from the earth, fodder for development. The quarry is the only site in Tyson's near environs that doesn't look natural. He told me that the owner of the quarry company had graciously created a berm and planted some trees that pretty much obscured the view of the quarry from Interstate 44, yet up here the view, he admitted, is somewhat diminished by the site. The presence of the quarry is a constant reminder that, although buffered by natural areas, the Tyson Research Center is never too far from the sprawl of the twentieth century. While it will take decades for the quarry to exhaust its supply of rock, Coles nonetheless wonders what will go in there when that time comes. He's pulling for something natural to accompany the woods and habitat over which he has been a vigilant steward for more than twenty years.

We stared out to the highway at a sight that Daniel Boone, who may have stood where we were nearly two hundred years ago on his last trek westward, would never have envisioned. The sun, hidden for much of the afternoon, returned feebly, lighting up the October trees. A hawk floated across the highway into the hills to the south.

"It used to be, in the spring, these woods were jammed with songbirds migrating northward," Coles said. "The noise was a cacophony, but a beautiful one. It was something like an orchestra in rehearsal before a concert, all the different instruments tuning up, discordant sounds, yet taken together, a beautiful, raucous sort of racket, promising harmony. That's probably gone forever now. I haven't heard that many birds together in twenty years. It was one of the most splendid free shows in nature."

Coles's vivid description had kindled my own memories. "I remember as a kid, there was a windbreak behind my grandparents' farmhouse. In the spring, there used to be a big gathering of birds out there, same time every year. I'd walk out and listen to them. I couldn't believe the racket. Those must have been the songbirds, right?"

"Yes," Coles said fervently, his eyes lively again. "Those were the songbirds. They still come back, but not as many. I'll bet that windbreak behind your grandparents' house doesn't see half of the numbers or variety it used to."

"Well, I'm not sure what's left of the windbreak or the farm," I said. "The farmhouse is still there, and so are some of the buildings, but a good portion of it is being subdivided."

"That's part of the picture I'm talking about," Coles said. "At least for the next few decades, a certain amount of development is inevitable, I guess. But we must be aware of salvaging *some*thing for wildlife. It would be a tragedy to lose the birds. But it would mean much more than an aesthetic loss to a bunch of nature fanatics. These birds are efficient, inexpensive insect eaters, for instance. They're a part of the natural system of checks and balances. Without them, agriculture and forestry both would suffer—more and more chemicals would have to be used to control insects. And that's risky business. It's costly and likely to be self-defeating in the long run. Of course, there's great promise of genetically engineered crop varieties to stymie insect pests.

I hope that is realized before it's too late. Still, it wouldn't find easy application in Latin America's tropical forests.

"Veteran bird-watchers and avian population researchers report that songbird numbers have declined increasingly throughout most of the country since the end of World War II. Now, perhaps you can put some of that blame on tropical deforestation, but the entire face of our country has changed in that span, and we're seeing the consequences now. Right here, in our own mad dash to settle the country, we've ignored a basic law of ecology: All things in nature are interconnected."

THREE RIVERS
Missouri Department of Conservation biologists Norm Stucky and Bill
Dieffenbach at the mouth of the Gasconade River joining the Missouri,
at Gasconade, Missouri. *(Courtesy of Tony Fitzpatrick)*

C H A P T E R   6

Three Rivers

"The river giveth, and the river taketh away," intoned Bill Dieffenbach, as if he were an old-time country preacher.

Dieffenbach looked at me balefully with dark, somber eyes. He is a middle-sized man, about fifty, lean and tough looking. He speaks in a hard-edged staccato voice that can be intimidating, yet behind its intensity is a timbre of commitment and sincerity. Lurking in his gaze is a smile waiting to happen. As now, as he speaks to me of rivers. "There are three big rivers in Missouri—the Mississippi above St. Louis, the Mississippi below St. Louis, and the Missouri. None of them are natural anymore. We've harnessed them so much that the natural process of giving and taking no longer occurs."

"In this century, especially since World War II, we've traded habitat for agriculture and development," said Dieffenbach's colleague, Norm Stucky, a tall, relaxed man in his forties, laid-back and handsome. Mr. Stucky's black hair is streaked with white, with a distinguished touch around the temples. His grin puts a visitor immediately at ease. Like Dieffenbach, Stucky was dressed in a short-sleeved white shirt and tie. But Stucky looks like a restless Missourian, as if he has his horse tied out back, and he can't wait to get out of this office and ride off into the sunset. "We've shackled our rivers to control them," Stucky went on. "Little thought was given to wildlife habitat. Now, as for what's left on most of the floodplains of Missouri's big rivers, well, a mouse would have to pack a lunch there."

It's summer in the Midwest. Not far from us, the river shimmers in the heat. We three were sitting at a conference table at the Missouri Department of Conservation Building in Jefferson City, the state capital. I was at the head of the long table, a view of the Lewis and Clark trail winding toward the Missouri River just a mile or so away, visible in front of me on this hot day in July. All I had asked was: What was the status of the big rivers in Missouri? I was just a curious—and admittedly a bit naive—reporter from St. Louis, but I had said the magic word, rivers. A most compelling word, and these two guys could run with it all afternoon. They had river tales to tell, and an education for any writer smart enough to stop awhile and listen.

Dieffenbach took over. "North of the mouth of the Missouri River, the Mississippi is controlled for navigation by twenty-six locks and dams that have become like a staircase, converting the Mississippi from a free-flowing river to a river-lake system. The locks and dams are essentially twenty-six huge bathtubs filling with sediment. South of St. Louis, the Mississippi River is channelized. It's a more free-flowing river, but in no way natural.

"As for the Missouri, there are six major dams on the entire river that control its flow. The lower 735 miles from Sioux City, Iowa, to St. Louis are channelized, except for a 55-mile stretch designated as a wild and scenic river area upstream of Sioux City. All 553 miles of the river in Missouri are channelized, paved with riprap. It's a prisoner bound in rock. It can no longer function normally."

The natural process of give-and-take, Dieffenbach told me, involves eroding banks and soil at one point and accreting silt and sediment at another, largely by the whims of nature, creating a healthy biodiversity with oxbows, sandbars, and islands. These are excellent habitat for waterfowl such as herons, egrets, cranes, ducks and geese, eagles, falcons, and cormorants. Natural give-and-take leaves deep pools for spawning fish, timber for songbirds, hawks, and deer. But after five decades of dam and dike construction and the placing of millions of tons of rocks to create the congressionally mandated navigation channel, roughly 9 feet deep and 300 feet wide along most of the river's course, the Missouri River has lost much of its biodiversity in exchange for easier navigation, flood control, and agricultural advantages.

That trade-off, to conservationists, represents a bigger steal than the Cardinals prying Lou Brock away from the Cubs for sore-armed Ernie Broglio in 1964.

In 1879, Dieffenbach explained, there were 640 acres of habitat per
river-mile along the Missouri River near St. Charles at Hall's Ferry
where the river was a mile across. More than one hundred years later,
there are only 140 acres of habitat per river mile at that stretch.
Similar decreases are seen throughout the state and throughout the
long, meandering course from St. Louis all the way to Yankton, South
Dakota, location of the first of six major reservoirs constructed by the
Army Corps of Engineers and Bureau of Reclamation to further control
the Missouri.

"The Missouri River today is a mere shadow of itself," said Stucky
in his broad, flat Heartland voice. "Sandbars and wetlands are going
or gone, displaced by land created through channeling the river. The
Lewis and Clark descriptions mention elk and grizzly, deer and
antelope along the river, geese, ducks, herons, and egrets darkening
the sky. That awesome abundance of wildlife is gone forever. We
couldn't possibly hope to restore it. And we're not just talking of the
big rivers alone, but their feeder systems as well. In Missouri alone
over the past eighty years, approximately 50,000 surface acres of water
have disappeared. There are lots of corn and soybeans there now.
That's made some people happy, but the environment obviously has
suffered."

Bill Dieffenbach sipped quickly from a Duds & Suds cup, put it
down gently, and smiled thoughtfully, to my relief.

"The river, the big river, is like an interstate highway," he said. "If
you travel an interstate, you don't see much real life on it. It's
convenient, it's efficient, but to get the real life, a meal, a motel, a
movie, a park, you get off the interstate. Same with the river. With
the Missouri River, what we have is an interstate highway—a nonde-
script stretch for convenient transportation. Backwaters, marshes, and
island complexes—the rest areas, motels, and Hardees of the river
world—are largely gone, but some remnants remain to remind us of
what was lost. The Mississippi and the Missouri are *not* biological
deserts or sewage canals, as some rivers in the country have become.
In terms of fishing and wildlife, they're both fairly decent, though
they've declined over the years. But they're interstates, really. That's
all we've got left, but at least we've got that."

In driving from St. Louis to Jefferson City, called Jeff by the natives, I had passed over the Missouri twice that day, the first time in an eerie, dense morning fog on an interstate (40) outside of Wentzville, the second time entering Jefferson City and its high, white, majestic limestone cliffs. Each time, as always, crossing the river was a thrill, albeit subdued. It offered visions of George Caleb Bingham paintings, Lewis and Clark, camps of Native Americans, and canoes of trappers and voyagers. Yet, listening to Dieffenbach and Stucky talk, I could see the river differently now, the striking sameness of its width at both sites, shorn of personality, the cloying reality of development along its shores and bottomlands.

Yet the river, be it the Mighty Mississippi or the historic Missouri, has its fierce pull, no matter the transgressions against it.

The wide Missouri River, although rimmed with colorful American history, has always suffered by comparison to the Mississippi River. William Warfield never sang a famous song about it, nor for that matter has Frank Sinatra. There are no Delta blues about the Missouri, though some mighty fine jazz came out of Kansas City. On the subject of rivers, Francis Parkman cannot stack up with Mark Twain, nor can any American writer, many believe. Huck Finn, Jim, and Tom Sawyer are more romantic (and interesting) to our psyche than are the noble Lewis, Clark, and Sacagawea. Throw in Injun Joe and the author himself as a river pilot, and there is simply no comparison. The Mississippi is the Father of Waters; the Missouri is the Big Muddy, courtesy of Pere Marquette. Its actual name comes from the Illinois Indians who dubbed the tribes living across the Mississippi as the *Missouri*, or "those who have canoes."

A decided edge in charisma, then, goes to the Mississippi. No major battles, such as Vicksburg, took place on the Missouri River during the Civil War, no generals, like Grant, emerged immortal. Yet, at 2,316 miles, the Missouri is the shorter of the two rivers by just 32 miles. In defining St. Louis, for one, as the Gateway to the West, the Missouri River has done more for that city than has the Father of Waters.

The Missouri River is a life force for seven states, the Mississippi for eleven. Almost 2 million tons of grain, fertilizer and other goods were shipped down the Missouri in 1989, compared with a whopping 26 million tons of goods ranging from coal and petroleum to grain and steel that passed through Lock and Dam 26 on the Mississippi the same year. The two rivers together, along with a small portion of the Kaskaskia in Illinois, comprise the Port of Metropolitan St. Louis, a seventy-mile stretch of riverfront on the Mississippi that is the nation's second largest inland port (first is Pittsburgh), capable of reaching twenty-nine industrial regions with a combined population of 90 million. The port is the northernmost point on the Mississippi that usually remains ice free, and thus navigable year-round. It handles the loading and unloading of between sixty and one hundred barges a day.[1,2]

The Mississippi, its myth aside, simply is favored logistically over the Missouri. Because it flows from the frigid north near St. Paul, Minnesota, to the Gulf of Mexico near New Orleans, the nation's largest international port, it has been the lifeblood of the Heartland for a century and a half. Ninety percent of Illinois's export soybeans and 77 percent of its corn is moved by barges down the Mississippi to New Orleans. One towboat that pushes 15 barges moves the same amount of grain, 22,500 tons, that 870 large semi-trucks or 2 trains composed of 225 jumbo hopper cars move, according to the Iowa Department of Transportation.

However, while the Missouri River plays second fiddle to the Mississippi in terms of transport, its economic and life-support clout is vital to states west of Missouri—Nebraska, the Dakotas, and Montana, as well as Iowa to the north, states that depend on the river for everything from agriculture and tourism to recreation and nourishing the massive Ogallala aquifer. Sixty percent of the population of Missouri, Dieffenbach told me, draws its drinking water from the Big Muddy. The river is more than just a highway; it is the water of life.

At the root of water problems and many environmental concerns in Missouri and other states reliant on the river is the series of dams, dikes, and reservoirs that was meant to be a panacea for the Heartland

---

[1]"Missouri River Causing New War Between the States," by Peg Couglin of the Associated Press, *St. Louis Post-Dispatch*, Sept. 15, 1991, pp. C1 and C6.
[2]"Developing Promise of Region's Waterways," by Christopher Carey, *St. Louis Post-Dispatch*, Sept. 23, 1991, pp. 1, 12, and 13 BP.

and the West. That is when the U.S. Army Corps of Engineers and the Bureau of Reclamation joined forces to tame the Missouri River, forever changing its face. It was called the Pick-Sloan Program, and it went into effect in 1944. Its history is one continuous story that begets many stories. It is a précis of development and the Heartland in the twentieth century.

"Nineteen forty-four," Bill Dieffenbach says, "is the date of death for the Missouri River."

For the corps, too, giveth, and it taketh away.

The impetus behind harnessing the Missouri River grew out of a series of natural disasters that left the Heartland and portions of the West reeling from one of the most famous droughts ever to hit a region, the thirties drought that created the Dust Bowl, followed by the opposite extreme, a multimillion-dollar flood in the forties along the lower Missouri basin that wrecked homes, flooded farm fields, and left many frustrated or in despair with nature's vagaries. Technology, it was decided, would be the cure of it all. Col. Lewis Pick of the U.S. Army Corps of Engineers, and Glen Sloan of the Bureau of Reclamation, put their heads together and put on a show that plays to this day. Their plan: The corps would build the major stem dams to control flooding and produce hydropower; they also would make the Missouri River essentially a navigation channel 300 feet wide, 9 feet deep, and stabilize the eroding basin's banks. The bureau in conjunction would use the corps' water stored behind the main stem dams to develop irrigation, which would relieve the drought-plagued Great Plains and construct their own dams along the Missouri's feeder streams to assist their plan. Thus, there would be commerce where plausible, and agriculture forever for the nation's breadbasket. Eventually, six mammoth dams were built stretching from Gavin's Point, South Dakota, at the lowest extreme, extending through Nebraska and the Dakotas, including Fort Randall, Big Bend, Oahee, and Garrison, and concluding with Fort Peck in Montana, the "biggest dam thing" in the world, 4 miles long, 250 feet high, with a reservoir 134 miles long spanning 1,525 miles of shoreline. The reservoirs were intended to control flooding and store sufficient water to maintain the navigation depth downstream. Hydroelectric turbines were added in hopes that the water would become electricity downstream and the river would nurture the arid lands in the Dakotas.

The Pick-Sloan program, nearing fifty years of age, has realized some of its goals but neglected or totally disregarded others. The Missouri River became a navigable stream, but, especially in its namesake state, an unnatural system. Flood control along the river generally is better than before. But 94 percent of the irrigation plans for farmers have yet to be delivered and, given tighter budgets on the horizon, probably never will be. Of the Missouri's 2,316 miles, fewer than 300 of them flow naturally.

South Dakota, all states considered, arguably may have suffered the most. Lake Oahe is the longest lake in the main stem dam system, with some 2,250 miles of shoreline. The Lake Oahe Dam near Pierre was completed in 1958, at a cost of $340 million, after nearly 500,000 acres of prime farm and timberlands were inundated. Yet, the "improvements" were felt on only 600 farms, which comprised less than 1 percent of the agricultural land base in the state. Finally, in 1980, the state decided to sell Lake Oahe water rights to Exxon of Houston for their Rocky Mountain Energy Transport system, which conveys a mix of Missouri River water with pulverized coal from the western states down a pipeline from Wyoming to the mid-southern states. The U.S. Fish and Wildlife Service reported a loss from the Pick-Sloan project of 309,000 acres of terrestrial habitat, 103,000 acres of aquatic habitat, and an almost complete elimination of all island and sandbars, accounting for a total loss of 474,600 acres of habitat.[3]

"So the state of Missouri lost a natural river and the upstream farmers never got their irrigation systems put in," said Dieffenbach. "Every mile of the Missouri River in this state has been touched by the 'men in the green suits,' as they used to call the corps engineers. But I don't want to make them sound like bad guys across the board. They became an easy scapegoat. Less than one-third of the planned levees from the Pick-Sloan Program have been done by the Feds. Because the Feds move so slowly, many local levee districts built their

---

[3] "There Once Was a River Called Missouri," Iowa Public Television documentary, 1981, Tom Moore, producer and writer. One of the best natural history video productions ever made.

own levee and drainage systems. Now, by law the government is required to provide floodways and wildlife corridors, letting us get our 'oar in the water.' The corps would set a levee back 500 feet for floodway and riparian purposes. Often, local levees, in the interest of agriculture, would set the levee very close to the river, and ignore floodway and riparian rights."

Norm Stucky leaned back and crossed his long legs. "In defense of the corps, the Pick-Sloan Act was authorized when people thought the earth's natural resources were inexhaustible. Now, since man has stepped on the moon and we've seen our own little planet from that perspective and we've learned how much smaller our own wealth is, we're seeing things differently. Today, all of us are much more willing to work with those we once considered adversaries."

Environmentalists for decades have viewed the corps with a wary, if not disapproving, eye, the way a traveler considers construction workers along a highway, ceaselessly on the job, yet forever leaning against their equipment, or gathering in groups for a coffee break. In short, they are always there, but the job is never done, the highways are forever being built. The corps, after all, built twenty-seven locks and dams along the Mississippi River, except for Lock and Dam 23, which was never built, but for which they account. It is good to have something in reserve.

Today, the Corps of Engineers, as if atoning for sins of the past, is constructing many of its projects with wildlife in mind. Environmentalists and naturalists throughout Missouri and Illinois extol the work of Pat McGinniss, a biologist who works with the corps just outside of St. Louis. Recent projects of the corps in the St. Louis area reflect a different awareness. For instance, adjacent to the new Mel Price Lock and Dam (formerly Lock and Dam 26), the corps has developed an environmental demonstration area. Wildlife—particularly water-fowl—response to the 1,100 acres of wetland and wet prairie habitat has been dramatic. Another recently completed project involved construction of a sediment-deflection device around Dresser Island, just north of St. Louis, in Pool 26. This two-year, $1.2 million project assures the future of critically important wetland habitat on the 940-acre island, which was in danger of silting in from the sedimental onslaught of the coursing Mississippi River. Dresser Island, which the corps bought to facilitate construction of the navigation dams, was turned over to the public in the fifties and became a prized duck-hunting area. But sedimentation has taken its toll, filling in the potholes, swamps, and lakes on the island, until Congress, as part of a compromise struck in the seventies to allow replacement of Lock and Dam 26, agreed to delegate some money to rehabilitate important riverine fish and wildlife habitat. Other similar projects are underway or planned in several other upper Mississippi River states. The sediment-deflection dike, extending five miles around the island, is a symbolic bow around a present to the citizens of Missouri and Illinois, who, the corps hopes, will take notice of that agency's preservation efforts.

As if the Missouri's three big rivers have not taken enough abuse in the century, another ill has been visited upon them in recent decades, one that has increasingly worried residents: Pesticides have been found in fish from the Missouri, Mississippi, Meramec, and other rivers, and analyses of drinking water drawn from the Missouri River have shown at times alarmingly high amounts of agricultural chemicals, primarily atrazine, a corn herbicide. Not a week goes by, seemingly, where there isn't a newspaper article about pollutants in the Heartland's rivers, recipients of pesticide-laced rain runoff from farmers' fields. The amounts sampled generally are highest in the spring, when farmers apply the herbicides. Heartland farmers apply as many as 300 million pounds of herbicides each spring, according to the U.S. Department of the Interior. Farmers are being urged to cut back or eliminate their use of chemicals as well as to use less toxic substitutes for atrazine, which is suspected of causing cancer.

Similarly, Bill Dieffenbach's and Norm Stucky's colleagues at the Missouri Department of Conservation have monitored fish in the big rivers throughout the 1980s to determine the extent of the pollution problem. Health advisories have been released from the department regularly since 1985. A whole soup of chemicals can be found in the rivers, generally at levels considered safe by the National Academy of Science-National Academy of Engineers criteria. Among the chemicals the Missouri Department of Conservation scientists looked for in fish samples were DDT, benzene, hexachloride, heptachlor, heptachlor epoxide, methoxychlor, mirex, aldrin, dieldrin, endrin, chlordane, and polychlorinated biphenyls (PCBs). Beginning in 1984, the scientists analyzed skinless fillets of channel catfish, shovelnose sturgeon, carp, flathead catfish, and late in 1987, crappie, bluegill, paddlefish, sauger, blue catfish, and largemouth bass for all these contaminants, but especially for aldrin and dieldrin, organochlorine pesticides used for termite and corn-insect control until 1975, when the EPA suspended their use. They also looked for traces of chlordane, a chlorinated hydrocarbon used for control of corn-, home-, and garden-insect pests until 1978, when its registration was suspended except for termite control (which was later suspended in 1988), and PCBs, used since 1929 in a variety of products, all nonagricultural, until its suspension in 1977. All of these chemicals were banned because of their toxicity and their degree of magnification in the food chain, as well as their permanence. Chlordane applied in 1978 that has found its way into water still persists in 1991, because chlordane, like the other organochlorines, has a fifty-year half-life. All of these chemicals are either known or suspected carcinogens.

Missouri Department of Conservation scientists found, over the course of their research, that chlordane levels generally decreased over the years in carp, catfish, and sturgeon taken from the Missouri River, but high levels in fish upstream of St. Louis in the Mississippi were found. PCB levels in fish generally declined since the discontinuation of the chemical in 1977. Similarly, aldrin and dieldrin levels found in fish generally declined with their discontinuation. Nonetheless, several health advisories were issued during the decade, cautioning Missouri's fisherman either not to eat carp, channel catfish, shovelnose sturgeon, and/or bigmouth buffalo fish taken from certain stretches along the two rivers, or to limit their consumption of the various fish to five ounces per week. The monitoring program goes on into the nineties, with chlordane the chemical that most bears watching.

Huck and Jim, then, in the closing years of the twentieth century, seemingly are best advised not necessarily to abandon their fishing poles, but, as Dieffenbach and Stucky suggest, eat river fish in moderation, not every day of the week.

"Hopefully, what we're seeing is the decline of these chemicals in the rivers," Stucky said. "The chlorinated hydrocarbons like chlordane are incredibly persistent, but they've been replaced in agriculture with other classes of pesticides called the organophosphates and carbamates, which break down more quickly. Still, we have to monitor from time to time. I eat fish taken out of the Missouri, but I want to know that the chemical levels are safe."

Dieffenbach lifted his cup, winked reassuringly, and toasted me. "I'm drinking Missouri River water right now. Would you like a glass yourself?" He chuckled. "No, we don't have any reports of blue babies in Missouri, like they've had in Iowa, for instance, where groundwater from private wells has been so contaminated with agricultural pesticide runoff that pregnant women have delivered oxygen-deprived babies. You don't see that here, that I know of, and I don't think you will."

He looked at his cup, as if for inspiration. "You have to look at things in perspective. It's easy to look at the negative. This cup's at the halfway point. I'd call it half-full. Norm, here, would say it's three-quarters full, even knowing it's half-full. He's that upbeat a person. But there are people, including some of our colleagues, who always look at things like they're half-empty. Chlordane in the water is a case in point. I'm glad people are concerned, but everyone has to remember where we've come from. In the fifties and sixties, the packing plants in Kansas City and Omaha were dumping raw sewage into the Kansas and Missouri Rivers. Globs of tallow and other wastes would float on the water. Who wants to fish those waters, who cares to drink from that mess?"

"Right," Stucky said. "In the fifties, few of the municipalities along the rivers had adequately sized sewage treatment plants, long-term pesticides were infiltrating the rivers, and the public was largely indifferent. Today, we say, 'damn, we've got chlordane in the water. It's so depressing.' But in thirty years, hundreds of millions of dollars have been spent for primary and secondary sewage treatment in our towns and cities. We're addressing that. That's a reflection of the environmental awareness that's come upon us. We have to maintain that awareness and take it several steps further. I'm not saying we don't have problems—we've got a peck of problems—but we're making progress."

Norm Stucky, as the Missouri Department of Conservation environmental coordinator, is involved with several major projects on the big rivers. Chief of these is the federally mandated Upper Mississippi River System Environmental Management Program, that addresses the enhancement of habitat, the reduction of sedimentation, the increase in recreation activities, the establishment of long-term monitoring of the river, and wise economic development along that stretch of the river. The willingness of the federal government to fund the Environmental Management Program is an affirmation that they see the Mississippi River as a nationally significant ecosystem, which must be preserved in partnership with any future economic development. Congress authorized $200 million for the project in 1986. To realize its goals, the program will need more funding soon, Stucky said, and in the five years of its existence, the biologist finds himself steeped, as he put it, in "biopolitics."

He came to the Missouri Department of Conservation in 1978 after nine years with the Nebraska Game and Parks Division of the State Department of Conservation. Norm Stucky is a native of Kansas, raised on the family farm outside of Newton on the western edge of the Kansas Flint Hills. His father introduced Stucky to hunting and fishing "from the time Shep was a pup," he told me. "As early as I can remember, I was a total nut about hunting and fishing. We went to town literally once a week, if that. I didn't care. I was outdoors from the word go."

When it became apparent that an older brother was preparing to take over the farm operation, Stucky found himself naturally inclined toward a degree in conservation at Kansas State University. After graduation, he thought of a career in physical therapy and was accepted into a program at Northwestern University when the opportunity came to go to graduate school in fisheries at Kansas State on an assistantship. Because he was about to get married, the extra money at Kansas State looked good, and Stucky's conservation career was launched. He has never regretted the choice.

Bill Dieffenbach shares a similar love of the outdoors, only the experiences that shaped his early consciousness of nature took place in another part of the country. The hard edge to his voice reflects a New Jersey accent silted in by a quarter century of life squarely in the middle of the country. Dieffenbach was born and raised in Jersey City, "a small town of about 500,000 about five minutes from New York

City," he told me jokingly. "I loved to fish for as long as I can remember. My goal at high school was to get enough money for a car and a boat so I could spend all my time fishing in the bays and ocean. After I graduated from high school, I wanted no part of college. 'Smart people go to college,' I thought. So I got a job in a factory and lasted about a year and a half when I realized that wasn't what I wanted to do with my life."

After a stint in the air force, Dieffenbach, the youngest of seven children, was invited to live with a brother in Colorado Springs, who, possessing an engineering degree and a master's in business administration, convinced his younger brother of the value of higher education. Dieffenbach took the cue, quit his job climbing poles for a telephone company, and enrolled at Colorado State University at Fort Collins, pursuing fisheries studies, his longtime love. After getting his master's degree, he accepted a job with the Missouri Department of Conservation in 1965. "We had one and eight-ninths children and I knew nothing at all about Missouri, except for the Department of Conservation's reputation, which was good. We moved here and have been here ever since. It's been great."

Dieffenbach has worked himself through the ranks of the conservation department's hierachy to his current position of assistant chief of the planning division. He supervises eight people in all areas of fish and wildlife conservation, including three highly regarded Ph.D. conservation planners, making his situation the envy of many counterparts throughout the country. Indeed, the Missouri Department of Conservation is considered to be in the top echelon of conservation departments in the United States. Some consider it to be the best. People like Dieffenbach and Stucky have built that reputation, which has also been aided, Dieffenbach told me, by the commitment the state has given the department.

Stucky reached behind him and produced a postcard. He placed it on the table and I examined it. It was in color, but faded, very old, looking almost like a watercolor painting, but was instead a photograph that had been colored in. The scene was of the Missouri River near Gasconade, a tiny town where the Gasconade River empties into the Missouri. In the picture, the river was vast, loaded with sandbars and vegetation. This, indeed, was "the wide Missouri" of song and story, about which we have all heard.

"I was poking around the archives a while back and came across this," Stucky said. "A railroad company—the Missouri Pacific—put this out in 1904 to promote ridership on its passenger service. Isn't that spectacular? See all the sandbars and how wide the river is? When I saw this, I thought, 'Boy, what a difference a century makes.' You can see the same sight today, only you wouldn't see anything quite as spectacular as this.

"A good part of environmental awareness is knowing what has happened to create our present situation. When the average American goes on vacation and crosses the Missouri River, he looks at it and thinks that's just the way God created it. But it isn't. It used to look like this. We ought to go down there sometime and see this. It's not that far away, and it's a beautiful drive."

Three months later, on a damp, chilly October afternoon, I kept the appointment in Gasconade with Stucky and Dieffenbach. Route 100, a beautiful, rolling drive, parts of it landmarks along the Lewis and Clark trail, passes through old Missouri Ozark hills, streams, and farm fields, the land undergoing the incessant Heartland transition from Ozark antiquity to what was commonly called in the seventies nouveau riche. Sprinkled throughout the "hollers" and hilltops are custom-kit log cabins and spanking-new split-level homes with views of crumbling barns and abandoned farmhouses, badly tended acres waiting to be sold to another urban buyer, and fields of milo leaning over in the rain, unharvested for more than a year. The St. Louis spillover extends far into the Ozark hills. Someone should make a postcard of these Missouri Ozarks as they look in the 1990s. On the other hand, Hermann, a charming, neatly preserved German settlement established decades before the Civil War, lends itself to a postcard. The old buildings have been preserved here, the citizenry proud of their heritage, their wines, and their quiet sense of order.

I followed Route 100 through cattle farms and bold hills, the highway repeatedly dropping the car thirty to forty feet down steep, winding hills and through lush woods. This was more like it, real

Ozark country. Gasconade rests like a tired hound dog across the bridge along its namesake river, which is wide and gentle as it approaches the Missouri. To the left of the bridge is a park, to the right a boat access. I went to the boat ramp, liking Gasconade, which shuns civilization, if not ignores it. Huck would like it, too. It's only fifty miles from Jeff City, a lively, modern place. I wondered delightedly what people here do for a living.

I got out of the car in the cold mist and walked the mussel-shell-strewn banks of the Gasconade, which arises deep in the Missouri Ozarks in the southwestern corner of the state and ends here. It's a green, friendly river, limestone bedded like most of Missouri's rivers that start in the Ozarks. Pickup trucks and jeeps with license plates from Georgia, Arkansas, and Tennessee were parked in the lot. Their owners were working on the railroad bridge that stretched across the river a couple of hundred yards downstream. One-hundred-foot-high bluffs stared at me across the river on its east side. Nothing but greenery garnished them.

Dieffenbach and Stucky pulled up in a dark late-model car, and I walked to them. They got out. I asked them what it was that had put Gasconade, modest as it is, on Missouri maps.

"The river, the railroad," Dieffenbach said, jabbing a finger at each. He had grown a beard since I had last seen him, the dark whiskers flecked with white. It looked good on him.

I told them I wanted to see the spot from where the postcard photo was shot. Stucky scratched his head. "To get an actual re-creation of that shot, you have to get on that bluff over there," he pointed downriver past the railroad bridge. "It was shot overlooking the mouth. To get there, we could walk over the bridge, I guess. Then there's a private road a little east of here. We'd have to get permission to access, but we could get up there or near there after scrambling for about a mile or so."

The wind picked up, the rain fell harder, and the railroad bridge looked slippery.

"Well, we should go to the mouth of the Gasconade," Dieffenbach said. "That's no problem. Let's do that."

We got into the warmth of the car and went through Gasconade, crossing the railroad tracks and a small group of men lunching around pickups, apparently fixing the track in town. The road took us past a slumbering bar and into a series of red-brick buildings, windowless and abandoned. They had the look of a company town to them.

"That's the old repair shops the corps used to run here when there were three or four dredges at Gasconade Harbor and they needed to keep the equipment in good shape," Dieffenbach said. "They look like old fire houses, don't they? The crews used to stay here for weeks, live there. They still use one of these buildings around here, I think. But they haven't done any serious dredging on this part of the Missouri for years."

Dieffenbach drove the car into a parking lot at a new facility the corps maintained on the river, the steel-sided buildings surrounded by a cyclone fence. He got out of the car and entered the building, coming out a few minutes later. "I thought I'd let them know we're here," he said.

We walked behind the corps buildings and onto the muddy beach. To the left was the Missouri, to the right the Gasconade. They joined behind an impressive, massive white limestone face that rose maybe 200 feet above the rivers. The bluffs were lined with railroad tracks at their base. A light was visible in the gray mist moving around a bend, an Amtrak train blaring its way toward the bridge. The passengers were in for a treat up there, just like the ones on the Missouri Pacific line decades before.

Stucky stood on a rise in tall grass and Dieffenbach joined him, Stucky pointing to the cliff. "Now, the big difference you'll see in the postcard and today is the size of the river," Stucky said. "Geez, it must have come way out north of here, taking all of that bottomland, and there were numerous sandbars and islands, too, in the river. Actually, there are more trees here today than there were then. But now, look, there's only one sandbar."

"I'll bet that sandbar's been here forever," Dieffenbach said. Then: "Do you hear that?"

Stucky brought out a tiny pair of binoculars and looked out toward the sandbar. "Yep, there are geese out there." He smiled. "It won't be long before there'll be a bunch of 'em out there."

The Missouri still looks wide at this point if only because the land that abuts it is broad and flat. In the gray, cold mist, river and land seemed blurringly as one. The Missouri, channeled though it is, still has the strong pull of the wild that I imagine all the different times I've crossed it. It was a splendid sight. Seeing it stirred a memory for Stucky.

"I'll never forget the first time I was on this river," he said, putting the binoculars away and looking off to the west. "This was 1963. I was a junior in high school. I was on a boat with a commercial fisherman out of Omaha named Emil Ducek, who also happened to be a professional wrestler. What a character he was. He only had one ear. One of his opponents took a dislike to him and actually bit off his other ear. Back then, wrestling was a little more real than it was fake. Anyhow, I'm on the river, and I'll never forget the power of that water while I was in the boat. Man, what a feeling! But here was this grand old river, and all around it was a putrid stench and gobs of tallow grease balls floating down the river. The packinghouses would just dump their refuse in the river. I want to tell you, the Missouri River was one stinking mess. You've got to say we've come a ways since then."

"In my lifetime," Dieffenbach said, "we've come from no recognition of environmental problems, to awareness, to actually doing something about them. From nothing to action. Sure, the river is not a natural force anymore. Neither is the Mississippi. But we've seen the errors that have been made in the past. I think we've learned from them. We're working together with some former foes, and some good things are going to happen. That's the only way to look at it."

I looked at the Missouri bluffs overlooking the two rivers and thought the scene still worthy of a postcard, or a book. Dieffenbach's words recalled those of the legendary river pilot and writer who shared the same visions. In taming the river, we gained something, and we lost something, as Mark Twain pointed out. And Mr. Twain also said there has never been a book as wonderful as the river. No book could ever encompass it all or hold our imaginations as this river still does.

EARTHWORMS TO THE RESCUE
Thomas Bicki, University of Illinois soil scientist. *(Courtesy of Robert Siebrecht)*

C H A P T E R 7

Earthworms to the Rescue

He wears an earring in his left ear. Not many soil scientists do, but Dr. Bicki is unfazed by convention. A powerfully built man in his middle thirties, Bicki is about six feet tall and swarthy complected. If he should choose to glare at you, he would be a truly frightening specter, a perfect pirate on Captain Hook's ship. But in the cornfields of Illinois, you might look long and hard before you find another buccaneer as likable as this one.

Thomas Bicki, Ph.D., is a Cooperative Extension Service agronomist at the University of Illinois at Urbana-Champaign. Bicki is a warm, friendly, outgoing man, eager to explain his specialties in soil chemistry, soil management, and erosion to anyone who lends an ear. As an extension soil scientist, he has traveled all of the state's interstates, most of its highways, and back roads to present his research results to farmers and farm advisers throughout Illinois's 102 counties. He's spoken in nearly every county, met thousands of farmers, worked with a steady group of colleagues at the university since 1982, and has rubbed elbows with scores of county advisers in that time. In recent years, he has averaged one hundred days on the road each year, like many an extension specialist, including solid travel from January through the middle of March at the county winter meetings, the equivalent of baseball's spring training season for farmers.

The Prairie State's flagship university was among the first of the nation's land-grant institutions, so designated in 1862 by order of native son Abraham Lincoln. President Lincoln established land-grant schools to promote agriculture and science education at affordable tuition rates for local citizenry. Each state in the Union has a land-grant university. The Cooperative Extension Service, established in 1914 under the power of the Smith-Lever Act, is the land-grant university's outreach organization that, through a network of offices in every county of the state and through research conducted at various experiment stations statewide, communicates research and information to the state's farmers, farm homemakers, and consumers in general. For decades, farmers and their families have relied upon the advice of extension agents and specialists like Bicki. Farm children are introduced to the familylike atmosphere of the Cooperative Extension Service through the famous 4-H clubs, valuable training grounds that provide youngsters opportunities to compete and learn as individuals as well as in groups. The extension service, an overwhelming success since its inception, has long been admired and imitated by other countries. However, like everything else in agriculture during the 1980s, the esteemed organization has undergone a topsy-turvy makeover.

The travel, the one-on-one teaching experiences with individual farmers, the painstaking attention to each county are no longer on Bicki's agenda, for instance, nor on that of other extension specialists in Illinois or, for that matter, in most other states. Agriculture, the nation's number one business, may have seen the most profound changes of any other industry in the previous decade, from seed salesmen to producers to advisers and all steps in between. Extension specialists can no longer operate like country doctors. Nowadays, Dr. Bicki no longer can hop into a university automobile, drive three hours to Collinsville, near St. Louis, give an hour-long talk on soil management and no-tillage practices, answer questions, then turn around and drive the three hours back. Instead, Bicki and extension specialists in agronomy, beef, pork, and poultry production, entomology, plant pathology, soil fertility, and weed science, will more likely spend their days training county regional advisers who will come to the Urbana campus several times a year to learn how to present the information to farmers in area counties. Because the extension service is funded three ways—through federal, state and county monies—times were very tough on it during the eighties. The federal government, with a deficit that has hit more than $352 billion dollars in the nineties, now makes a meager contribution to the extension service; state budgets are always strapped, and individual counties in Illinois have resorted to special referendums to keep funding the extension service. Some counties have voted it out, and extension county advisers, accustomed to a system so well entrenched that it has become a way of life, have had to scramble to get another position somewhere else in the state or else leave extension altogether. In just a decade, one of the most admired hierarchies ever assembled has been pulled apart, piece by piece.

"It's been obvious throughout the decade that the extension service couldn't survive the way it had for years. And it couldn't be a static organization," Bicki said from behind his desk on the third floor of Turner Hall, the agronomy building on the University of Illinois campus. "The new trend is a shopping-mall sort of philosophy—gather all the information, put it in one place where lots of people will come and get it, and make sure the information is current and up to date. To be honest, I really won't miss all the travel. I'll miss the farmers, though, because you keep your finger on the pulse of what's happening when you visit the farmer. But I'm probably more valuable here writing manuals, researching my plots, and training the regional people."

Farming was awash in changes during the eighties, a decade that, in Illinois alone, saw the state's pool of farmers decline from roughly 100,000 in 1980 to 84,000 in 1990. Dr. Bicki has ridden with the changes, and played a major role in the adaptation in Illinois of one of the most dramatic changes in farming practices, no-tillage, whereby a farmer no longer tills the soil, but plants into the previous crop's residue, saving topsoil, fuel, and time, all the while leaving the soil in place and harvesting crops that yield nearly as much as those planted conventionally with extensive tillage. As a futurist in a somewhat tradition-bound profession, this agronomist has posed several concepts that do not always sit well with his colleagues.

"It's funny I should mention shopping malls," he told me, a faint trace of his East Coast accent still audible after years of Midwest living. He leaned forward, folding his dark, powerful forearms, obviously warming to his topic. "Because I think they are at the core of a land-use ethic that we never address: Is it right to take another forty acres of some of the best prime prairie farmland in the world at the edge of Champaign, Bloomington, or Decatur and turn it into another shopping mall, and at the same time take another forty acres of highly erodible, sloping soil in southern Missouri, pay that farmer to keep it in production, and allow the shopping mall to be built? Should the government allow land in central Illinois that produces 200-bushel corn to be sold off to developers, all the while continuing to pay, at taxpayers' expense, subsidies to the farmer on highly erodible soil that at best will produce 100-bushel corn? I'm terribly concerned that we're losing too much good soil and protecting marginal soil.

"My feeling is to keep that good land in farming, tear up all the cities, take all the good land, and get everybody the hell out of here. We could produce most of the corn needed in the country right here in Illinois if we planted the state from border to border. Instead, the citizens of this country are supporting poor farmers to grow crops on poor land. Nobody gains a thing from that. I know that's a pretty revolutionary idea because it involves a much larger land ethic than what we're operating on now. How do you tell people in Illinois that you can't build any more shopping malls?

"We don't need any more people here in Illinois," he says emphatically. "Think about going to the worst of the Third World countries where people are starving and telling them to take their best farmland and build a big city on it, then go out to the poor farmland and grow food. That's exactly what we're doing here in the Midwest."

Dr. Bicki leaned back in his chair and stroked his beard, swiveling back and forth, then stopped and looked straight ahead with his dark, piercing pirate eyes.

"This is a national ethical issue that nobody has addressed because it's not in our tradition to approach problems systematically. Instead, we do everything haphazardly, we fight fires here and there. A few years back the government put hundreds of dairy farmers out of business, bought off their cows, and slaughtered them because we were producing too much dairy products. Now, what do we do but encourage the development of bovine somatotropin, a hormone that increases milk production in cows—it makes supercows. Didn't we kill off the cows because we produced too much milk? Is there any sense to that kind of policy? We still produce more than we need now.

"I would love to see a systematic approach to environmental problems instead of flitting about from one issue to another with little long-term vision. We need to look at all facets of the environment, not single ecological events."

Bicki can analyze the most arcane of soil management problems, such as the distribution of calcium in a soil profile and the runoff of pesticides from topsoil into groundwater. Those tasks he performs every day. But clearly this agronomist has great notions about big pictures. Bicki loves the soil as much as any farmer and he knows considerably more about it than most farmers. He has developed intriguing concepts about the environmental aspects of soil management and stewardship.

Imagine a Heartland as it exists today, with its ubiquitous corn, soybean, and wheat fields, except added to that landscape are buffer zones, large areas of vegetation stripped through the cropland like fire lanes through the woods, "ecological fire lanes," as Bicki calls them. These corridors are the home of natural predators that reduce or eliminate the populations of harmful insects like the European corn borer, corn rootworm, the bean leaf beetle, the black cutworm, wheat aphid, and many others. Many of the plants grown on the ecological fire lanes are native prairie plants, deep-rooted perennials or biennials that are excellent for soil tilth and soil placement. The plants serve also as a purifying zone to stop water-carrying pesticide and fertilizer runoff from going into streams. The natural predators would lessen farmers' reliance upon insecticides, the most toxic of all pesticides to humans, while the plants in the ecology lane would check soil erosion and filter out water-transported contaminants.

Bicki envisions this as a real possibility in the future on a large scale—he'd like to try it on a small scale—and with some colleagues he wrote a proposal to the National Science Foundation (NSF) Long-Term Ecological Research program to sponsor a twenty-year experiment whereby he would take a section—640 acres—of prime farmland and plant 120 acres of it with the ecology-lane plants and then monitor the success of the system each year in terms of yield, soil quality, insect, weed and disease control, and runoff control. A limiting factor of his proposed system may be one of priorities: Does the system offset the amount of crop production value taken out of the 120-acre ecology lane? Would it be worth it for a farmer to plant the ecology lane and sacrifice 150 bushels of corn or 50 bushels of soybeans per acre on the 120 acres?

"The system addresses every environmental aspect of agriculture, and I really believe it will work," he said. "NSF found the proposal too production-oriented and suggested we go to USDA. They said, in effect, it didn't solve any immediate problems. So that puts us in a Catch-22 position. That's often a problem with ideas that are so innovative that people are afraid of them."

Bicki has been a major player in Illinois's most radical departure from tradition, the no-till movement. Though heralded by a core of agronomists in the seventies, no-till was practiced by few farmers on any sort of scale at all in Illinois at the dawn of the eighties. In 1982, when Bicki joined the University of Illinois faculty after two years at the University of Florida, the notion was just taking hold. In 1991, there were more farmers practicing no-till in Illinois than in any other state in the nation.

No-till is the most extreme measure in a tillage-reduction bag of tricks known as conservation tillage—in effect, using little or no tillage in crop production to save soil, time, and money. Methods vary in descending extremity from no-tilling, to ridge tilling, in which farmers plant seed into ridges built up on their soils with specialized equipment, to chisel plowing, plowing fields with an instrument that only slightly disturbs the soil instead of turning it completely over. Conservation tillage is a component of integrated pest management (IPM), an umbrella term hatched from various USDA agencies, which are farming practices designed to make best uses of pesticide and fertilizer inputs through crop rotation, crop scouting for weeds, insects, and plant diseases, and the wise and timely use of pesticides only as needed. Today, nearly every Illinois farmer practices IPM to one extent or another, and the concept has caught on nationwide. More and more farmers also are joining the no-till bandwagon. But at first the notion of leaving crop residue—cornstalks, soybean, and wheat stubble—on the field instead of plowing it eight inches beneath the ground each fall was as alien a notion to a midwestern farmer as changing from a protein-based diet to one rich in complex carbohydrates was for a veteran weight-watcher. It seemed implasuible. America, after all, relied on those who *tilled* the soil.

In the traditional Thanksgiving drive in the country for dinner at grandmother's house, city folks in the Heartland were accustomed to seeing deep, black, rich furrows in the earth, exposing the hearty gumbo of soil that made the area the most productive agricultural region in the world. Seeing the neat display of turned-over soil was part of the Thanksgiving tradition, a sign-off to another crop year, a signal that a farmer had done a good job, and an act of pride as well— nothing other than a tall-standing corn crop revealed the beauty and wealth of Heartland soils than the after-harvest furrows from fall and winter plowing.

Farmers tilled the soil because it was standard. Fall plowing cleaned up the residue—"trash," farmers called it—and most importantly it buried weeds and their seeds deep enough into the topsoil that they could not germinate and grow in the spring. The instrument used in deep plowing is called a moldboard plow; its name was derived from the characteristic curved board aligned behind the plowshare, the board lifting up the soil and turning it over. The inventor of the steel moldboard plow was none other than John Deere himself, who sold them by the hundreds in the 1850s and ushered in the settlement of the prairie.

The moldboard plow and its counterparts—other deep tillers such as the gang plow and rider plow—accomplished their tasks admirably. In less than 150 years, of 37,000 original square miles of prairie in Illinois, only 2 square miles remained. The soils of Illinois and other Heartland states were routinely moldboard plowed in the fall and winter, perhaps again in the spring, then disked or harrowed to break the clods in the spring, and planted with grains in exceptionally "clean" seedbeds. As the crop emerged, farmers routinely cultivated with rotary hoes or disks to let the soil breathe and to knock off the weeds that were bound to show up. Steel slashing soil was the perennial way to work the land. The rotary hoe, in fact, had its own jingle: "When the weeds begin to grow, get out the steel and hoe, hoe, hoe."

The big problem with moldboard plowing was that it left the soil completely vulnerable to water and wind erosion. A cadre of Illinois agronomists in the late fifties and early sixties grew concerned with the amount of topsoil loss, especially on sloping soils. These agronomists, among them the late George McKibben, William Oschwald, former Illinois Cooperative Extension Service director, and William Walker, professor emeritus, all from the University of Illinois, foresaw that the forces of wind and rain, combined with clean tillage, were moving tons of topsoil off the land into ditches, streams, rivers, and lakes all throughout the Heartland. Mixed in with the topsoil are other important commodities, fertilizer, plant materials and nutrients, and, with the increasing use of chemicals in farming, pesticides. Pesticides and nitrates from the fertilizer were reaching surface water supplies, at times in concentrations that were potentially hazardous. By the early 1980s, the admonitions of the soil savers were proving to be correct: In Illinois, 6.7 tons of topsoil per acre was being lost to wind and rain erosion each year, according to the Illinois Environmental Protection Agency.

That, it would seem, is a lot of soil gone with the wind, washed out with the rain. And it is, especially if it is an amount consistently being lost year after year. But the picture of topsoil fading away, lost forever, is a bit misleading, says Bicki.

"I have real problems with the notion of losing soil," he said. "In one sense, it is not so much the loss of soil but the redistribution of it that we're talking about. For instance, there's all sorts of erosion going on right here in Champaign County, but a lot of it is a part of a natural cycle in the development of a mature landscape. Let's say you have a piece of land with a summit a few feet higher than the low area around it. The natural process is to erode the highs, fill in the lows, and you end up with relatively flat plains. That's really what's going on with soil erosion to a large extent, but some portion of these eroded soils eventually finds its way to streams, and *that's* where the problems come in. Even though it's only a fraction of the total amount of soil redistributed, that fraction has a tremendous dollar value from the standpoint of fertility loss, clogging of waterways, transportation loss from silting, and even the occasional death during a dust storm. That's infrequent, but it happens."

A typical uneroded prairie soil will have a topsoil that is between twelve to eighteen inches thick. Soil scientists refer to the topsoil as the A horizon; beneath the A horizon, logically, lies the B horizon, or subsoil, typically descending from eighteen to about sixty inches into the earth. Beneath that is the C horizon, or "parent" material, either the original material laid down by prevailing winds that swept across the Heartland, loess, or glacial drift, the original material deposited by the glaciers, from which the B and A horizons are nurtured. The A horizon developed from the addition of organic matter—from plant materials—from the top down; the B horizon formed from the bottom up by modifying the physical and chemical properties of the C horizon. Thus, when the glaciers receded in Illinois and northern Missouri, they left behind a parent material, the C horizon; when plants began to grow on the parent material, the A horizon developed; through the process of weathering and soil development, the B horizon developed.

Although there are more than 400 different soil types in Illinois, classified by various chemical constituents and the number and arrangement of soil horizons, and named after place names where they were first described, there are two simple prototypes—forests and prairie. In Illinois, 60 percent of the soils are prairie; in Missouri, there is an almost even split. The prairie soils are so fertile because the plant litter that covered them for so many thousands of years retained the soil's relatively high pH, and a very healthy dose of basic nutrients such as calcium, phosphorus, potassium, and magnesium, which were constantly recycled through the process of annual plant growth and death. In forest soils, though, the organic matter incorporated into the soil came almost exclusively from leaf litter, which, after decomposing, is typically acidic. As the trees grew, nutrients removed from the soil were stored in the timber. When the settlers came and cut down the trees for firewood and houses, they essentially took away all the nutrients that would have been recycled back to the soil as the trees died and decayed naturally. The prairie soil, in contrast, was like an organic-matter-and-nutrient bank account, adding interest to the principal; the forest soils, once devoid of trees, became a plundered bank account.

The topsoil on uneroded forest soil, at about six inches or less, is one-half to one-third of the topsoil of its counterpart prairie soil. Erosion, which occurs much more rapidly on forest soils because they tend to be found on more rolling landscapes, happens when the A horizon is gradually whittled away, exposing the B horizon. Typically, on moderately eroded forest soils, some of the subsoil will be incorporated into the A horizon after plowing. In rare cases, although they do occur in Illinois and Missouri, more so in Missouri, the entire A horizon of the soil may be lost.

"Let's say two inches of A horizon in a forested soil are eroded and a farmer moldboard plows the soil about six inches deep," Bicki explained. "What he's actually done is plow four inches of topsoil and two inches of subsoil. If he stops to look he can see by the color and texture that there is some subsoil mixed into what he's turned up. Now he's got a moderately eroded soil that will only get worse if he continues moldboard plowing. On a prairie soil, with a twelve-inch topsoil, a farmer has to lose eight inches of topsoil to incorporate two inches of subsoil to have that same classification of moderately eroded. What we've seen in Illinois and throughout the Midwest until just a few years ago was the constant use of the moldboard plow and the gradual wearing away of topsoil."

The biggest loser in the soil erosion process is the Heartland's streams and waterways. The runoff ends up in the backwaters of the state's major rivers, the Illinois, Mississippi, Ohio, and Rock. For instance, in 1900 the average depth of the upper Peoria Lake, a large body of water that is an extension of the Illinois River at Peoria, was between eight and ten feet. Ninety years later, the average depth was not quite two feet. The lake, which is fed by creeks originating in agricultural watersheds, is in danger of filling up with sediment by the beginning of the next century. The same situation is occurring all along the major rivers of Illinois and Missouri. All of the backwater lakes that serve as a sediment basin for the Illinois River, for example, once they fill up, will spill their contents into the Illinois and ultimately clog up that mighty river.

Thus, Illinois needs to save soil from that environmental angle. But as for the loss to the farmer, Bicki thinks it's wise to keep the situation in perspective. For years, soil scientists have talked about "tolerable" topsoil loss, referring to the amount of soil loss from erosion that does not exceed the soil's ability to sustain its productivity. A farmer, for example, who erodes two tons of topsoil per acre may seem to be rapidly depleting his resource. But one acre of land six inches thick, Bicki explained, weighs a staggering 2 million pounds—1,000 tons. If a farmer erodes two tons of soil per acre, that's actually one five-hundredths of the 2 million pounds, or .012 inch of soil that is lost, about one one-hundredth of an inch of soil.

"If you have eighteen inches of soil in the A horizon, think how long it would take at two tons per acre to remove six inches of soil," Bicki said. "Let's say the guy's been farming for fifty years, and he's losing soil at that rate during that span. By the end of his tenure on the land he's lost a half an inch of topsoil. It's really hard to lose twelve to eighteen inches of topsoil. Some people have managed to do it, but it's hard nonetheless."

While conservation of soil is one of the motives for reduced tillage, especially no-till, Bicki said economics is the overriding reason more farmers are practicing it. No-tillage requires far fewer trips across a field, saving time as well as soil. A farmer who practices no-tillage uses less, though more modified, machinery, including a special planter equipped with coulters—narrow wheels that cut the soil residue in preparation for the seed—disks that create a furrow for the seed, and firming wheels that cover and place the seed firmly in the soil. While in 1980 many of the no-till planters available were farmer-modified conventional planters, the agriculture machinery industry, always a kinetic business, was quick to respond to the interest, and a wide array of no-till planters are easy to find today.

Another reason for the adaptation of no-till is the Food Security Act of 1985, the Farm Bill. Farmers with highly erodible land who are enrolled in price-support programs—a vast majority of farmers—are required to practice conservation. There are programs, such as set-aside programs, where a farmer agrees to take land out of grain production, plant it with grasses or legumes to provide soil cover, and collect payments for not working the land. Another such program is the Conservation Reserve Program (CRP), an ambitious, ten-year project where farmers take highly erodible land out of production and plant trees or other crops to protect soil, making farmers necessarily more conscientious about conserving.

"The rules and policies of the federal government have provided the necessary push to get no-till and other conservation practices going," Bicki said. "Frankly, it was needed."

Each year farmers are strapped by the vagaries of weather, market prices, economic policies, and the uncertainty of insect and disease problems. They shoulder an enormous amount of risk. As a rule, farmers are very conscious of what their peers are doing. To try something new on a large scale puts them on trial, in a sense, in front of their neighbors and friends. No one wants to fail, and in the Heartland, one bad year has ruined many a farmer. So when no-till was first being viewed as a viable, exciting way to farm, many farmers were curious to try it, but few were willing to take the plunge. Wisely, the pioneers, modifying their conventional planters as best they could, began planting twenty acres or so in no-till and seeing what they could come up with.

The original no-till farmers found it difficult to get good stands with high populations. They solved that problem with adjustments to the planters and planting with drills instead of broadcasting the seed. They feared the residue into which they planted would be attractive to insects and diseases. But, especially by rotating crops and scouting their fields religiously, insects and diseases are no longer any more of a problem with no-till than they are with heavy tillage systems.

A drawback is that no-till makes a producer solely reliant on herbicides for weed control. The no-till farmer cannot avoid using them. The conventional farmer will use them, too, but he shouldn't need to use them nearly as much as the no-till farmer because his deep plowing buries weed seeds, preventing them from germinating, and he can cultivate to control germinated weeds in inter-row areas.

The dilemma of farming in the post–World War II era boils down to what we want to save. Conservation tillage saves many resources and is environmentally friendly, but it requires the steadfast use of pesticides. Since Rachel Carson's *Silent Spring* was published in the early sixties, all of the informed public have considered pesticides suspiciously. A groundswell of organic farming sentiment has swept the country since the seventies, and it continues unabated. The Environmental Protection Agency released data in 1991 that showed many of the commonly used pesticides in farming can be detected in small amounts in rainwater, a sort of "Old McDonald's rain." Agricultural pesticides and nitrates from fertilizers have been routinely monitored in groundwater supplies in Iowa, parts of Missouri, and Illinois in the latter part of the eighties. The fear is not so much of an immediate poisoning, but of the deleterious effects after constant exposure to trace amounts of the chemicals found in pesticides. The more the public knows, the more incensed they are likely to be, and the person most often castigated for environmental excesses in recent years is our country cousin, the farmer.

"If you're willing to pay six dollars for a bag of corn chips that were produced pesticide-free, the American farmer can produce corn without pesticides," Bicki remarked about this dilemma. "But if you want to buy the chips for sixty-nine cents a bag, you'll have to have them with pesticides applied at levels the EPA says are safe. Farming could go back to the days when farmers lost half of their crops to insects and diseases, but if you want bread at ninety-five cents a loaf instead of six dollars a loaf, that's what you have to live with. No farmer knowingly wants to grow a crop with residue on it, but you have to balance some amount of residue on food that's not a health risk with the cost of producing that food."

With the emergence of no-till, the increasing experiments with natural predators to control insects and diseases, and the blossoming of the overall theme of the 1980s—sustainable agriculture—there is a move toward bringing a measure of simplicity back to agriculture. Bicki, as he has been with many issues in agriculture at the University of Illinois, is in the middle of this movement.

Consider the lowly earthworm, *Lumbricus rubellis*. Dr. Bicki has, in a very systematic way, and he is trying to understand how such a simple creature can be incorporated into farming plans as much as the applications of fertilizer, the use of herbicides, and the saving of soil.

By the late 1980s, Heartland farmers, ranging from conventional to no-till innovators, had started to reach a plateau with yields. This was the culmination of years of research that first presented better crop varieties through smart plant breeding, better yields through the introduction of first fertilizer and then herbicides, then higher plant populations through the introduction of better planting methods and selection of disease-resistant varieties. Corn yields of 150 to 200 bushels per acre and soybean yields of more than 40 bushels per acre are the norm now and they seem to have leveled off. The next big hurdle, Bicki believes, involves water and soil management.

"The big question now is: Does the physical condition of the soil have a limiting effect on yield? If so, we can't do much with water other than irrigate, and that's very expensive, or perhaps seed clouds, and that's not proven to be effective yet. The Europeans for a long time have shown that earthworms can increase the fertility of the soil by taking plant-available nutrients from the B and C horizons and redistribute them into the A horizon. Primarily, their research has been done on marginally productive soil with little fertility. Very little has been done on highly fertile soils like we have here.

"It's a curious fact that I've heard over and over again from no-till farmers that it takes about eight years for no-till soils to come back and produce good yields. That may mean it takes that long for the earthworms to come back and improve the soil. We don't know. But it may mean something as simple as a healthy earthworm population is what it takes to make no-till work."

Earthworms themselves are not soil fertilizer. They instead aerate the soil, improve its structure, recycle nutrients, and increase infiltration of water into the soil. Cultivation of Heartland soils throughout the century has dramatically decreased the population of earthworms. The plows and cultivators literally chop up and kill the worms and bury the residue that is the natural habitat for earthworms, surface-feeding creatures that burrow into the soil for organic matter banquets. If there is no residue for them on the fields, when they burrow upward in search of food, they die in the sun from exposure to ultraviolet light—there is no shade for them to crawl under. City dwellers have seen this form of annelid suicide after a heavy rain when the soil becomes saturated with water and the earthworms are flooded out, crawl onto the pavement, and die from prolonged sunlight exposure— many a boy has gathered fishing bait in such a manner.

No-till is a natural system to reincarnate earthworms into midwestern soils. The residue provides a fine shade, there's plenty of organic matter for sustenance, and moist soil prevents their dessication. But the other part of the one-two punch that has knocked out earthworms on the prairie soil is pesticides, especially a class of insecticides called the carbamates, used on a host of insect pests, particularly the corn rootworm, which tends to plague cornfields that are not rotated. Oddly, herbicides applied at normal field application rates have little or no effect on the earthworm mortality, although more research is needed. Another class of insecticides called the organophosphates have shown varying levels of toxicity ranging from no effect to high, and yet another class, the organochlorines, no longer legal to use, has a toxicity ranging from low to high. DDT, the infamous organochlorine, has shown little toxicity on worms, while chlordane, used for years to kill termites and other insect pests, is high. Exacerbating the problem is the long life of the organochlorines in the soil; although they are no longer permitted to be applied to cropland, they can still be found from applications made as long as twenty years ago.

A typical, uncultivated tallgrass prairie may have as many as 1 to 2 million earthworms burrowing in the soil per acre; a long-term pasture fertilized naturally with manure may have as many as 2 to 2.5 million earthworms per acre, all doing what comes naturally and helping to improve the soil. The earthworm could become a farmer's cheapest production input.

"As soon as you start cultivating the soil, the population drops dramatically," Bicki said. "In intensively tilled soil with no application of pesticides toxic to earthworms, you might have a quarter- to a half-million worms per acre. Add the wrong pesticide and their population is likely to be decimated. It's interesting to think that the key to unleashing the next stage of productivity for midwestern crops might be found in a schoolboy's bait bucket. A hurdle to overcome is how to reestablish earthworms in some uniform way throughout a field."

An entrepreneur farmer in central Illinois raises earthworms and has patented a process to encapsulate an earthworm cocoon in a capsule. The capsules can be mixed with seeds in the planting hopper. At planting time the cocoons are incorporated with the soybean seeds and can be uniformly "planted" in the field. While his notion has drawn chuckles from some area farmers, there are others willing to try it— the value of the earthworm is an old farmer's tale passed down from fathers to sons for generations.

Bicki wants to add credence to the farmer's tale. On four acres a farmer has loaned to him near Elliot, Illinois, a tiny community about twenty miles north of Champaign, Bicki is studying the effects of earthworms on soils. The farmer is himself an earthworm aficionado, with more than 160 acres of his croplands having been introduced to earthworms that he raises himself in a nearby facility. Bicki has subplotted the four acres into one area where no earthworms have been introduced; another area where a quarter-million earthworms have been added; another that has a half-million; and a last where one million earthworms are squirming through the soil. At the University of Illinois experiment station outside of Perry, in west-central Illinois, he has a similar, though smaller, experiment afoot. The two studies differ, essentially, in the type of tillage systems used; at Orr Center the plots have been planted no-till or else chisel plowed. At Elliot, they are no-tilled or else para-tilled—a system where the plow lifts and disturbs soil beneath the surface but essentially leaves the soil residue intact. Over the years he will take note of crop yield, soil conditions, and the status of the earthworms themselves as they work, gratis, for the state's farmers.

Thomas Bicki is a native of Rhode Island, graduating with a degree in agronomy in 1978. He was originally interested in becoming an engineer, but took an elective in botany and found himself increasingly drawn to the plant and soil sciences. Upon the advice of a professor, he switched his major from engineering to agronomy, only, he said "because I was told that botanists never get jobs." He went to Iowa State University, a mecca for agriculture majors, to enter the M.S. and

Ph.D. programs in agronomy with an emphasis on soils, their genesis, morphology, and physics.

Bicki spent a happy childhood as a "child gentleman farmer," as he puts it; he raised horses, baled hay, and did enough chores to get a taste of farming and a perspective on it. His grandfather had nine sons, none of whom he wanted to become farmers, and so he worked hard to send them away to colleges or to the city. Although Bicki spent a good deal of time on farms as a child, and later married a girl reared on a farm, he considers himself a city kid, having grown up in an urban area of Rhode Island.

"The whole idea of sustainable agriculture came out of the Northeast," remarked the former New Englander. "There are a lot of small, diversified farms in that part of the country. Sustainable agriculture is spreading here and may find a niche. Maybe some excitement about earthworms, something as simple as that, can help change ideas about the importance of some of the more fundamental things in agriculture."

Looking out over the hundreds of acres of crops and experimental plots at the University of Illinois South Farm, one sees every imaginable type of experiment in all the varieties of plants—from soybeans to sunflowers—that can be grown in the Prairie State. All the different tillage experiments involving machinery costing thousands of dollars and all the diverse chemical treatments developed by the nation's crackerjack chemists to ensure a pest-free crop are represented here. Meanwhile, miles away from Urbana, deep in the soils of Ford County and the Orr Center in Pike County, Bicki's earthworms are wriggling their way through the A horizon, seeking the microorganisms and organic matter on which they thrive, doing their thing for the soils of Illinois.

AN ILLINOIS FARMER
Earl Hesterberg shows the radar gun linked to a computer in his tractor cab, which together coordinate an even distribution of chemicals and fertilizer on the acres he farms near Gifford, Illinois. *(Courtesy of Tony Fitzpatrick)*

C H A P T E R   8

An Illinois Farmer

Earl Hesterberg is both a gentleman and a farmer. He has no
livestock on his farm, but he does have earthworms, lots of them.

He owns 200 acres of fine silty loam soil near Gifford, Illinois, in
agriculturally endowed Champaign County. Hesterberg's home sits on
a country road, one mile outside of Gifford (population 800). The
house is near a creek and sheltered by a fine grove of oak and maple
trees across the road, a perfect windbreak from the cold north winds
that blow all the way from Canada across the broad, flat prairie. In
1976 and 1977, Hesterberg had the roomy ranch house built, a
windfall for his wife, Sue, and children, Stephanie and Chad, courtesy
of the last big boom years in American agriculture, the 1970s, when,
as Hesterberg put it, "it was real hard to lose money farming. Prices,
especially for soybeans, was so good then. I'd fed my family. I had
money left over, so I thought we'd start the house we'd been planning
because the house we were living in on the rented farm was old and in
need of much repair. So we had the house built and later we bought
our first piece of ground in 1977. That was ten years *after* I started
farming."

It was a hot, sunny June morning and Hesterberg and I had gotten
into his Chevy pickup and toured his fields of corn and soybeans
during a dry spell. Corn was heading into pollination soon; the tassels

on the plant containing the pollen that would scatter throughout the fields (landing on the cornsilk, each strand of silk responsible for forming one kernel of corn), had not sprouted yet. This is one of the great "white knuckle" stages of farming, a crucial time when farmers pace the yard or floor or just drive alongside their fields looking skyward, hoping and praying for a nice long, steady, soaking rain. Drought will send an agnostic farmer to church on Sunday; that, and bad weather during planting and harvesting, the other two gut-twisting times on the farm. But Hesterberg, a placid man, was not worried. He wanted to show me the worm holes in his bean fields.

Hesterberg stopped the truck on a hauling pathway along a bean field and got out of the truck. He is a big, easy-going man, six feet two inches or better, solidly built and strong. He wore work boots, Dickie overalls, and a long-sleeved shirt. A seed cap tilted upward on his head revealed blond, ruddy features and eyes as calmly blue as the sky after a storm. He stopped in a narrow row of soybeans and pulled back a plant. Near the base of the plant by a dusty minipile of decomposing corn stalks—last year's crop—he brushed aside the pile and revealed a neat little hole made by a burrowing earthworm. He bent over another plant, showing several more; two rows over, he moved more residue and showed me other worm holes.

"I planted these beans right into last year's cornstalks, never made one pass to clean up the residue," he said, smiling a warm, open smile. "And I didn't use any insecticide on beans following corn because you usually don't find many insect problems with that kind of rotation. I've got earthworms all over my farm."

Earl Hesterberg is a master no-till farmer, one of Champaign County's first big-time no-tillers. He harvests respectable-to-excellent yields year after year using a system that old-timers in the county first laughed at. No-till farmers were considered lazy at first, certain to be courting financial ruin, two assessments Hesterberg heard constantly until about two years ago. Then one day a county elder crossed the road and approached Hesterberg as he took a break from planting and told him, enthusiastically, he was doing the right thing.

"Fella said, 'Earl, you're on the right track, no matter what anybody else says. If I was startin' over, I'd go your way.' Then just this morning I was having coffee downtown and a young fellow asked me some questions about no-till. I don't think he farms erodible land, because he lives in Flatville, but he wants to cut costs. More and more guys are asking me about it. You see, up here in this area, we're always looking for ways to cut costs. About all that's raised anymore is cash grain, and there aren't many sidelines. We're always happy for ways to improve our methods, but we're conservative in our approach."

Hesterberg's corner of Champaign County, which is noted generally for its flat, fertile prairie soils, is one of the few portions of the county where the ground is rolling. Champaign, after all, comes from the French, meaning an expanse of level, open country. He estimates 80 percent of the land he farms is not just rolling, but "highly erodible land," as classified by the Soil Conservation Service (SCS). He learned his conservation methods early on from his father, who ran a dairy farm just three miles from Hesterberg's place, and from his brother Leonard. His father, he recalled, hated to waste anything. If he tore up a piece of ground doing chores with his tractor, he'd go back in and fill it up. Older brother Leonard, with whom Hesterberg began farming in 1967, hated the sight of eroded soil so much he felt a moral repugnance at seeing streaks in the soil from sheet and rill erosion after a heavy rain. He almost quit farming because he felt he was mistreating the soil. They were moldboard plowing then. Leonard passed away in July 1971 in a boating mishap. Earl hired a man and continued farming. He and his helper began chisel plowing cornstalks, a rather new practice in the early seventies. He and Leonard already had adopted the practice of not tilling the fragile soybean fields the previous year. Then, in the early eighties, Hesterberg got the itch to try no-till.

His first concern was weeds. The second was machinery. He thought it over for a couple of years, then bought a no-till planter and, after consulting with various herbicide companies and visiting a herbicide company research farm, developed a herbicide program that evolved into the basic one he uses today for corn: an application of herbicide to the soil immediately after planting, lightly incorporated into the soil by rainfall instead of machinery, which would destroy the protective residue. The herbicide becomes activated when the rain falls, setting off the chemical ingredients that go about killing weeds that pop through the soil, but allowing the corn to grow without the moisture-robbing competition of weeds.

For soybeans, each spring he'll kill the existing weeds with a contact herbicide (so-named because of its quick kill) before planting. Then within one to three days, he and his help will plant the soybeans at 200,000 to 225,000 seeds per acre. After the beans have emerged and are in the second or third trifoliate stage, he'll spray again to kill any new weeds that have grown with the soybeans. From this stage on, the canopy of the soybean takes over, providing enough shade to keep any new weeds from growing and becoming competitive with the soybeans for the soil nutrients and soil moisture.

There are more than fifteen registered soybean herbicide products in any given year; for corn there are about twenty. Every year or every other year another product is introduced and an old one drops off; Hesterberg will try the new ones on a tentative basis. Sometimes, depending on what kind of herbicide he uses, he'll mix it with his fertilizer—a ration of nitrogen, phosphorus, and potassium. He plants corn in thirty-inch rows, as he has for many years; he plants soybeans in just eight-inch rows with a grain drill attached to a no-till coulter cart. The grain drill approach to soybeans is a relatively new planting method for that crop, developed to encourage more plants per acre and more shading of weeds by the plant canopy. Drilling beans, he told me, also increases yield potential by as much as 15 percent. The thicker canopy that drilled soybeans provides also helps protect the soil from erosion, another major benefit.

After the corn has been planted and it stands about three to six inches tall, he'll inject anhydrous ammonia, a form of nitrogen stored as a gas in a long tank, on his corn ground to boost the nitrogen content of the soil, the most needed and most depleted element of soils planted in corn.

Hesterberg drove the truck on a country road, pointing out his fields. He raises only corn and soybeans, although he is considering planting eighty acres of wheat on one of his more highly erosive pieces of land. His landlords include a German woman who lives in California, from whom he rents 320 acres, a Champaign family from whom he rents 640 acres, and a local family who have arranged for him to farm 140 acres. His rental arrangements are all a fifty-fifty split with the landowner, each paying 50 percent of inputs such as fertilizer, herbicides, and seed and each receiving 50 percent of the harvested grain. The landlord has the investment in the farm and the tenant offsets that investment with his own contribution of labor, management, and machinery.

At the top of a hill high enough to give a commanding view of land for miles around, Hesterberg stopped and pointed southward. "In the fall, I'll be harvesting this ground and look out south and see all these Flatville farmers harvesting all that flat ground from row to row and don't have to worry about miles of terraces and waterways. I told one of them the other day, jokingly, not everybody can farm all that easy land. Some of us has to have a challenge."

The area around Flatville and Royal, two tiny farming communities, is so flat, low-lying, and barren of anything besides elevators and crops that it appears to be below sea level. The Flatville blacktop, accessible off Interstate 74 and, more directly, off Route 45, which dissects the eastern slice of Illinois from Brookport near the Kentucky border to near Antioch on the Wisconsin border, has been made famous in paintings by Billy Morrow Jackson and in photographs by the late Art Sinsebaugh. On a gloomy November day, a person gazing very long at the black harvested earth joining the gray sky can become disoriented on the Flatville blacktop, the way one feels looking out the window of a banking airplane. There is no telling where earth stops and sky begins.

Hesterberg pulled off the road and drove down a grass waterway that snaked between healthy stands of corn. Nearly two miles of waterways cut through the land Hesterberg farms; he has put them in himself, or else remodeled existing ones, as well as built terraces, to halt water runoff from the sloping soils and to curb soil erosion. The waterways are common practices among grain farmers but often unnoticed by travelers along the interstate. From an automobile, the waterways often can't be seen or else look simply like a piece of ground the farmer chose to ignore or else a boundary between properties. But they are there to control water and save soil, and Hesterberg is proud of them for the job they do, although he finds them vexing at harvest and planting time because they slow him down. But he's also seen pheasant, fox, and quail in the grassy corridors, which he mows three or four times each growing season.

"Once you build terraces, you have them forever," he said. "I could chisel plow this ground with a straight-shank chisel every two years if I put in more terraces, but I prefer no-tilling and keeping the waterways. When I harvest beans, the first thing I do is cut around the waterways very carefully. Without them, I could go straight through the rows and be done more quickly. But it's a good feeling to know they're holding the soil."

Hesterberg shares the cost of building waterways, terraces, and drainage ditches with SCS, a branch of USDA with a regional office in Champaign. He will tell them of his plans to farm and between them they will reach an agreement over which waterway or terrace plan to follow for the type of tillage system he'll use.

He brought the truck off the bumpy waterway onto the blacktop and into the driveway where the original farm was. He conducts all of his business inside one of two large equipment sheds. The red-and-white one close to the road houses his office, tractors, planting equipment, combine, sprayer, and other equipment. The other one across the drive about forty yards away is rented out to a local fertilizer dealer for equipment and storage. To the south of his equipment shed, five grain bins sit side by side. To the west of the grain bins and equipment shed another forty or fifty yards away lies a pond, about an acre wide, fringed with cattails, its water shimmering gently in the hot sun. The land lies nicely here; there is a peaceful view of the rolling fields of corn to the west, giving ever so slightly a sense of elevation in a flat land.

Livestock buildings used to be part of the place, as well as an old farmhouse that Hesterberg and his family lived in before he built his new house. When the land changed possession from one owner to the

Champaign owner, Hesterberg tore down the livestock buildings, unused and in bad repair, in the late sixties, and the house went later. We walked into the machine shed, an airy, spacious, squeaky-clean building. A huge, shiny red CASE-IH 7130 tractor, the second-largest two-wheel drive tractor that company makes, was parked in front of us a few yards away. Its thick tires reach nearly five feet tall, its enclosed, air-conditioned cab is equipped with a computer-controlled monitor with radar that will adjust the rate of herbicide and nitrogen he wants to put on the soil in relationship to the speed that the tractor moves across the ground, ensuring a uniform distribution of herbicide. Beyond the CASE-IH 7130, which has 175 horsepower, there is a spacious area with a basketball hoop and net, and a doorway leading to the second part of the shed, which houses his second big tractor, a CASE-IH 7110, which has 130 horsepower, two smaller tractors from the forties and seventies, the McCormick "H" a veteran of the farmers' drive to Washington, D.C., in 1969. They're not very powerful for the kind of farming done today, but Hesterberg keeps them for small chores. Everything is so smooth, so clean, there's hardly a trace of the timeless country smell of gasoline, grease, wood, and rusty steel. There is no rusty steel on Earl Hesterberg's farm.

Hesterberg's office is a bright paneled room with a big picture window that gives a southern view; there is an old couch near the window and a long desk and a chair on the north side of the room. Hesterberg explained part of the reason he was able to afford the two new CASEs.

Until the fall of 1990 he had used the tractor shed as headquarters for a business he and two brothers started several years ago. The brothers invented a device they called a chaff spreader; rotating blades that are attached to the combine's rear axle, the chaff spreader prevents soybean chaff from piling up between rows and distributes the residue more evenly across a field. At the time, Hesterberg and his brothers saw the trend toward conservation tillage looming—and the coming adaptation of no-till—and realized that the piece of machinery they envisioned was totally absent from the combines being manufactured. They developed the item, tried it out on their own combine, spent a winter making more, and sold a few, at first through word of mouth.

Then a major agriculture magazine got wind of it, ran a piece on the Hesterberg invention, and, as so often happens with farmers who glean every bit of information on things that will save them time and labor, they started buying it in droves. The tractor shed was operating headquarters during those years; the parts were built and stored there, orders were taken at his office, and marketing brainstorming sessions held there as well. Sales of the item, which in 1991 retailed for approximately $600, took off from an average of between 150 and 800 in the first three years to more than 1,600 in 1990. Meanwhile, Hesterberg ran the farm from his office as well, and found himself running two jobs 365 days of the year. In addition to two brothers in business with him, Hesterberg hired one part-time worker during planting and harvest for the farm, and several part-time workers for the spreader business. Things, he realized, were getting out of hand. So that fall he sold out his share of the business to a younger brother who drove a semi-truck for a local food distributor and had been having back trouble. That brother is now managing the spreader business. Now the tractor shed is used entirely for the farm. His other two brothers farm a lesser amount of land than Earl, and thus have more time to devote to the business.

"I'm far more relaxed now," he said. "Life's too short for all that hassle. But the machinery business was very good to me."

His position now is in sharp contrast to what it was in 1967, when he started farming with his brother Leonard. The two started with 840 rented acres, borrowed money, and the intense drive to farm. They worked eighteen-hour days, farming scared.

"We'd a' been a lot more scared than we were if we'd kept the kind of records we do today," he laughed. "But here I was twenty-two, just married, a thousand dollars in the bank, and with the knowledge I had gained working with my dad. I'd only had one other job before that, working at the Kraft factory in Champaign. We wanted to farm so bad we just kept our nose to the grindstone."

Despite their ardor, they had a bad year off the bat. The land the brothers worked had been completely farmed out; it was low in lime and other nutrients, and they faced enormous weed pressure plus a very dry year locally. That harvest averaged only seventy-nine bushels of corn per acre, which they were able to sell for only ninety-seven cents a bushel. Yet they persisted. They limed the soils, bringing up the acidity and building up the fertility bank of nutrients in the soil. They gradually started turning a profit. In 1969, they rented another 320 acres.

"Efficiency," Hesterberg said, and he pursed his lips tightly. "The only thing that keeps farmers going is their efficiency. The rest of society has not kept pace with the farmer's efficiency. I say that with many exclamation points behind it. Fifteen years ago, I got a dollar more for a bushel of corn at three twenty and two dollars more for soybeans at about eight dollars than I do today. Yet in that time all my inputs, fertilizer, herbicides, machinery, hired labor, and all, they've all gone up. And I'm paid less for what I produce. It's a very serious problem, a big reason you see so many guys lose at farming these days. What other segment of society has to deal with that? It's very difficult to turn a profit in farming these days."

Hesterberg brought out a rating sheet assessed by Farm Bureau Farm Management (FBFM), a program launched in conjunction with the extension service designed to promote efficiency in farming. He showed where, among other costs, his use of fuel was much lower per acre compared to other farmers who work comparable acreage and soils; so, too, were his costs for parts and repairs. In all, the assessment showed that, on a three-year average, he netted approximately $44 per tillable acre more farming his 1,300 acres than the average farmer did farming a similar-sized farm with his soil type.

"I don't want to make it seem like I'm bragging, but I'm proud of that," he said sheepishly. "I owe these figures almost entirely to no-till. No-till makes you far more efficient, and it adds to my desire to become as efficient as I can."

Hesterberg has known heartbreak and happiness in the quiet country of east-central Illinois. One year that really hurt was 1980 when he suffered poor yields during the great drought of that year. The best he could do was raise 55-bushel corn on land that normally averaged 130 bushels per acre. That year he did some forward pricing on the futures market, a common practice where a producer contracts to sell a crop at an agreed-upon price. For corn that year, the price was $2.35 per bushel. The crop year looked like a great one until the end of June when the drought set in for most of the rest of the summer. He had forward priced about 20 percent of his expected crop at the contract price, his yields declined 60 percent. But what it actually amounted to was 60 percent of the corn he harvested that year went at the contract price. Meanwhile, because of the drought, prices went much higher for corn than the $2.35 per bushel he had contracted. "But," he said with a shrug, "a contract is a contract and you have to deliver. Farmers take gambles like that every year."

In 1971, Hesterberg's partner and brother Leonard, whom he idolized, died. He was staggered by the loss, but kept farming, and developed a close working relationship for years with a hired hand, Rick Uden, whom he first met when the future farmer was a kid in the Sunday school class Hesterberg taught. Rick, who was an ace mechanic in addition to being a savvy crops man, grew to think so much like Hesterberg that it seemed the two were developing ESP. Finally, Hesterberg urged him to go elsewhere because he couldn't afford to pay him the salary that Uden was worth, and the young man would learn more at another place with more responsibility on his shoulders. Uden's abilities, as Hesterberg put it, "were greater than I could challenge him."

When he speaks of his family, Hesterberg proudly talks of his wife, Sue, who still drives a tractor each year at harvest, his daughter, Stephanie, now a student at a college in Iowa, and son, Chad, an eighth grader who helps him with lots of chores around the farm and shows a high interest in farming, but isn't ready yet, his dad feels, for the critical jobs, the anhydrous ammonia or the pesticides, although Chad helps a lot with harvesting and other tractor-driving jobs. There's a joy in working closely with someone with whom you can share ideas.

Hesterberg, with difficulty but great strength, speaks of son David, who was killed at the age of seven riding his bicycle along the road beside the farm.

"I'll share this with you because it's part of what's happened to me as a farmer here these twenty-four years," he said, his blue eyes unblinking. "But he was killed in June. . . . " He paused. "He'd be twenty-two now if he was alive. This happened between when school got out and when vacation Bible school started. The Thursday prior to the day he died we said grace before supper and David said to me, 'Dad, I know what heaven's like.' And I said, 'What's that?' And he said, 'In heaven, you sing to Jesus and you're happy all the time.' and I asked him, 'Who told you that? Did you learn that in Sunday school?' And he said, 'No, I just know.'

"I'll never forget the words he said. Within a week, he was dead. Now, some people have said to me that he knew what was going to happen to him. And I say no, he didn't, but God did because God is all-knowing, and he permitted David to share that knowledge he had with us and that helped us cope with things. A lot of people say, 'I don't know how you could ever cope with that.' But it's like the scriptures say, 'when there's strength that's needed, God gives you the strength.'

"I'll share something else with you. After it was all over I went through every stage they say you go through. I pounded my fist on the table at God many times. I said, 'You took my son, the only one I had. My brothers have their sons, but you took mine.' Then I even questioned my wife. And I'd say, 'Why did you let him go out on the road?' My wife and I had always been very close, but during this whole thing we became even closer because we were able to talk to each other and share our feelings with one another. Our Christian faith grew."

At the time the road belonged to the state and was infrequently mowed. It wasn't as big or busy as it is now, he explained. An older cousin had left on a bicycle and David persisted in asking permission to follow her on his bicycle. Sue gave in finally, but told David not to go beyond the break where a field driveway intersected, and to come back when he made it to the break. Hesterberg was out in a field with teenagers he had hired to pick up rocks in the field. David had asked to come along, but Hesterberg thought he should stay at home to play with his cousins. An older farmer driving down the road in a pickup, probably gazing out the window at the crops as farmers are wont to do, never saw David for all the tall bromegrass and did not immediately realize he had hit the child.

"So I was mad at myself, too, for not letting him work with me. He was kept alive on life-support machines, but the doctors told us as far as they could tell he'd never make it. His kidneys had stopped functioning. His heart had stopped functioning on its own, and because of massive head injuries he was classified as brain dead. So we had to make the decision to take him off the machines. We decided to let him go. Afterwards, I second-guessed that decision so many times. I wanted to go up and hug him, see. Later, I'd say to myself, 'If you hadn't decided to turn the machines off, maybe there would have been a very slight possibility that he could be in a nursing home somewhere and at least you could hug him.' Then, you have to grab yourself and say, 'Earl, you're just selfish. If you truly believe in Jesus Christ, in heaven, and that it is perfect there, and that we should all want to go there, let the poor guy go.' That was the hardest thing, second-guessing myself, thinking if I had given him a little more time, maybe a miracle could've happened."

He stopped and stared bemusedly at the floor. A smile spread across his face. "But I've been blessed so much, I truly have. I have great kids, a good and loving wife, and a healthy family. Farming's been good to me. I've been fortunate to do what I really love."

Outside, we looked at the pond glimmering in the midday sun; a hot breeze rippled through the corn leaves. Hesterberg declined an offer for lunch, but recommended J.R.'s or the Longbranch Saloon in town for a good plate of fish.

"Gonna need a rain pretty soon," he said, nodding toward the crops. "They look good now, but in a few weeks the leaves'll start curling up on the corn if they don't get enough moisture. The plant does that to protect itself from the heat. You know, sometimes I look at that pond and wonder if I might stock it with catfish. I'm always looking for a niche to add to the operation. Maybe a little catfish farm would go hand in hand with the other crops. But I'm always thinking like that. Every year when I'm done harvesting. I'm ready to add another 200 acres. Then when I plant I say, 'How am I going to get all this done?' "

Hesterberg has the strength do to whatever he sets out to do. It's a comfort knowing the soil in this niche of the Heartland is in his hands.

POND WISDOM

Owen Sexton, Washington University professor of biology, holding a bullfrog tadpole too big for the fish in Railroad Pond. *(Courtesy of Joseph Angeles, Washington University Photographic Services)*

CHAPTER 9

Pond Wisdom

Henry David Thoreau gave us Walden Pond, the concept of man's oneness with nature, the tradition of civil disobedience, and so much more; his ideas became the bedrock for philosophers ranging from Mahatma Ghandi and Martin Luther King, Jr., to hosts of writers from John Steinbeck and Jack Kerouac and the Beats to, unconsciously perhaps, the entire Woodstock generation. We did not want to end up, after all, fantasizing our way through lives of "quiet desperation." We desperately wanted, instead, "to do our thing," a vulgar, though apt, précis of Thoreau's salient themes. His musings on life at Walden imbedded into our minds the ethos of rugged individualism; his soothing, yet defiant, words limned a quaint, yet urbane rebelliousness. Of all he gave to the world, though, his most enduring legacy is an image: a pond, a sunrise or sunset, a person meditating on the shore. Ironically, in the late 1980s, the original Walden was the target of developers who wanted to construct an office mall there in another of the endless drives to develop the nation. A group led by pop singer Don Henley, who claimed that reading the philosopher during his college days influenced his thinking, played concerts and scheduled events to save Walden Woods.

A part of the American Dream is to have a private place of one's own where nature still thrives in some form or another. Shades of Thoreau's pond live on today in at times garish circumstances: housing developments in suburbia everywhere in the United States, hacked out of woodlands, wetlands, or farmlands, seemingly are incomplete unless the developer scoops out an acre or two or three and inserts artificial ponds to add to the aesthetics of already sterile environments. Between 1986 and 1988, according to the United States Department of Agriculture, nearly 20,000 acres of ponds were built across the nation on farmland alone for farmers who shared the cost with the government to enhance conservation efforts: An impoundment, as they are called by the government, can help block soil erosion, helps cattle farmers' water supplies in times of drought, and depending on how they are managed, can attract a panoply of wildlife. Untold thousands of such impoundments, ranging from a quarter acre to several acres, are gouged out of the land each year by developers or nouveau Thoreaus seeking their own re-creation of Walden's pond.

Americans, in the latter part of the twentieth century, are retaking and reshaping the country. According to USDA, in 1988, 64 million Americans, about a fourth of the population, lived in rural areas, which the agency defines as open countryside and settlements under 2,500 residents not in the suburbs of large cities. Of these millions only about 5 percent live on farms, a group that makes up a mere 2 percent of the entire U.S. population. While it would seem that rural areas are receiving a boost from this influx of population, the reverse is actually true: Many rural areas, in the Midwest at least, have suffered grievously during the economic downturn of agriculture in the 1980s. USDA demographers characterize the types of people moving to the country as affluent urbanites who are purchasing a second home, or else disgruntled city dwellers willing to commute long distances to work. The shift of urban flight to rural rebirth is a deceptive one; demographers say the real trend behind the numbers is the slow but inexorable spread of suburbia. Many of these areas labeled rural are on the outskirts of suburbia and by the first decade of the next century may become engulfed in vast sprawls of communities with only patches of countryside left between them.

The Heartland is chock-full of ponds. According to the Illinois Department of Conservation, the central United States has just slightly more acreage in ponds, 78,351, than its closest competitor, the South, with 75,861 acres. The South, however, has nearly double the number of ponds, 44,462, than the central region's 24,218. That the South should lead the nation in this arcane category is no surprise: The region was the major focus of United States Department of Agriculture's (USDA) drive to halt soil erosion on farmed-out cotton lands during the Depression. But that the nation's Heartland should be dotted with so many ponds is unusual—one doesn't automatically associate these bodies of water with the midwestern biogeography. A closer look, however, shows that, according to the Illinois Department of Conservation, most of the ponds in Illinois, 84,459, are artificial. A mere 4,265 were fashioned from the glaciers or other natural processes. The rate of pond building is advancing at nearly 500 per year in Illinois and Missouri, according to both states' departments of conservation.

Thoreau, it would seem, would be happy. At first glance, the emergence of so many ponds seems to be only a boon to conservation—aesthetically pleasing, ponds also control water and soil runoff, provide a habitat for wildlife, and make great fishing holes. In fact, most ponds that are constructed are stocked with fish. Both the Illinois and Missouri conservation departments will stock a pond for free with bass, bluegill, and catfish and provide landowners a management plan to keep fish populations healthy. Landowners can realize their dream of woods, fireflies, the chorus of croaking frogs, and bass jumping in the pond at twilight.

But those intent on creating their version of Walden Pond can't have it all. If they stock their ponds with fish, they'll have few or no frogs. Fish eat the amphibian young, an illustration of one of nature's most basic laws—the predator/prey relationship. So, the noveau Thoreaus might ask, who cares if you don't have frogs, salamanders, and newts in your pond, just so long as the fish are spawning each year and you're pulling out bass in the gold ol' summertime.

Owen Sexton, Ph.D., professor of biology at Washington University in St. Louis, cares. He and other ecologists throughout the world wonder what may be happening to amphibian populations. In the late 1980s a mysterious phenomenon swept across the world: Biologists from such divergent places as Peru and Costa Rica, California and Oregon, Australia and much of Europe reported declining numbers of frog and toad species. An international conference held at the University of California, Irvine, was hastily convened in February of 1990 to address these trends. Alleged contributors to the decline range from any number and combination of factors that include acid rain, pesticide runoff, harvesting of the animals for food and, ironically, scientific research, and fish preying on amphibians. The consensus, as so often is the case with science, was not firm. The trends and evidence were not clear-cut enough to say conclusively what is behind the losses and what the losses mean, although at the heart of the matter is the undeniable role of human disturbance of habitat. Pessimists think the decline may be, on a major scale, an indication of ecological doom: They insist that—because amphibians live in dual habitats—the species may be succumbing to the consequences of acid rain, pesticide runoff and reduction of habitat, clear-cutting of old-growth forests being the prime example. Because amphibians occupy such a vital spot in the food chain, their demise could be linked to our own, their disappearance around the world another analogy of the miner's canary—one that croaks, in more ways than one.

Sexton is not prepared to offer that view and, in fact, is skeptical about what is commonly known as "the balance of nature," a notion he considers to have become somewhat mythologized through the years. He believes the "balance" we've all come to grasp as a primary driving force in all of nature often is subject to mere whimsy far more than we ever think. Yet he staunchly believes in the importance of amphibians—he's spent a career as one of their greatest champions.

"If you tinker with the ecosystem on the microscale or the macroscale you're changing a whole host of interactions with potentially far-reaching implications," Dr. Sexton told me as we walked along a dusty road at Washington University's Tyson Research Center in southwestern St. Louis County on a blistering June morning. "There is no doubt in my mind that every time a pond is built, for whatever reason, and it's stocked with fish, you've eliminated habitat for amphibians."

Sexton is a tall, lean man, sixtyish, ramrod straight, and, with his neat silver goatee, noble looking. He was dressed in work boots, khaki pants, and, despite the heat, long sleeves as he showed me Antire Creek, its bed dry now during a droughty month. The stream is a tributary of the Meramec River into which it empties slightly more than a quarter mile away from the northern boundary of the Tyson Research Center. Sexton is a world-class ecologist who has studied ecosystems throughout Central and Latin America and other parts of the world as well as Missouri, where his varied research interests include amphibians, reptiles, the endangered collared lizard in Missouri's glades, and the Missouri prairies. He is a pioneer member of the Missouri Prairie Foundation, having served as president and vice president of that organization, which has preserved and expanded the state's native unplowed prairies in the southwestern corner of the state. A modest, quiet man, Sexton has influenced the course of conservation in this part of the Heartland as much as any other ecologist in the region. He started Tyson's Wolf Sanctuary with Carol and Marlin Perkins in the early 1970s. He has had a hand in many major studies in the state since joining the Washington University faculty in 1955. He has successfully reintroduced the wood frog, an endangered species in central Missouri, in Tyson's ponds, and his contribution to the understanding of glades, "pauper" prairies existing in ever-decreasing numbers as dry, shallow-soiled islands between limestone hillsides, has been so profound that his name is automatically linked to the term—like Budweiser is with beer.

In the late 1980s, he published a paper in *Transactions, Missouri Academy of Science*, that may be the most dramatic argument of fish predation on amphibian populations ever written.

The study, as so often happens in science, was an outgrowth of serendipity. In the late 1960s, Sexton had three small ponds built at Tyson to study amphibians. He named them Railroad Pond, New Pond, and Salamander Pond. He deliberately left the ponds free of fish to see what the population of amphibians was at Tyson and what different species would colonize the ponds. Although Antire Creek runs through a small portion of Tyson and various natural potholes fill with water after heavy rains, there were no true ponds at Tyson at the time. Sexton, his graduate students, and Washington University developmental biologists had had to use a venerable pond in the woods across Interstate 44, originally called Forest 66 for the famed highway but since called Forest 44, to study amphibians.

After the ponds were built, Sexton found that fourteen different species of frogs—among them, the tree frog, bullfrog, green frog, and leopard frog—salamanders, including the tiger and spotted salamanders, and newts, a kind of salamander, lived in and near the ponds in various stages of development. For ten years, Sexton and his students collected data and conducted studies on amphibian populations. They were surprised by some developments. They knew, for instance, that the spotted salamander bred at Tyson, but they were totally amazed to find that the tiger salamander and the narrow-mouthed salamander invaded the ponds to breed, an indication that for years there had been a dwindling population of these amphibians just hanging on in the Tyson woods using whatever pools they could find for their breeding sites. In those years, the amphibian populations in the three ponds thrived.

Then, natural disaster struck in the spring of 1979. A deluge of rain spilled the Meramec River over its banks, the flood introducing several of the eighty-nine species of fish found in the river, the highest number of fish inhabiting any stream in the state, into Antire Creek. The creek itself expanded over its banks almost into the road alongside Railroad Pond. The fish made their way through outlets and feeder rivulets into not only Railroad pond, but New Pond a quarter of a mile up the road. Salamander Pond, more than a half mile from either of the other two ponds and isolated on high ground away from any feeder stream, was untouched. Three years later another flood immersed an outlet of Railroad Pond, but left the other two ponds unaffected.

By 1983, twelve of the original fourteen amphibian species no longer could be found in Railroad Pond. Bullfrogs and cricket frogs are the only remnant amphibians left in that pond, which still harbors six different species of fish introduced by the spring floods. The frog species survived because the bullfrog tadpoles are larger than those of the other species as well as distasteful to the fish; the cricket frog tadpoles survive because they have cleverly adapted to life along shorelines—they don't swim out far enough to be eaten by the fish. Other species make the fatal error of swimming too far. At New Pond, a much smaller impoundment, fish populations are erratic because the pond sometimes dries up and the species introduced during the flood, minnows and shiners, are not such voracious predators. The impact of the flood on Railroad Pond's amphibian population has been devastating for more than ten years.

Showing the extent of the floods that year, Sexton pointed down the road to the viaduct where a deer bounded up the dry creek slope to a point where the creek saunters toward the Meramec, then he turned and motioned with a sweeping gesture to the road as it bends onto the main drag of Tyson. "So that year the creek was really up and spilled green sunfish, bluegill, bass, bullheads, minnows, and golden shiners into the ponds," he said, walking back toward the road where it parallels Railroad Pond. "The bluegills and the green sunfish are the major predators. The green sunfish is a pioneer species and just a voracious amphibian predator. From the standpoint of science, the ponds were an experiment waiting to happen—the flood provided a perfect, uninterrupted experiment—two affected areas with a control, Salamander Pond, to compare them with. We had a good handle on what was in the ponds. Although there had been a few papers done on exploring the relationship between fish and amphibians, there hadn't been very much on introduction of species. I think the study shows without doubt that fish will wipe out amphibians and that if amphibian populations truly are down throughout the world, the practice of stocking ponds with fish is an undeniably logical factor in reducing amphibian habitat. Remember, we didn't introduce any amphibians into Railroad Pond—they came in from the woods of their own volition. This is a case of the imbalance of nature and it was a total fluke. Total flukes happen a lot in nature."

There is a long history of the accidental introduction of one species into an ecosystem that ultimately changes other aspects of that system. Take the gypsy moth, for instance, introduced into New England in the nineteenth century when a few of the moths escaped from a scientist's laboratory and then spread first throughout the Northeast, where it defoliated thousands of acres of trees, then, in the twentieth century, westward all the way to Missouri. The moths spread as egg masses attached to furnishings of people making long moves—they were, in effect, hitchhikers. In the early 1980s, outbreaks of the gypsy moth in the Chicago suburbs and in various other counties in Illinois had specialists worried that an epidemic the size of the Dutch elm disease of the 1950s might occur. A timely spraying program, in most places, has halted the nuisance, but not before thousands of acres of trees, primarily in the Northeast, had been defoliated. On a more widespread scale, the introduction of rats from European ships to places like Hawaii and New Zealand wiped out many bird species there. And Kudzu, the Japanese perennial introduced into the Deep South during the Depression, now grows as far north as St. Louis County, Missouri.

On the microscale, fish have been introduced into ponds by fishermen emptying bait into the water as they bring home their day's catch. On the macroscale, in recent years no more dramatic illustration of Sexton's point exists than in Africa's Lake Victoria, the world's third-largest lake. In the 1960s, British colonists introduced a tasty species of perch, the Nile perch, to boost the fishing industry and tourism, and instead brought a nightmarish predator into the ecosystem that today threatens the very existence of the lake. The Nile perch can grow to six feet in length and feeds on all species of fish, including the tilapia, small delicious fish that fishermen are able to preserve simply by letting them dry in the sun. The Nile perch ate other fish that were algae feeders; the algae then grew uncontrollably in the upper water, dying, then sinking to the bottom of the 270-foot-deep lake. This left the bottom 110 feet of the lake deprived of oxygen and drove all of the fish out of that zone, more readily available as prey for the Nile perch. Now that the population are dependent on the Nile perch, they are deforesting the shoreline to smoke the fish, which are too big and oily to dry in the sun. As a result, the deforestation and soil erosion are serious problems for the lake, which is vital to three African countries, Tanzania, Uganda, and Kenya.

Owen Sexton led me through a fringe of waist-high bromegrass, Johnson grass, and cattails near Railroad Pond and we walked around its perimeter. It is a small pond, less than a quarter of an acre, almost perfectly circular, picture perfect in the mind's eye of what a pond should look like. At its deepest, in the middle where Sexton purposefully had had a depression scooped to serve as a reservoir to hedge against severe drought, the water is about five feet deep. Along the banks it is less than a foot deep for a couple of yards out. Dragonflies hovered over the water; in the blue sky above turkey buzzards floated overhead. Large circles emanated mysteriously from the invisible interaction of snapping turtles beneath the surface of the water. Algal blooms dotted the water; bushy green patamogeton plants held their own, having been introduced from migrating waterfowl or else by winds. Clumps of green sagittarius arrowhead plants, which Sexton introduced to encourage amphibian immigration and as protection against fish predation, rounded out the aquascape. As an example of the kind of research Sexton and his students conduct at the ponds, he mentioned the work of Dianne Seale, who regularly seined the pond and determined the amphibian populations. Seale, now a professor at the University of Wisconsin, Milwaukee, studied the nitrogen metabolism of the pond as mediated by amphibians and determined by the volume of ammonia the amphibians excreted. The creatures play a vital role in nitrogen turnover and metabolism in the pond, which is crucial to the entire pond ecosystem.

"This pond has been a very nice place for my study," Sexton said, looking across it with satisfaction. "It's never dried out, there have always been species to observe and study. We seined a bass once that was fifteen inches long, the biggest fish we've found here. Most often we've found green sunfish at about six inches and some catfish that get that big. The fish get stunted here because they have no predators to keep their population down and not enough room to thrive. As a result, they overpopulate the pond and deplete the resources. Frankly, I'd like to get rid of them."

Sexton harbors no animosity toward fish and finds no fault with people who build ponds and stock them with fish. It's just that he has seen firsthand the impact fish have on amphibians and other species and he has developed a special feeling for some of nature's most underrated, overlooked, and misunderstood creatures. Plus, he is convinced that most landowners are ignorant of the kind of wildlife they could have if they had a fishless pond.

Amphibians were actually Sexton's secondary interest: Reptiles were his first love from boyhood when, at the age of twelve with the encouragement of his mother, who was also a snake devotee, his family surprised him for his birthday by sanctioning the building of a snake pit in his backyard. There he kept black snakes, pine, water, and king snakes, anything he could find in the woods and fields near his suburban Philadelphia-area home, which was situated then at the edge of the country. He'd bring home snakes he captured on hikes on his cousins' Pennsylvania farm or on trips to the New Jersey seashore and pine barrens. He went on to Oberlin College for his bachelor's degree in biology and to the University of Michigan for his graduate and doctoral work. It was there, as a teacher at the University of Michigan's biological station in northern Michigan that Sexton became a Hemingway fan after a friend loaned him a copy of Hemingway's Nick Adams stories, many of them set in upper Michigan. He became so enthralled with Hemingway's fiction, his style, his love for nature and the juxtaposition of drama with nature, that Sexton conducted his own informal inventory of the area, took pictures of many settings he could identify from the text, interviewed people who knew the author, and visited many of the natural settings for Hemingway's stories. Using his keen insight into the natural world, Sexton made a close study of Hemingway's descriptions of the natural areas and what he calls the "incredible imaginary flights" from the actual setting to fictive conveniences. The result is a biologist's look at Hemingway, a rare insight into one of the world's most studied writers.

Papa Hemingway aside, it was during this period when Sexton began to appreciate the importance of amphibians as they relate to reptiles. As the first semiterrestrial organisms, amphibians of course preceded reptiles. Scientists believe they have inhabited the earth for far more than 100 million years. There are three forms of amphibians extant: salamanders and their relatives, including various kinds of newts; frogs and toads and their many relatives; and caecilians, tropical amphibians about which little is known. Amphibians start life in the water in egg form, advance to the larval stage as tadpoles, and as adults live out their dual lives on both land and water. In the larval stage, frogs and toads are largely herbivorous, eating phytoplankton or simple plant material; when they metamorphose into adults they switch their eating habits to include protein, consuming a wide assortment of insects, and changing from what are known as primary consumers to secondary or higher-order consumers in the food chain. Salamanders, on the other hand, in both larval and adult stages, are carnivores, consuming insects as well as certain species of aquatic arthropods and crustaceans. In Missouri, there are presently approximately twenty different species of amphibians, most of them viable populations, although, as in the case of the wood frog some years back, that has not always been the case.

A typical Missouri pond, sans fish, might include crustaceans, zooplankton, water fleas, daphne, a green shrub, various aquatic worms, turtles, and exotic species such as byrozoans, slimy, jellylike masses of tiny invertebrate animals that cling together and may reach the size of a basketball. Their coloring can range from translucent to brown with occasional greenish or yellow tints caused by algae and bacteria that grow on the community. Although people often find byrozoans unsightly, their presence in a pond is actually a good sign because they cannot exist in a polluted environment.

While amphibians do a yeoman's job of eating insects, Sexton is reluctant to say their presence in the ecosystem is precisely to keep insect populations in check.

"It's obvious that amphibians depress insect populations and that if we were to lose them or seriously repress their populations, insect numbers would probably go up, but then there might be other species that could pick up the slack," he said. "I think the strict interpretation of the 'balance of nature' scheme we hear all the time is a bit overblown and shouldn't be encouraged too much. In fact, strictly speaking, it's a myth. Amphibians are of interest to me because they are fascinating creatures with a right to their habitat. In terms of the 'balance of nature,' well, they're part of an interacting system and it often depends on whether the other components are interacting with them. I am concerned when I hear of depleted populations, but to get a true handle on the situation, you really need a series of long-term monitoring programs—work that might take twenty or more years to conduct accurately. That kind of science is hard to get funded and then to conduct. One scientist may not want to devote twenty years of his career to a monitoring program."

As we turned to leave Railroad Pond, Sexton suddenly bent to the ground and picked up a box turtle, female, he pointed out, because of its brown eyes and concave underbelly. It was now the tail end of terrapin mating season, with migration at its peak, and the turtle seemed intent on a refreshing dip in Railroad Pond. Sexton cooed at her, calling her a beauty as her feet kicked from side to side. Seeing the box turtle spurred a story that obviously troubled him.

He had recently returned from a month-long trip to Paris where he had visited a daughter and had done some research at the Paris Museum of Natural History. On a walk to the famed Paris Right Bank one day, he passed a long open market that catered to the French interest in exotic animals. To his amazement—even though he had heard reports of these activities from his colleagues—he saw that most of the exotic animals for sale were some of the more mundane American animals, including garter snakes, king snakes, various lizards, and the common box turtle which he now held in his hand. What was more astonishing was the prices: the equivalent of $65 for a garter snake, $400 for a king snake, as much as $100 for a box turtle.

"Can you imagine," he asked, "how many of these turtles you could harvest during migration with little trouble and then ship overseas, and what a profit could be made? It's a thriving, but little-known black market, although, to defend the French, they're buying out of love for animals and not out of any greedy impulse. If that kind of activity continues unabated, it could make a dent on species populations in the United States."

For nearly thirty years, Sexton has researched a fifty-acre area in nearby Jefferson County that is the northernmost edge of range of the collared lizard, a species native to the Southwest and that by all logic should be extinct in Missouri. A surprisingly thriving and adaptable population of the lizards inhabits the glades in the Missouri Ozarks and have been isolated from other populations for more than 4,000 years. They share the dry glade habitat with a host of reptiles, including Great Plains rat snakes, racers, black rat snakes, hognosed snakes, fence lizards, blue-tailed skinks, and even scorpions. The collared lizard faces seemingly imminent extinction because the glade habitat itself, constantly being edged out by forests over thousands of years, is rapidly becoming extinct. Yet they not only persist but persevere. In the mideighties, a reporter from the *St. Louis Post-Dispatch* wrote an article about Sexton's work and ignored his request to keep the location of his research area out of the story. Within weeks, much of his population of collared lizards had been raided by locals who had read the article and seen the pictures of collared lizards—sharp-looking reptiles with bodies about five inches long and tails twice that length—and had followed the explicit directions in the newspaper article. The misguided desire to possess something rare and wild, the same urge at work in France with people seeing American "exotics," could destroy his research and wipe out a rare population. Nowadays, he'll reveal no more about the location than to say it's in rural Jefferson County.

Up the road at New Pond, we circled the tiny pond and observed a phoebe perched on the dry limbs of a cottonwood tree, swooping across the pond as it hunted dragonflies and other insects; two common northern water snakes gliding across the surface, their eyes all that were visible, like a submarine's periscope; and leopard frogs making their surprisingly fast, bold leap into the water from the shoreline.

"Everything you see here, you wouldn't see in a pond with fish," Sexton said. "The fish will eat almost everything but the phoebes. This pond has seen a drop in amphibians populations, but not a whole lot because the minnows and shiners primarily are vegetation feeders. Every spring it's generally fish free and amphibians breed successfully. In many ways, it's the most interesting pond out here because many ponds in nature are in a similarly equivocal position—they sometimes dry out."

Sexton noted that colleague Richard Coles, the director of the Tyson Research Center, brings inner-city school children to the pond to wade and seine it for wildlife. The disturbance has never bothered his research.

"This is really a dime-sized pond," he observed. "Now, you can have a lot of fun with small places like this that support a real aquatic system in nature. Most pond builders want to construct miniature lakes. If people want to put fish ponds in the country, that's fine, but I should think that they should also have one or two places like this on their property, and they'll see lots more wildlife."

About a half mile away from New Pond, up a small hill and a trail leading into the woods, lies Salamander Pond. We parked the car alongside the main road and hiked up the hill. Along the trail were various wooden slabs Sexton and Coles keep to observe snakes in the warm months. The cool earth beneath the planks attracts mice, a staple for snakes. Sexton lifted each board he passed, revealing dark, moist soil but no snakes until we reached the final one. There a sleek black racer lay coiled, darting its tongue at his sudden exposure. This snake sells in France for one hundred dollars, he reminded me, and gently placed the board atop the reptile's snuggery.

Salamander Pond, flanked by woods, is an hourglass-shaped body of water, slightly larger than New Pond and not quite the size of Railroad Pond. A hut constructed for data collection and shelter in inclement weather is situated off the trail to the southeast; a thermometer, reading 88 degrees in the shade already this morning, is nailed to a tree. The pond was decorated in lacy green duck wheat, a wispy, ethereal plant that lent a misty aura to the surroundings. The pond is surprisingly small and shallow, yet productive for a researcher—in more than twenty years, it has never dried out. Sticks of varying lengths and thicknesses stand throughout the center of the pond, placed as part of a study to determine what size of twig females of different amphibian species prefer to lay their eggs on.

Salamander Pond has the largest number of breeding amphibians species of all the Tyson ponds, with an estimated 1,800 individual spotted salamanders and 500 pairs of wood frogs. The pond is the most successful of the three Tyson ponds and the scene of one of Sexton's greatest ecological triumphs. The population of the wood frog, *Rana sylvatica*, scattered throughout Missouri in the midseventies, was dwindling; in the St. Louis region and northward, there were no known populations, although records indicated that they were abundant in that part of the state at the turn of the century. In 1980, Sexton joined forces with Missouri Department of Conservation herpetologist Tom R. Johnson in reestablishing the wood frog in Salamander Pond. Johnson knew of a thriving population of wood frogs south of Tyson and brought the egg masses to introduce to Salamander Pond.

We walked around the eastern perimeter of Salamander Pond as Owen Sexton pointed out a fence of aluminum sheeting about a foot high; trenches, lined with plastic, were dug on either side of the fence, which wrapped around the pond's northeastern edge. Sexton introduced just eleven egg masses in March of 1980. Seven years later, he and his colleagues built the fence and trenches as traps to count the population of wood frogs. Those collected on the outside of the fence were counted as immigrants; those on the interior of the fence were emigrants. At the end of the breeding period in April of 1987, the researchers counted 311 immigrants and just 46 emigrants—a classic ecological success story that shows, said Sexton, "where you supply suitable habitat, you draw decent wildlife populations." In 1991, Sexton estimates, there were more than 500 breeding pairs of wood frogs in Salamander Pond. It's the only pond at Tyson where the wood frogs maintain a population because there is no pressure from fish. The wood frog reintroduction has been so successful that the animals ironically have emigrated from Tyson, across bustling Interstate 44, to the old pond at Forest 44, more than a mile away, to breed there as well.

"I think it's a great example of reintroducing an endangered species at a very low cost compared with efforts to reintroduce other more tantalizing species, let's say, the peregrine falcon," Sexton said as he cleared leaves and organic matter out of a section of the traps. "People put so much emphasis on saving the noble species, but you don't hear much about those that aren't cute and fuzzy. They're all important to save, but you'll never see a newspaper campaign to save the millipede. Amphibians play a very significant role in the ecosystem—as predators of insects and as prey for other animals such as snakes. They're just too often ignored."

On cold wet nights in late winter and early spring, Sexton pointed out, spotted salamanders by the hundreds trek through this part of Missouri for a mating rendezvous at impoundments wherever they may find them. People who live near populations of the creatures could spend their whole lives ignorant of the fact that they could witness this incredible migration. Salamanders seldom make the headlines.

We walked about Salamander Pond back toward the trail, our footsteps rustling leopard frogs out of the grass along the shore. The amphibians, no more than two inches long, make bold springboard leaps from the edge, every bit as remarkable, on the microscale, as divers leaping off the cliffs of Acapulco. As they dived toward the hospitable waters of Salamander Pond, landing with a minikerplunk, all seemed well in Missouri. Thoreau would approve.

LIGHTS ALONG THE MERAMEC
Farmers Carol Springer and David Curtis on their Missouri Ozarks farm near Bourbon, Missouri. *(Courtesy of Sara Fitzpatrick)*

Lights along the Meramec

arol Springer, a sturdy, blond-ish woman, looks past the gravel drive to a pasture dotted with cows and their calves, the lifeblood of her farm; 400 feet beyond, a hedge of oak and cedar trees borders a fence along the gravel state road adjoining her place. There she sees a big, unobstructed patch of Missouri sky. Turning to the left she can see the ancient limestone cliffs ranging more than 120 feet above the road and overlooking all her 460 acres; the Meramec River; the whole of Crawford County; and much of the central Missouri Ozarks, all the way to St. Louis some 75 miles away. Returning counterclockwise, she can inspect the grove of trees flanking the driveway that snakes up from the road and catch sight of the one-story house made of wood chopped and sawed from the cedar trees on her land by husband, David Curtis, and her father, Clark. Thus, after she gets two-year-old Andrew settled in for his afternoon nap, Carol Springer sometimes takes a break from her endless chores by sitting on the porch outside her 110-year-old Missouri Ozarks farmhouse and gazing out the screens at vistas she has known and loved all her life.

The cedarwood house, built in 1988, is the only new sight in this panorama; an annex to the main house, it serves as bed-and-breakfast quarters, a sideline to the farm. She and David take in as many as 300 boarders a year on the farm, a second occupation for both that helps pay the feed and other bills and keeps them permanently bound to the farm. On warm days, she hears little more than the bawling of cattle, the rustle of the wind through the trees, and the electrical zing of a hummingbird as it approaches the feeder outside the porch. To the visitors at her farm boarding for the night, this spectacle is heartbreakingly beautiful, so bucolic as to be unreal. To Carol Springer, it is a comfort: it is home.

Every now and then at times like these, Springer will look up at the porch ceiling and shudder at the suffocating thought that if the U.S. Army Corps of Engineers had had their way a dozen years ago, the whole piece of real estate about her now would be thirty feet under water. All the memories of sweat and toil, love, joy, sorrow, and tradition would have been submersed under the dammed-up Meramec River, which meanders for more than a mile along her land. Then memories of her friends and neighbors who fell victim to the scheme to turn the last 50-mile stretch of the 190-mile-long stream into a vast recreational lake by selling their land to the government will creep into her consciousness. She'll get so angry at the turn of events, she'll leave the porch and find some chores to do until the bad feelings gradually subside.

Carol Springer came within receipt of a registered letter—announcing condemnation of her property—from losing the farm she owns, a piece of property that has been in her family for more than 150 years. Scores of her neighbors had lost their farms to the federal government by power of eminent domain. Twenty-eight thousand, six hundred acres had been gobbled up, the houses and buildings torn down, surveying stakes driven through the earth, people displaced from lands they had worked all their lives in an episode that unfolds like the holocaust of the Ozarks. Springer and her land survived it.

Baseball immortal and native Missourian Yogi Berra famously noted that "it ain't over till it's over." But Springer's story adds a new dimension to the saying, leading one to wonder when over really is over, or if over is ever over.

The story really begins before Springer was born. In 1938, in the Great Depression and the unprecedented involvement of the federal government in the affairs of the American people, plans were set to build a series of dams on the Meramec River, a limestone-bedded stream that is a scenic and ecological marvel. During the decade, the government had constructed more than 200 dams on the Mississippi and Ohio rivers and their tributaries for the usual reasons—to control flooding and to boost commercial navigation along the super rivers. This, after all, was in the era of the Tennessee Valley Authority, the prototypical massive Depression-era project that ultimately brought electricity to backwoods farmhouses, jobs to hard-luck workers, and money to local economies all through harnessing the power of water. After a series of false starts in the forties and the early sixties when the public and various conservation agencies balked at the prospects of the native countryside becoming transmogrified into a gigantic lake, people finally were swayed by the logic that increased tourism to the area would mean more dollars to folks unaccustomed to money, and careful conservation would provide an enhanced wildlife for all. Then, too, the Meramec was prone to flooding, and people, especially those downstream, who lived along its banks had been inconvenienced in the past by the occasional outburst of nature. In the late sixties, with hedging support from the Missouri Department of Conservation, the Meramec Dam got the go-ahead and land acquisition commenced. The cost to taxpayers was estimated at $250 million.

To understand the depth of the story is first to comprehend the character of a river, an intangible so deep as to be nearly indescribable. Louis Armstrong, when asked once to explain the meaning of jazz, replied, "Man, if you got to ask, you'll never know." Ask a person who has grown up on or near a river, fishing, canoeing, or merely hiking along its banks, what that river means to him or her, and the question will elicit a similar response.

The Meramec—its name comes from the Indians, its meaning is not clear—begins its haphazard course in the wooded hills of the south-central Missouri Ozarks, flowing northeastward of its own whimsical volition and entering the Mississippi River just south of St. Louis. By no means pristine—arguably, there are no pristine areas left in either Missouri or Illinois—the Meramec nonetheless hosts an abundant, diverse wildlife. Deer, raccoon, muskrat, beaver, fox, coyote, squirrel, and dozens of other species visit its banks, sandbars, and waters. The river otter, newly reintroduced, is making a comeback here. The endangered pink mucket, so rare as to occur only in about ten other streams in the Midwest, and other species of mussel live in the entire river stretch, filter feeding along the limestone bed and absorbing, as they must to survive, the dissolved limestone in the river to build their shells. Trout and smallmouth bass are plentiful in the upper portion of the river, which is fed by cold springs branching out of the Missouri Ozark hills and a half dozen or so smaller streams. Among these are the Bourbeuse River and Courtouis (Cote-away, by the locals) Creek, legacies of the French, Big River (a misnomer) and Huzzah (Hoo-zaw) Creek and Dry Fork. Hickory, oak, sycamore, and cedar trees brood over the banks; hawks, wild turkeys, and blue heron perform their fly-bys. The water, free of the silt arising from such rivers as the Mississippi and Missouri, is a pale green.

Never very wide, the Meramec begins as a narrow channel not far from the small town of Salem in Dent County, picking up reinforcement from its tributaries. Upstream, as the river widens, stately limestone bluffs, at times spectacular, line the banks. More than 200 caves—including Meramec Caverns and Onondaga, advertised on farmers' barn roofs and billboards nestled in the hills—are known to exist in its valleys. The river itself is ancient, its sedimentary rock bed formed from a sea that covered the entire Ozark region roughly 500 million years ago. The cycle whereby the region was submerged below, then elevated above, the sea over millions of years laid the foundation for the river and the Ozarks themselves. The subsequent erosion of rocks caused by the cycle created what is known as the Ozark uplift.[1]

Ernest Hemingway, in his classic short story, "Big, Two-Hearted River," wrote of a river that in spirit was much like the Meramec. The Meramec is neither big, nor two-hearted, although it can be argued that, through no natural influences, the stream is actually two rivers. From its source to roughly thirty miles from St. Louis, it runs through narrow valleys, sparsely populated regions devoted to crops, livestock, and trees, true Missouri Ozark country. As it nears Times Beach, a recent settlement that sprouted up as resort area in the 1920s, the character changes. The closer to St. Louis, the fewer natural areas, and the more clubhouses, industries, and floodplain development.

The lower end of the river has been popular among urbanites

---

[1]*Passages of a Stream: A Chronicle of the Meramec*, James Jackson, University of Missouri Press, 1984.

seeking sanctuary from the city for decades; the real estate pages of the *St. Louis Post-Dispatch* are forever advertising lots, acreages, abandoned farms, and other intriguing properties. Except for the confederacy of wildlife areas consisting of Tyson Research Center, Castlewood State Park, Lone Elk Park, Beaumont Boy Scout Reservation, and Forest 44, clumped defiantly in western St. Louis County against urban sprawl, the lower stretch of the Meramec more and more is characterized by the intrusion of the sameness of suburbia.

It's not that way, not yet anyway, in Carol Springer's neck of the woods, but the flavor of her environs has definitely been seasoned by the battles of the decades to reshape the country into a plaything of the government, politicians, and developers. Most of her neighbors are absentee landowners from St. Louis; swept out with the land buy-outs were the true Ozark farmers, who moved to neighboring Bourbon, Sullivan, Steeleville, or, broken by the struggle, died early deaths.

"That's what I'm living with now," Springer said as she walked along the fence in the front pasture on her farm. "I'm still bitter about my neighbors being bumped. Then, when the dam project was finally defeated, they lost the chance to buy it back because they didn't have enough money to purchase it. I have nothing against my *new* neighbors—I just don't see that many of them. But the people I worked with, and lived with, all my life were displaced by the whole project. And some of them went to their graves early, because of that."

The series of events unfolded like this: In 1968, when Springer was a high school junior, the government started buying land in preparation for building the dams along the Meramec. The largest dam was to be built not ten miles away from her farm near Sullivan. By then, the government had begun building a grandiose visitor's center, called the Hickory Ridge Conference Center, on a lush hilltop overlooking the proposed site for the enormous earthen dam. They began purchasing property throughout Crawford and Washington counties through the dubious power of eminent domain. After issuing a condemnation notice, the government, through the local courts, would determine the value of the property, then, with minimal margin for negotiation, pay off the people whose land was condemned.

Once it became obvious that the dam project seemingly was going to happen, Springer and her friends who treasured the area made a point to explore the hills and waters as thoroughly as they could. They would ride horseback throughout the hills, float the Meramec at every available opportunity to further etch the region in their memories— each trip, they feared, might be their last. Springer at times would ride alone on old logging trails from her farm to her parents' place, passing ancient cemeteries, abandoned buildings, and other remnants of a previous civilization that was thriving even more, she realized, at the turn of the century than in the 1970s. She winced at the site of an old schoolhouse and post office razed by court order to make way for the dam. In the back of her mind on these solitary rides was the dire thought that she and her friends might someday have to sabotage the dam. Clandestinely, she'd pull out of the ground stakes the Army Corps of Engineers had driven for their surveys—anything to upset the applecart. In the midst of the great natural beauty was the constant, sickening specter of leveled buildings.

"The places didn't have to be leveled that early in the project," she said with a disdainful shake of her head. "I think they figured the earlier they tore them down, the less the population might resist. Many of the people couldn't receive full payments for their lands unless the buildings were removed, like a deposit withheld. The corps said they wanted the buildings out of the way to reduce the hazards of floating lumber once the area was inundated. To me, it was pure psychological warfare."

The standard method of paving the way for the dam was to bulldoze buildings and burn them.

"If you sold out willingly, then they might have rented your land back to you," said David Curtis. He is a slender, relaxed man, about forty, with the sharp, angular looks of a young Peter Fonda. "If you butted heads with them, they'd tear everything down. You can protest, go to the courts and spend money to resist them, but ultimately they have the power to condemn your place. They get it and you don't."

It was through the political inferno of the dam that Curtis met Springer in 1977; he had recently graduated from the University of Missouri in Columbia with a bachelor's degree in forestry and had been active in opposing the dam in one of the few hot political issues on campus in the disco-laden midseventies. He took a job with the Department of Natural Resources in nearby Sullivan, Missouri, where the intense issue was coming to a head. He heard of Springer's battle, and met her. Soon, he joined forces with her, the Ozark Chapter of the Sierra Club, and other area conservationists. They married in 1980, and city boy Curtis, who grew up in suburban St. Louis, became a farmer with his wife by his side, as in a reincarnation of a certain Grant Wood painting, 1980s style.

Springer's farm was dangerously close to falling into federal hands with those around it when she, her father, and the Sierra Club, became coplaintiffs in a suit that challenged the U.S. Army Corps of Engineers' original environmental impact document, a double-spaced, seven-page statement that was, according to Curtis, "just a joke, a completely inadequate document, the kind of thing a high school student could have put together. It was easy to challenge in court." That procedure stalled the condemnation process for a couple of years until the Missouri legislature reluctantly authorized a referendum in thirteen eastern Missouri counties, including St. Louis, that was to be voted on in August of 1978.

"Right before the referendum, I was suffering a lot of sleepless nights," Springer said. "If the voters didn't vote it down, then we're gone. I think that when you've been the underdog for so long, you don't have much self-esteem anymore. You get a Don Quixote complex. We never dreamed we'd have the support we got. It was great to think, after the long struggle, that it was the public that saved us."

The vote ran two to one against building the dam, much to the surprise of its opponents, who feared voter apathy in a late-summer election and the unknown sentiments of the public. Locally, for instance, Crawford County had the highest vote for the dam, with nearly 60 percent of the vote in favor of it. All of the other counties but Washington County, which for years had the highest unemployment rate in the state, voted against the dam. Ultimately, neither Springer nor Curtis believe the public was outraged at the destruction of nature and the displacement of people from their homes so much as they were grateful for the opportunity to vote down another dip into the pork barrel. The referendum gave voters the rare chance to veto personally the expenditure of millions of dollars for a dubious project. In the inflationary 1970s, that opportunity was an attractive one.

Although Springer and her farm survived, the notion of building a dam, like a demon in a horror movie, kept creeping back. The referendum was nonbinding, which cast an uneasy pall around the farm. It was not until President Reagan signed a deauthorization act to rescind the project, paving the way for resale of the condemned properties, that the nails were driven into the coffin. Still, dam proponents in the eighties, dying hard after the defeat, tried to resurrect the idea with scaled-down proposals for a smaller dam.

Meanwhile, from the time the case got stalled in the courts to the present, Springer and Curtis made both enemies and friends. In Bourbon, a sleepy, picturesque village of 1,259 a few miles from the farm, there are people in favor of the dam who haven't spoken to them for a decade. On the other side, they made lifelong friends with many conservationists, such as St. Louisans Jerry Sugerman, a canoeing enthusiast, and Don Rimbach, a former employee of nearby Onondaga Cave, which, like many other natural beauties, would have been inundated. They worked out a pleasant relationship with neighbor Emma Ware, who, with her daughters, was a dam fighter and bought back some of the condemned property and allowed Springer and Curtis the use of the farmland. And, ironically, they even benefited from the buy-outs: In the early eighties, a hazardous time for beef producers, with the price of beef very low and inflation still rampant, they were able to rent pasture from the government and thus stay in business.

By 1986, the Springer farm was an island in a sea of federal lands; it was, said Curtis, a curious, almost spooky area to be in. There was plenty of farmland available, but few people left farming it. The Corps of Engineers gave former owners or their heirs the first chance to buy back the land at an inflated, nonnegotiable price. Few were able to repurchase. Then, in 1986 and 1987, a series of auctions were held to sell the land. In many instances, more than a decade had passed since the original owners had lost the land; inflation had taken its bounding leap, making repurchase out of the question for most; the buildings, which to country people are every bit as much landmarks as street signs and billboards are to urban dwellers, had been cruelly razed.

"Before the auctions, Congress had mandated that the land be offered back to the original owners at fair market value, set by the corps appraisers, take it or leave it," Springer said with a burst of cynical laughter. "That was the real final twist of the knife. Hardly anyone could afford to come back."

Springer called the cattle, and the cows and calves came trotting toward the fence. They were predominantly russet-colored Herefords and black Angus. The type of operation she and Curtis run is called a cow-calf operation. They generally have about 180 head of cattle on some 300 acres of pasture; they own about 85 cows and a few registered purebred bulls that they selectively breed year-round with the cows. The cattle are kept out in the pastures all year; when the pregnant cow is ready to give birth, she does so usually without assistance in the pasture in the shelter of cedar and hickory trees throughout the farm. The calves are nurtured by their mothers and turned out on their own after a few months. They are sold, either at auctions in nearby Potosi or Cuba, or else to farmers in northern Illinois and Missouri, when they are yearlings. They weigh about 600 pounds then, and Springer and Curtis make anywhere between sixty cents to a dollar twenty-five per pound on each yearling. The yearlings change status at these sales when they become feeder cattle fattened up for a little more than three months on corn and soybean rations. They are then sold to the big meat-processing companies and end up on dinner tables and in fast-food restaurants throughout the country and the world.

In addition to the pasture grasses, Springer and Curtis feed their cattle high-quality hay they raise and bale on the farm; they intersperse the hay feedings, which are the animals' staple, with protein pellets comprised of mixed corn and soybeans pressed into little cakes. Because they don't raise any cash grain, they buy these pellets.

Springer's farm is typical of many Missouri Ozark farms, a livestock operation that makes best use of the topography—the sloping land generally is too steep to grow the staples of the Midwest—corn, soybeans, or wheat—the soil, consisting largely of a clay base, too rocky. Thus, the nature of farming here is far different from that which has commonly evolved throughout the Midwest since the end of World War II—intensive row-cropping of corn and soybeans to sell as cash grain or else to drive vast hog or feeder cattle operations. That is the type of farming done in Illinois and most of northern Missouri.

In the 1990s, about 2 million Americans make their living off the land—that's about 2 percent of the entire population. At the turn of the century, according to the USDA, 37.5 percent of the American workforce consisted of farmers or their hired hands. Just fifty years later, only 11.6 percent of American workers were on the land. In 1989, just 2.5 percent. Industrialization and rapid settlement of the continent, which brought new opportunities to the country's workers, fewer hours of work through the burgeoning powers of the unions, and ultimately a more predictable, stable lifestyle, increasingly drew many people away from the farm. Still, agriculture, composed of agribusinesses such as the fertilizer and chemical industries, transportation, food processing, and so forth, is the nation's largest business, generating $830.6 billion in 1989, and producing 15.8 percent of the nation's gross national product, all of this from a core of workers who only comprise 2.5 percent of the population.

In that same year, 195,000 women either managed or operated farms in the United States, out of a labor pool of more than 53 million women. Women consist of just .07 percent of the country's farmers, making Carol Springer something on the order of what Mary Bacon had been to horse racing and Shirley Muldowney to race-car driving, rare as a fresh buffalo head nickel.

"It's not something I tend to think of too often," Springer said, gazing out at the cattle. "I can do anything a man can do on the farm. I was born and raised in the country and farmed with my dad long before I took over this place. But it's something I am proud of—being a woman who farms. I wish I were a little better with machinery. But on this place, that's where Dave comes into the picture."

It is difficult, it might be argued, to distinguish between women who are farmers and women who live on a farm, because farm wives are essential partners in any farming operation. In addition usually to being matriarchs of a household, farm wives traditionally have kept the books, assisted in livestock care, and planting and harvesting.

Girls raised on a farm do all the chores that their brothers do, including, in recent years, operating machinery. But the strict definition of "woman farmer" that the USDA uses is predicated upon ownership or management. Since the early 1970s, the farm Springer has worked, which belonged to her grandfather, has been her operation solely. Before marrying Curtis in 1980, she had farmed the place on her own with help from her dad for four years. She did everything—from raising cattle, chickens, horses, and hay—on her own.

Curtis smiled slowly. "I never thought I'd end up living here," he said. "I knew I didn't want anything to do with the city, but to end up a farmer in the Ozarks, it certainly wasn't anything I had planned. I owe it all to the politics of the dam."

Growing up in Kirkwood and Webster Groves, southwestern suburbs of St. Louis, Curtis was, in his words, a "shade-tree mechanic," who began buying broken-down cars and fixing them from the time he was sixteen. On the farm, he's in charge of the machinery, preparing the three tractors, the hay mowers, rakes, and balers in early spring prior to the series of hay cuttings—alfalfa fields are cut two to three times—that begin in May and extend sometimes into September.

"Anything that's mechanical is fair game for me," he said. "Carol's specialty is the cattle. I've learned an awful lot from her, and a lot from her dad about carpentry, but I could never make up the knowledge she's gained from living here from the start. Between the two of us, we operate as a partnership."

There is a dirt road that runs behind the house leading to an aluminum shed to the left and branching off to the right toward two old barns, one that stores bales of hay, other feed, and supplies, and another that shelters the three horses Springer and Curtis keep. By the shed sit a well-used, medium-sized Allis Chalmers tractor and various other machines; inside the shed was an old Porsche that Curtis was working on, rebuilding trashed Porsches being a passion he's carried since his youth. The barns, which Springer estimates were built in the 1870s, were being rehabbed, their wooden beams and trusses laid bare, and new siding piled up on the ground alongside. The buildings had been neglected during the period of indecision about the dam. But in recent years Curtis and Clark Springer, Carol's father, had been renovating the buildings, giving them new status as they neared a second century of existence.

Between the barns and the shed, the path leads to a beautiful, slightly sloping spread of seventy acres of bottomland that fronts the Meramec River. Looking out upon the green sea of Kentucky fescue, wheat, alfalfa, and red clover mix, one cannot see the river. The edge of the field is lined with tall oak and hickory trees, one of the key natural boundaries that keep the valuable, deep riverbottom topsoil in place and out of the river. Beyond the sentry post of trees, out of eyesight, is a five-acre island of trees that sets in a low-lying area prone to flooding. The island serves as a buffer between floodwaters and the long corridor of trees bordering the hayfield. Many of the trees were left uncut by Springer's forebears. And Curtis, carrying on the tradition, has planted new trees in a gap-toothed area where some trees in the boundary caved in to the pressure of the December 1982 flood, which some river veterans say was the worst flood ever to hit the Meramec.

"The most important thing to do on a streamfront property is to maintain a corridor of trees along your bottomlands, or else you'll lose a lot of the edge of the field," said Forester Curtis. "You're looking at what is easily the best soil on the place. Carol's grandfather, who died in 1972, had a lot to do with the farm looking like it does now. He put in the series of terraces you see out there that help keep the soil from eroding away."

The terraces are elevated mounds of soil, fashioned by a tractor and scoop shovel and compacted along key places in the field. When it rains, especially when it rains heavily, the terraces stop the runoff of soil as it slides down the gentle slopes in the bottomland. Throughout the grazing land on the farm, Springer's grandfather had constructed terraces to keep those soils in check, too. In combination with the Kentucky fescue grass, seeded originally in the 1960s more for its soil-holding capacity than its feed quality, the terraces ensure that there is scarcely an eroded area on the entire farm.

Because Springer and Curtis do not grow grains, they never rely on herbicides to control weeds. Every several years, they renovate pastures, seeding clover or alfalfa into the old stands. By and large, they keep the land—and the river—free of chemicals. The maintenance of the hay land is vital to their operation, because the richer the hay, especially the higher the protein content, derived mainly from the alfalfa and clover, the less they have to rely on the protein pellets. The pellets become expensive, especially during the winter, when the farmers may feed out as much as fifteen tons of supplements.

While summer is a critical time on the farm, during which Curtis, constantly at the whim of the weather, is under great pressure to get all the hay cut, baled, and stored, winter is a crucial time as well. He and Springer spend lots of time and money getting cattle through the winter. They haul feed to the pastures then, on average, one hundred straight days. They try to tailor the size of the herd so that it is at its smallest during the winter, to keep feed costs and calf losses low. They sell off as much of the herd as they possibly can in the fall, and they try to arrange that most of the cows are giving birth in the spring and fall to avoid having the calves go through the harsh weather.

In the spring and fall, Springer vaccinates the calves and weans them from their mothers. At about three months Curtis "cuts" or castrates the bull calves, a rite of passage that brings them the status of steer and ultimately seals their fate as food on the table. The farmers breed the cows with one of two bulls to try to ensure that the cows will give birth between February and May. The Angus bull is paired with the Hereford cows; the Hereford bull with any of the other "exotic" breeds—Simmental, Charolais, Brahma, and mixes of these breeds. The bulls are bluebloods; their papers reveal intimate details of their bloodlines and the expected quality of their progeny. Thus, if there are any calving difficulties, the blame is placed on the bull because he is supposed to be a known commodity.

There are two major roundups each year where Springer and Curtis will handle every animal on the place, moving them to different pastures. For the most part in the summer, the animals are entirely on pasture, so they don't tend to them much. At that time, they're busy harvesting and putting up hay.

"A lot of what I do here is education," Springer said, sitting at the long, old oak table in her dining room. Outside the window to her left fifty yards away past a grove of trees was a pond where she raised ducks, the ducks gone now after a raid by a pack of coyotes, a visceral reminder that they live in near wilderness. "When Dave first came here he didn't know a steer from a heifer, and now he can run the place. Every day our guests are always asking what I do as a farmer, and that just brings out one question after another."

Springer recalled how the bed-and-board business started. During the peak of the dam controversy everyone from Governor—now Senator—Bond and John Danforth—soon to become senator—and TV news crews visited the farm because of Springer's active role in stopping the dam. While the beauty of the place did not change opinions, everyone unanimously praised the quaint house and gorgeous surroundings. One day her father Clark jokingly suggested charging a fee to visit because, after all, they weren't getting any work done. That set the wheels spinning, and shortly after marrying, she and Curtis hatched the plan to operate a bed-and-breakfast inn.

It's rare for an Ozark cattle farmer, as it has become for many other farmers, not to hold down a second job in town. It is rarer yet for farmers, especially in the Ozarks with its lack of industry, to find any job that pays above minimum wage. Springer and Curtis have mitigated that fact of life with their enterprise, which they call Meramec Farm Bed & Board, and in so doing have further pledged their troth to the land. Springer is forever baking and cooking, which she has mastered as deftly as she has her animal husbandry. She and Curtis are constantly the affable hosts, who will spend time with guests if the guests so choose, or leave them to their own devices, the hiking, fishing, and sight-seeing which abound in the area. Some guests seldom leave the cabin, using the getaway for a romantic tryst. Others have become personal friends with whom the couple have kept up a correspondence.

"We have guests nearly every weekend, and in the summer and fall we sometimes have them through the week," she said. "This kind of work is not for everyone, but I like it, and one of the things I like is the chance to give people an experience that shows them just how beautiful this country really is. I hope that impression will stay with them."

The dam controversy seemingly is behind them now, but Springer still worries that people do not cherish the land as they should.

"You can see development right around Bourbon, people parceling some of this lovely area into housing plots," she said. "One of the things that riles my curmudgeonly nature is the development in St. Charles County, north of here. They're turning some of the best farmland in the whole country—those soils developed between the Missouri and Mississippi rivers—into suburbia. Someday someone's going to say, 'Where did all the good soil go?' I favor some kind of zoning to protect the soil. That's not so much a problem out here, because we're in no way near suburbia, but it's a sad thing that it has to happen up there simply because all that great land is situated where everybody wants to live."

In the early 1980s, Springer and others lobbied the Missouri legislature rigorously to get a scenic easement law passed that would prohibit cutting wood or building new structures within 600 feet on either side of the Meramec River. The bill passed, but, throughout the valley, she sees the law being broken as each year passes. Out-of-area owners, wanting a dwelling with a view, continue to break the law until it's become so common that no one, neither the Department of Natural Resources nor the state Department of Conservation, wants to tackle those who are ignoring the law.

"I don't know why, but no one wants to stand up to them," she said. "I'm going to hate to see all these trailers lined up along the riverbanks. I've been fighting the system for twenty years now, and, yes, we stopped the dam from being built, but to see this sort of thing happen, well, everything has made me a bit cynical."

In the past ten years, looking out into the night, she can see lights dotting the landscape about her, requests from the absentee landowners to the power company to let all those about them know that someone is at home. But real country people don't leave their lights on at night. The message the city owners are actually sending is that there is a place here that has a locked gate—day and night—and nobody on the premises. The lights are perfect accessories to acts of vandalism. The Missouri Ozark nights Carol Springer grew up with as a girl were as dark as India ink, or else lit only by a reflection of the moon or maybe a million stars. The country nights were as peaceful and dark as a church after evening prayer meeting.

THE EYES OF THE WOLF
Vicki O'Toole, director of the Wolf Sanctuary, at her trailer office on the Tyson Research Center grounds. *(Courtesy of Sara Fitzpatrick)*

C H A P T E R   1 1

The Eyes of the Wolf

At the turn of the century, Illinois and Missouri were both completely settled; Indians had long been pushed westward, buffalo, elk, and cougars driven out as well. The last vestige of original wildness that La Salle had breathlessly witnessed on his journey down the Illinois—wolves—were very nearly altogether gone, too, except for a few remnant stray wild packs and loners that farmers, fearing loss of livestock, poisoned or shot.

Two hundred years ago, both *Canis lupis* (the gray), and *Canis rufus* (the red), ranged not only the Heartland but all the lower forty-eight states. By the nineteenth century, only a subspecies of the gray wolf known as the Great Plains or buffalo wolf, was left in Missouri and Illinois. By 1926, the buffalo wolf was declared extinct in the region; forty years later, it was listed as an endangered species in the United States. While experts say to a person that it was extremely unlikely that there were any thriving wolf populations in the bistate region beyond 1900, if you talk to enough people born in the first quarter of this century who lived in the country, you will undoubtedly hear tales, apocryphal or sworn, of wolves dashing through cornfields, woods, or pasture, ravishing everything from cattle to chickens or simply fleeing, in bafflement, from the encroachment of civilization. Red wolves or gray, they were the stuff of family legends rather than authenticated sightings.

On the other hand, in the first decade of the century, untold thousands of Mexican gray wolves, beautiful, sleek animals, about twice the size of a coyote, ranged the great American Southwest and the northern half of Mexico. These wolves ran in small packs or singly in search of their prey—deer, pronghorn antelope, rabbits, and other small animals. They hunted in the characteristic circular pathways of wolves, similar to the popular image of Indians surrounding a wagon train; the circles extended as far as one hundred miles in diameter. As the region gradually became settled and cattle more and more dominated the dry, barren landscape that had been the wolves' home for millenia, the tentacles of civilization made the wolves' natural prey scarcer. They added cattle, a convenience food, to their diet. Wolf experts believe that the Mexican wolves traveled in small numbers— packs of between four and eight. Because they were not accustomed to large game, they would pick off livestock singly, or in pairs. The sight of wolf-ravaged cattle sickened and disgusted southwestern cattlemen, lone wolves themselves, isolated from the rest of the country, prototypical Marlboro Men. The cattlemen thought nothing of shooting a gray wolf or coyote on sight. For recreation, they would form a sort of wildcat posse, riding for miles and wiping out den after den of wolves, at peace with themselves that they were thinning out a nuisance population that was only taking money out of their pockets.

By 1915, three years after Arizona and new Mexico were admitted into the Union and not long after the daring Apache warrior Geronimo had given up his struggle against the Long Knives in Arizona and Mexico, the ranchers and the Federal Bureau of Biological Survey, the precursor of today's U.S. Fish and Wildlife Service, teamed together to control the nuisance. Gray wolves and coyotes, long considered open game, were now indiscriminately targeted with poisoned bait and leg-hold traps; the predators, noting the circular runs of the wolves, found their prey easy marks. Whole packs of wolves died agonizing deaths after eating strychnine-laced meat or getting their powerful hind legs snared in steel; their carcasses became carrion for buzzards and vultures, their bones a satisfying reminder to a cowboy on horseback of a job well done.

Biologists were scarce, if nonexistent, in that part of the country then. Government reports and private journals are all the literature ever to document the Mexican gray wolf. This evidence indicates that the peak of the control program—a euphemism for eradication—occurred roughly between 1910 and 1925, although concentrated efforts were still being launched in the 1950s. While the extant literature gives no evidence of how many Mexican gray wolves existed at the time, it shows how effective the early measures were. Fifty years later, after just a few decades of eradication, the Mexican gray wolf was put on the Federal Endangered Species List. Today, although tiny populations are rumored in northern Mexico, it is considered extinct in the wild in that country and the United States. Only thirty-nine of the animals—all in captivity—are known to exist, making them one of the rarest mammals on earth.

The fate of the Mexican gray wolf in the wild rests largely on the slender shoulders of Vicki O'Toole, in Missouri. She is the director of the Wild Canid Survival and Research Center, also known as the Wolf Sanctuary. Ms. O'Toole is in charge of slightly more than one-fourth of the world's population of Mexican gray wolves now confined to a few acres of fenced-in pens hundreds of miles out of their natural range in the placid Missouri hills of Washington University's Tyson Research Center, less than thirty miles west of St. Louis. She oversees the care of eleven Mexican grays, including five breeding pairs, the highest number of breeding pairs anywhere, plus seven other wolves, Iranian, tundra, and red wolves.

The Wolf Sanctuary's goals are to breed endangered wolf species and prepare them for their eventual release into the wild. It was founded in 1971 by the late TV icon Marlin Perkins, then retired director of the St. Louis Zoo, his wife, Carol Perkins, and Washington University wildlife biologist Owen Sexton. The impetus for its conception was Perkins's haunting conviction that the wolf, badly misunderstood and poorly portrayed to the general public, had a legitimate niche in nature that had been wantonly erased. Marlin Perkins died in 1986 and never saw the first blush of success of his creation. In 1986, Brindled Hope, a female red wolf bred and raised at the Wolf Sanctuary, was released with seven other red wolves at the Alligator River National Wildlife Refuge in North Carolina, a coastal marsh and forest that was carefully selected for its prime habitat and seclusion from civilization as a perfect release site for the red wolf. Brindled Hope and her pup were still alive three years later, and the breeding and release program for the red wolf has become an unqualified success, with additional releases in the late 1980s on off-shore islands in Mississippi, Florida, and South Carolina. The red wolf program has become a paradigm for the Mexican gray wolf program, but the Mexican gray wolf and its backers, working with only a tiny core population of extant wolves and fighting a strong ranching lobby, have tougher hurdles to overcome.

One is the propagation of a reliable breeding stock, which falls directly in Vicki O'Toole's bailiwick. While she had a hand in the success of the red wolf program, and she continues to breed red wolves at the sanctuary, O'Toole's focus is the resurrection of the Mexican gray wolf, and it is a vision that is as powerfully focused as a wolf's wild, intent eyes on its prey.

O'Toole's office is a simple trailer near the main grounds of the Tyson Research Center. The motif is all canine; posters and pictures of wolves adorn the walls; a stuffed tundra wolf prowls inside a glass enclosure in the center of the trailer. Copious canine literature is stacked everywhere.

The wolf lady is a strikingly beautiful woman, diminutive, olive skinned, hazel eyed, and ageless. Her features, starting with an aquiline nose, are classic. Dressed neatly in designer jeans, knee-high boots, white blouse, and scarf, she doesn't look like one who wrestles with wolves; rather, with her flawless diction and warm manners, she has the appearance of the ideal TV news anchor.

How, I asked her one day, did she become so prominently involved with the preservation of one of nature's most violent predators, perhaps the most ambiguously symbolic animal America harbors?

"It's the howls," she said, laughing. "I became addicted to the howls; and their eyes, they have the wildest, most beautiful eyes. They're a truly beautiful animal. There's lots of howls going on now, it's their mating season."

Wolves howl, O'Toole explains to the many who ask, for a variety of reasons. They howl to gather the pack for a hunt, to express territorial boundaries to other packs, or, as the plaintive sound might indicate, to sing the blues. The howling during mating season, which starts about November and lasts through spring, is related to territorial rights.

The beauty of the beast is key to O'Toole's attraction to wolves. A dog lover since she was a child growing up in St. Louis County, she started at the Wolf Sanctuary in 1980 as a volunteer working with then director Bill Malloy, who taught her much of what she knows about wolves and their handling.

"I was looking for an art mentor," she told me. "Instead I found a nature mentor."

Though since remarried, she had recently moved back to St. Louis from New Orleans after a divorce and had been raising her two young daughters on her own. She had a degree in sociology from Tulane, but art was her metier. As time allowed, she painted portraits in oils and charcoal, selling a few of her works. Working with the wolves started as an avocation, then in 1986, when she took over from Malloy, a vocation, and now, as the opportunity looms closer to release the Mexican gray wolf in the wild, an obsession, fraught with political tussles.

"I've seen the reaction to the Mexican gray wolf swing from one of indifference and even outright contempt—a lot of people considered it just a varmint—to fawning admiration in less than five years," she says. "For years, people thought the Mexican gray wolf was just another gray wolf—not very genetically distinct. But recent genetic advances show it to be one of the purest of all wolf species, older and more distinct than the red wolf, for instance. We fought for the Mexican wolf from the start; I can't tell you how strange and wonderful that makes me feel at the same time. People are starting to pay attention. The Mexican gray wolf has become a hot item."

Very few facilities in the country were willing to provide space for the Mexican gray wolf in 1980. The Wolf Sanctuary in Missouri opened its doors to the beleaguered animal, taking on as many breeding pairs as it could handle. By the late 1980s, two Washington

University geneticists, Dr. Alan Templeton and Dr. John Patton, using the latest genetic sleuthing techniques, determined the highly refined, pure genes of the Mexican gray wolf, showing that the wolf exhibited no traces of hybridization with other canid species, notably the coyote. Their tests not only woke up environmentalists to the need to propagate the rapidly disappearing animal, but it also confirmed O'Toole's conviction that the Mexican gray wolf be given better treatment. Now zoos and other facilities are wanting to join the Mexican gray wolf bandwagon by offering holding and breeding space.

Breeding efforts are crucial to the success of the program, which now has a full-time recovery coordinator, Dave Parsons, a wildlife biologist appointed by the U.S. Fish and Wildlife Service in Albuquerque, New Mexico, whose job it is to monitor the success of breeding programs and find a proper site for reintroduction into the wild. White Sands Missile Range in southern New Mexico, for decades a government testing site for missiles and other projectiles, has been proposed as a likely habitat, being remote, with adequate water and ample prey.

While thirty-nine wolves might seem a reasonable number with which to start a release program, the process is far more complicated and involved. When a breeding pair is released into the wild, for instance, biologists automatically assume that the two will not survive for long, and bank, instead, on their offspring to provide a population. That is why when the red wolves were released in 1986 eight breeding pairs were placed in the Alligator River Wildlife Refuge. Also, biologists have found that a breeding pair released with a litter stand a better chance because they instinctively stay with the litter. Left alone, a pair might wander off, perplexed by alien surroundings and, reverting to their former human imprint, actually seek civilization. The crux of their survival and development is to retain their wildness, a difficult task.

"We want to maintain wild wolves, so that when they're released they're afraid of people and won't wind up on peoples' back porches and get shot," O'Toole told me. "The true nature of the wolf is to be afraid of people, and that's the behavior we attempt to preserve. We want them to truly pass on wolf behavior to their offspring. We only have a couple of years to do this. That's the critical nature of what we're doing."

The wolves at Tyson, for instance, are fed Purina Dog Chow, gratis from Ralston Purina Company, based in St. Louis. The wolf in the wild, of course, is primarily a carnivore, shunning grains unless it must resort to them. Weaning a captive wolf off dog kibble and onto wild prey is a stepwise process. When a pair of the Mexican grays O'Toole cares for is deemed ready for wildlife acclimation, they will follow the same program the red wolves undertook. They will be shipped in crates to a site near their intended release, where they will be isolated in a holding area called acclimation pens. Here, it is hoped that they will breed and raise a litter. Gradually, they will be introduced to prey by providing them fresh road-killed animals; eventually, as they become accustomed to road-kills, wild prey will be introduced to the acclimation pens. Ultimately, the wolves will be retaught (in a hands-off manner) that they are, indeed, carnivores, that dog chow is not their meal of choice.

Wild wolves run in packs from as few as four to as many as thirty or so, although studies indicate that fewer than one pack in one hundred have as many as ten members. The pack is the wolf social structure, with a dominant male and female who generally remain paired for life as pack leaders. As in an army or municipal government, the other members make key, though descending-order, contributions to the structure. The pack is essential for hunting purposes. Strength in numbers helps the animals bring down their game. While myths have propagated the notion of wolves being deadly, calculating hunters, studies have shown them to be less than efficient—only about 10 percent of the prey they stalk are captured. They often prey upon the weaker of the animals they encounter, which also often happen to be those that carry disease or poor genetic traits. In doing so, they perform an ironically noble service to nature: Through their kills they strengthen the genetic stock of their prey by culling out the weak genes. The remains of their prey provide food for other predators such as coyotes and buzzards. In a balanced natural setting, such as northern Minnesota where about 1,700 gray wolves live, they have been shown to keep deer and moose herds in proper balance, and, importantly to their champions and fans, wolves have seldom preyed upon farmers' livestock.

While wolves may not be the ruthless killing machines that their myth suggests, they are formidable predators nonetheless. An adult male averages about eighty pounds, although it can weigh in the one hundred-pound range. Females generally weigh twenty to thirty pounds less. Consider a Labrador or German shepherd of similar size: The wolf's strength, as measured by its jaws, is three times that of those breeds of dogs. Its syncopated trot is about five miles per hour, a little less than the speed of the average jogger. Yet it can reach bursts of speed of up to thirty-five miles per hour and has been known to maintain that speed for as long as twenty miles. A single wolf can bring a deer down by itself, although wolves nearly always attack as part of a pack.

At the Wolf Sanctuary, every effort is made to minimize contact between O'Toole and her assistants and the wolves, not out of deference to their strength, but for fear the wolves will become pals with humans, dependent on them. The only interaction with humans the wolves receive is when they are brought in or shipped out and when they get vaccinations from a Washington University veterinarian. O'Toole tries hard to coordinate these occasions so that the wolves receive their shots just prior to departure or immediately upon their arrival. This caregiving yet isolationist attitude toward the wolves' existence has made O'Toole, by her own estimation, a bit schizophrenic.

"I love the wolves, but I *want* them to hate me," O'Toole has said. "People tell me all the time how fortunate I am to be so close to such a rare form of nature, but they generally have the wrong idea about what I do. The wolves are not pets, they're predators. I love them so they can be released in the wild."

Vicki O'Toole runs the Wolf Sanctuary like a miniranch. At five feet four inches and one hundred pounds, she is smaller than her hired hands and not much bigger than the wolves themselves. In addition to dealing with the animals, she oversees the maintenance of the sanctuary, work that is physically demanding. She has removed trees herself from the enclosures, sprayed the area to control ticks, and has hauled everything from scat to feed. Transfer from the Wolf Sanctuary to zoos or release sites and arrivals from Lambert Airport to the sanctuary often come at odd hours of the night or morning, requiring O'Toole and her assistants to work in near-pitch darkness and varying weather conditions. She recalls slipping and sliding in mud at 3:00 A.M. during a raging thunderstorm to crate a wolf due out on a 6:00 A.M. flight to New Mexico. If O'Toole misses the flight, she goes through the whole process over again.

O'Toole is assisted by three part-time keepers, all men, who undergo a six-month training period and study a manual she has compiled. One of the keepers is a former Topeka zookeeper and accustomed to animal care, but the other two are not professionals in that sense of the word, merely interested in the animals and their welfare. They come out to the Wolf Sanctuary three times a week to keep feed and water supplies adequate, clean and check the scat areas for evidence of worms, and help her with general maintenance. Wolf handling, she points out, is not for everyone, which the training period brings out in people. Sometimes a potential handler will think he can deal with a wolf the way you deal with a domestic dog—in a master-servant relationship, with a lot of force behind it—but O'Toole highly discourages what she calls "the macho thing," because, she reminds the keepers, the animals possess unknown depths of wildness in them.

She recalled her first time in a pen with wolves as "an exciting, mystical experience, which is renewed every time I get in with them." While she cannot remember an incident when she ever felt fear in their presence, she insists she has a "healthy respect" for them. The wolves are kept in a maze of pens on the fifty acres, separated from the different species by gates. Water, an important staple in a wolf's maintenance, is pumped into ponds. Sheds, like cattle sheds, provide shelter. Food is placed in corner pens within the enclosures.

When O'Toole and her handlers need to capture a wolf for shipping or veterinary care, she spends days plotting out a method to isolate the wolf from its mate or pack and drive it into a holding area. Sometimes they will chase a wolf; other times they need to use a prodding stick to move it where they want. The shipping crate will be placed inside the holding area so the wolf will be more easily inclined to be driven into it. When the veterinarian vaccinates an animal, O'Toole and her helpers will hold the wolf and the veterinarian will approach casually, administer the shot, and then back off from the wolf slowly. The wolf's behavior during these times is unpredictable, ranging from hyperactivity and defensiveness to outright cowardice. The volatility makes each situation unique and O'Toole's game plan needs to stay flexible, predicated on what she calls an instinctual response to the animal's behavior. Usually the wolves get into the crates with minimal physical handling; occasionally they balk so much at being moved that a handler has no other choice than to pick it up and place it inside. Such a last-ditch tactic, she admitted, isn't any fun but is sometimes necessary.

Outwitting a wolf in captivity is not an easy task. While their intelligence is hard to quantify, all specimens at the Wolf Sanctuary are wily creatures, and keeping them in the enclosures is something O'Toole constantly works on. Wolves are territorial animals with different temperaments: the Iranian species show the most territoriality and orneriness—they constantly fight among each other—and the Mexican gray wolves show the most intelligence.

"The Mexican gray wolves are problem solvers," O'Toole has observed. "If they know a vet check is coming around, you can see they're thinking how to get out. They canvass the area, look all about them. It's as if they're anticipating the problem. I think some day it might be wise for anthropologists to study not just primates but wolves also because obviously we were animals that had to solve similar problems at one time. We evolved from creatures that hunted in packs, like wolves, and I think there may be something we can learn about ourselves by studying their behavior."

If wrestling with wolves can be a daunting task, it pales in comparison with political tussles the Mexican wolf has brought O'Toole and others in the preservation camp. Myths about wolves in general often foster a distrust and fear of the animal that is absolutely unfounded, yet maintained throughout centuries by diverse mythologies ranging from familiar fairy tales to adolescent horror stories.

While public opinion polls show a strong majority of people favor wolves being released in the wild in national parks such as Yellowstone, one sectarian group—ranchers—remains staunchly opposed to the idea. Their anxiety is perpetuated in many cases by the oldest form of communication: talk. O'Toole showed me a newsletter from a western organization dedicated to keeping wolves off public lands. I scanned the introduction and was struck immediately by the author's reference to cattlemen's tales decades ago of the wanton bloodlust of wolves, their love of killing cattle for sport, their alleged attack methods of going for the hind legs of their prey. The sources for many of these tales, the author readily admitted, were cowboys passing through the high plains, holing up for a few days at a rancher's house and spinning yarns to ease the loneliness of their existence. No one knows how many corks were pulled from countless bottles during these sessions, but the myth of the ravaging wolf, was perpetuated, forever etched on the minds of ranchers who have today become the key stumbling block to reintroduction of the species into the wild.

That wolves will prey upon cattle is an undeniable truth. But research repeatedly shows that wolves attack livestock only if they are readily available. The Minnesota situation is the strongest testimonial to wolves living in harmony with their ecosystem; if farmers there should lose any livestock to wolves, they are reimbursed financially by the state Department of Conservation. Similarly, Defenders of Wildlife, a national conservation group, has pledged a $100,000 fund to reimburse ranchers in the Yellowstone area for loss from predation. And they have begun a similar program in the Southwest for the Mexican gray wolf. Still, the point is moot for the Mexican gray wolf, O'Toole said, because of an abundance of vast, remote areas in the Southwest that is the historic range of the Mexican gray wolf. But the voracious wolf myth lives on.

"There are all sorts of self-serving myths out there," says the wolf lady. "They're connected to a fear by some ranchers that they will lose their lifestyle." For years, she explains, many southwestern ranchers have been able to graze their livestock cheaply on public lands. So their anxiety about the reintroduction of the wolf onto these and adjacent areas may be tied in to their fear that they may lose some of these rights as much as, if not more than, their worry about potential loss of livestock.

"But this 'not in my backyard' mentality is ridiculous. Sure, wolves are predators. But they kill to feed themselves and their families. There's nothing demonic about that. Nonetheless, I have to deal with opponents of reintroduction all the time. And I have to be very careful how I deal with them. As the time gets closer to release, I'm going to have to sway them more convincingly into our camp. The Mexican wolf is the most political of animals. But I've found you just have to stand your ground, get beyond all the egos, and do all you can for the animals because things could fall apart at any moment. Any hang-up in the program could mean extinction."

O'Toole has seen incidences of cancer and other diseases cropping up in the wolves she handles at the Wolf Sanctuary and other sites. Whether the diseases are linked to captivity or are also evident in the wild is uncertain, but it is a troubling backdrop to her goal. In the winter, a female Mexican gray died of renal failure, reducing this unique breeding population to five pairs. The previous year, the Wolf Sanctuary Mexican grays produced no litters, although a whopping litter of nine was born at a site in New Mexico. The mating ritual for a captive wolf is tricky at best, compounded by the fact that instinctively the animals are wild and in the wild only the alpha female mates with the alpha male. Thus, the wolves need an extended courtship at the Wolf Sanctuary to be comfortable with each other so they can best take advantage of the female estrus, a scant four to eight weeks in the year. The Mexican wolves at the Wolf Sanctuary had been paired together since November, although O'Toole had hoped to pair them even earlier because, she has found, their ritual is even more elaborate and time-consuming than those of other species she has handled.

O'Toole told me of a blue-sky plan to release red wolves in Illinois and Missouri someday. Habitat in the south of both states could support small populations. In Missouri there is already a tiny population of black bears in the Ozarks near the Arkansas border. There are occasional reports of bobcats in the southern tip of Illinois and in Missouri. With the introduction of wolves, the area could move one giant step closer to being what it was hundreds of years ago. The musing spawned a question that had puzzled me for years: Were there enough wolves in the area in the early years of the twentieth century to justify the number of sightings I had always heard? My father, father-in-law, and grandfather, countrymen each one, told of occasional wolves roaming the countryside. My grandfather even pointed out the site—the cattle pasture west of the farmhouse—where he'd seen them back in the twenties and thirties. They saw wolves! O'Toole said that it was possible, though unlikely. To this day she gets calls from people spotting "wolves" in suburban subdivisions and throughout the countryside. What they see, she said, are feral dogs or coyotes, or hybrids of the two, but nothing with the true genes of a wolf. The same was probably true of the early-century sightings, although there *were* tiny remnants of packs at that time. Because feral dogs are often mistaken for wolves, they give the wolf a bad name, she points out. These wild dogs have lost their fear of humans and have become a troublesome and at times a hostile nuisance.

I accompanied O'Toole on a visit to her wolves. She unlocked the gate to their sanctuary, and we walked up to a loading dock, remnant from the war years, climbed the stairs, and surveyed the area. To the left a pack of about four Iranian wolves, tawny and lithe, trotted a worn area inside a square pen of about an acre; ironically, I noted that they trod the familiar circular hunting pattern as best they could with what little range they had. In the center enclosure, a black tundra wolf came to a pond to drink, then beheld us with its steely glint. Far to the right were the Mexican gray enclosures.

O'Toole whispered as toads near the pond, awakened from their winter hibernation, sang an almost birdlike song in anticipation of their own breeding season. "The big tundra wolves are more like what we've been accustomed to think wolves look like," she said. "The pendulum is coming back. One hundred years ago, people hated wolves until they were almost gone. Thirty years ago, people wanted wolf hybrids as pets. It might have been a sort of precursor to Yuppie ambitions. But that notion was wrong. The wolf is a predator. We don't have to justify its existence by making a pet out of it. It doesn't belong to us. We don't have to possess it or harness it. It should be out there, existing in harmony in nature. That's the concept that people are just now getting excited about."

I looked, transfixed, at the tundra wolf and remembered that the only wolf I had ever observed closely before had been one kept in a small pen on a northern Illinois game farm at Yorkville near my home. It had paced the small area neurotically, lonely, and anxious for its freedom. It had had no business being on display in a tiny pen like that. I had felt a kinship with its plight and now wondered if our fascination with the wild, narrow eyes of the wolf were not really a reflection of our own yearning for freedom; that what we saw in the wolf's eyes was the entrapment of a wild creature, and with it our own capture.

O'Toole pointed to the right. "There's Don Diego and some of the other Mexican wolves. We can go a little closer."

We walked down the platform along a path leading toward the Mexican enclosures, passing the indifferent tundra wolf and its feeding area. About fifty yards away, up on a tree-shaded hill, two Mexican wolves bounded throughout their pens; farther back, two other pairs trotted the enclosure. Directly ahead of us a lone wolf halted and regarded us almost quizzically; it was no more than thirty yards from us, and we still had enough room to walk right up to it.

This wolf was Don Diego, sire of at least a dozen offspring at the sanctuary, and, like Uncas in *The Last of the Mohicans*, the last of his kind to have been caught in the wild. Last year, he produced no offspring, and O'Toole feared that he had become sterile. At fourteen, he is a grizzled though noble specimen, his muzzle now white and his coat shaved to help treat tumors that were removed from his back last year. Though his time is short, O'Toole assured me he was still a macho guy.

We took in the whole area encompassing the Mexican gray wolf enclosures. O'Toole nodded to the top of the hill. "Maybe some of their offspring will be free. Wouldn't that be something?"

I assured her that it would, and, looking at Don Diego, who still regarded us nonchalantly, I asked if I could get a little closer to him. She said okay, so I walked slowly toward Don Diego, who almost seemed to be smiling. Moving slowly, I held a steady gaze on the wolf, and I felt a tremendous desire to be in the pen with him, to pet him, to see if he'd fetch, to wrestle him as you would a dog.

"That's far enough," O'Toole said firmly. "Don't go any further."

At a distance of ten yards, I bid the last of the wild-caught Mexican gray wolves my respects.

RESURRECTIONS
Prairie restorer Robert Betz at a young Fermilab prairie, remnant of the Big Woods in the background, Batavia, Illinois. *(Courtesy of Tony Fitzpatrick)*

Resurrections

This was a real farm. It smelled of metal, straw, gasoline, and manure. You found it driving Route 34 to Mendota, La Salle County, Illinois, crossing Route 51, a long and scenic road stretching from Minneapolis to New Orleans, on a road that took you past Classen's, a local family supermarket, past elegant homes on the outskirts of town, a show farm to the left, a working hog farm to the right. At the crest of a hill, the road turned to gravel and from the top, if the corn was not too tall, you saw my grandfather's farm to the northwest, on the right, less than a quarter of a mile away. It was a humble but exciting place. At the intersection of another country road, the farm began with an east pasture that wrapped around the barn. When the price of hogs was good, my grandfather Harry kept hog houses and feeders out there, feeding out hogs by the dozen.

The east pasture adjoined a cement feedlot on the south side of the barn with a well there to water the hogs. The pasture was open to the feedlot, but closed to another feedlot and cattle shed directly east of the barn, where Harry fed out his cattle. If he was feeding out both hogs and cattle, the east pasture was closed to the cattle; they were routed into the pasture north and west of the house, in all, about ten acres of hilly land. The land beyond the northwest pasture was usually in corn or soybeans, mostly corn, though, to feed the livestock. Just past the intersection you went up the long gravel driveway leading to the garage, tool shed, and grain bin to the northeast. Harry's flower garden was to the right of the driveway, an acre or so of pasture was to the left. Fenced off from the cattle pasture and wrapping around the house to the north, this piece of land Harry kept trimmed with a dozen or so sheep, a flock housed in a shed to the northeast of the house.

In the recesses of my mind, there is a blissful dearth of memories of our living arrangements in the quaint old farmhouse that contained just two real bedrooms and seven people. However, there was a plethora of sensual delights, the warm breath of cattle in the wooden feeding trough in the barn as they ate corn shelled by our own hands; the lurking shadow of a rat scurrying through the corncrib alongside the barn; the bawling of a Jersey cow as Dad, on a stout wooden stool, milked her with us kids giggling and shoving each other behind him; his remonstrances to me to stay behind and avoid the cow's tail and then feeling the sharp sting of it on my cheek, much more powerful than it looked, and the burning of tears at the pain; my sisters' laughter; the squish and hiss of warm milk from the udders; the taste of that milk an hour later, warm, fresh, thick, and sweet, smelling and tasting, too, of the barn. There was manure from four different types of animals—cattle, hogs, chickens, and sheep. Thus, fertilizer from all but the hogs. The aroma was the smell of money, as grandmother Kay Kay said. There was the sound of money, too—the lowing of cattle, the squeal and snort of pigs, the clang of the hog feeders.

Once, lord of the feed lot that I was, I rode a hog in the hog lot— briefly, for it is difficult with nothing but bristles to hold on to— while Harry and Dad leaned against the fence laughing. Digging potatoes in the rich soil behind the house in Harry's garden, finding the jewels as they're lifted with the spade; the tremendous clatter of birds in the tall oaks and hard maples in the spring that I heard from boyhood to adulthood in the north pasture behind the garden, a feeling of awe that these birds collectively were somehow a force much more powerful than humans; walking with Harry and Dad into the chicken yard behind the house to collect breakfast, Harry stooping to walk inside where he would gather a half dozen or so brown- or white-shelled eggs in a pail, the hens, squawking and flapping, clucking and cooing, the dusky smell of guano and feathers, not a place to play in. Harry said he lost his hair here when he hit his head on the chicken coop and it all fell out. For the longest time, we believed him.

Only once do I remember anything other than sheep in that pasture. Once he rented it to a farmer who wanted to pasture his Angus bull there. All of the grandchildren, mischievous as we were, were cautioned to keep a good distance between us and the bull, and, heeding the gory stories of charging bulls, we did. Not so, our feisty grandmother Kay Kay. One day, while Harry was in town, she took some trash out to burn behind the vegetable garden and the bull took notice of her. Kay Kay never revealed if she said something to the bull or if she made a gesture to which the bull took offense—which could not be ruled out either—or if the bull did not take well to her scent, but he pawed the ground, snorted, huffed, and charged—to Kay Kay's surprise and dismay. Trash, kitchen matches, and grandmother flew in all directions when she knew the bull was going to make it through the barbed wire: the fence didn't stop him. Kay Kay took refuge in Harry's toolshed, where she slammed the door shut, prayed to the Blessed Virgin, and waited for her heart to calm down. The bull, meanwhile, kept her hostage; he found the grass around the toolshed to his liking and idly grazed it, perhaps smugly savoring his victory over humanity. Eventually he sauntered off away from the toolshed, and Kay Kay, dashing pell-mell to the garage, made good her escape. While none of her fourteen grandchildren ever witnessed the event, it's a good bet that many of us wished we could have been there ourselves.

This menagerie Harry maintained on only 120 acres—whether he was farming it or renting it out. In his prime, he farmed it and about 100 acres of another farm his sister Annie owned a few miles away. He drove Cadillacs the last twelve years of his life. He died at eighty-six, a proud, tough old man, a successful farmer, even though his schooling had stopped at the eighth grade. Many of us baby boomers in the Heartland had grandfathers like him.

After he died in 1972, the farm was sold, following the great pattern of the Heartland in the past three decades, to a larger farmer in the area. There was no one in the family, after all, who could farm it or manage it, and Kay Kay, who died in 1976, was well into her seventies, not wanting to live alone far from her family. Until very recently, the last time I had seen the farm was the year my grandmother died, 1976. That day, fifteen years ago, at the top of the hill, I had stopped the car and looked forlornly at the house being built in the west pasture, close, too close, to the farmhouse. I stayed at the top of the hill for a long time, not wanting to go any farther, and turned the car around in the driveway of the hog farm on the crest of the hill, the reassuring sound and smell of a farm accompanying my senses back to the present. I savored those prairie memories.

About 175 miles southeast of Harry's farm, the South Farm at the University of Illinois in Urbana-Champaign is a vast complex of experimental fields and pastures, barns and livestock-holding facilities, where agronomists, veterinarians, dairy and livestock specialists, and entomologists have conducted experiments for decades to advance agriculture. A myriad of experiments involving every conceivable kind of crop and farm animal associated with the Heartland have been performed here; Heartland farmers and the world's consumers have greatly benefited from the research. The focus here is almost entirely on the future.

In 1983, two men, John Bouseman, an entomologist with the Illinois Natural History Survey, a department of the state's Division of Energy and Natural Resources, and Ken Robertson, Ph.D., a botanist with the survey and professor emeritus of botany at the University of Illinois, petitioned the head of the Natural History Survey for a one-and-a-half-acre plot at the South Farm to grow plants that were indigenous to Illinois—tallgrass prairie plants. The two men wanted the plot of prairie plants as a convenience for students to study Illinois's natural heritage, the lush carpet of wildflowers called forbs and tallgrasses such as big and little bluestem, Indian grass, prairie dropseed, and switchgrass. Except for the restored prairies, such as at the Morton Arboretum in Lisle, and the Fermilab near Batavia, and the one large natural gem, the Gensburg Markham prairie near Markham, all of them western or southern suburbs of Chicago, the little native prairie left in Illinois could only be found in old, abandoned pioneer cemeteries scattered throughout the state and along railroad tracks. Both habitats hung on for obvious reasons, but using them as living laboratories provided several drawbacks.

"Students can't get any sense of scale from looking at isolated plants along railroad tracks," Ken Robertson told me. "And it makes for a long, difficult day, chartering a bus to take students to the Chicago area to see a prairie. We wanted one here, in the middle of the Prairie State's best-known university."

"We never thought we'd get the go-ahead," added John Bouseman. "There's so much competition for research space out here. But the ghost of Black Hawk or someone must have been with us."

We stood on the eastern perimeter of the South Farm prairie in the late afternoon of a hot June day. Dr. Robertson, equipped with a camera, is a wiry, lithe man, barely gray at the temples, looking far younger than his years. Plants are his passion, the prairie a love he can never forget. He is a board member of the Grand Prairie Friends of Illinois, an organization of professional and amateur botanists who are propagating prairie throughout the state. He still holds an appointment with the Illinois Natural History Survey and teaches an occasional botany class at the university. He received his Ph.D. at Washington University in St. Louis, and for a number of years was a curator at the Arnold Arboretum at Harvard University before coming to the survey and the University of Illinois.

Bouseman, dressed in khaki hiking shorts and shirt and vest, lacked only a pith helmet, although he has worn one on many occasions. A veteran of thirty years researching insects and their habitat for the Natural History Survey, he has been in the far corners of the world, from Latin America to Africa, when, as he puts it, "they truly were the far corners of the world—the habitat was still intact, the relentless deforestation had barely begun." Bearded, his hair sprinkled with white, he has a rugged appearance, though he is gentle, slow-talking, and witty. It had been some months since the two had been out to the plot, and they were anxious to see it.

The tiny piece of soil that is the South Farm prairie is a budding replica of what the 22,000 square miles of original tallgrass prairie looked like in Illinois in the early 1800s. Today in Illinois, at best, ecologists estimate that there are only four square miles of prairie intact, after centuries of cultivation and development. Settlers, farmers, and developers all the way into the last few decades of the twentieth century rapidly erased the prairie from memory and nearly from existence; even botanists ignored it until a handful in the 1960s realized that the seed stock of many native Illinois plants was in danger of extinction, and the state that called itself the Prairie State might never have any inkling at all of what it was named after.

Bouseman filled his pipe with Captain Black, blowing out billows of white smoke, and looked with pleasure at the plot, set amidst an apiary and an orchard of apple trees. "The first spring, 1984, it looked like a big crop of weeds, didn't it, Ken? Now we're just beginning to get what you might call a prairie."

Dr. Robertson was a few yards into the plot, snapping a picture of rattlesnake master, *Eyringium yuccifolium*, a spiraling, fuzzy-headed forb the settlers used to think was a natural snake deterrent. He and Bouseman were surprised to find it in their plot because they had not planted it. They surmise that it came in courtesy of a bird or else was blown in on flatland winds from patches of remnant prairie along the Illinois-Central tracks just south of Champaign. That its seed survived at all and landed in a hospitable environment was something of a miracle; it had a much greater chance of landing in a corn or soybean field where it certainly would have died upon contact with herbicides.

Ken Robertson came out of the tallgrass, grinning. "That's a very healthy-looking plant," he said. "We'll be doing better once we get more forbs into the plot."

Each year, Robertson and his prairie-buff colleagues try to add more forbs to the mix of grasses and wildflowers that constitutes their prairie. Presently, they have about thirty different kinds of grasses, wildflowers, and herbs. A full-blown, large-scale prairie will support 150 different species of the mix. John Bouseman, busy with a project that finds him surveying the deer tick population of Illinois, has not been as active with the prairie plot as he has been in the past, but is looking forward to analyzing the insect population in the plot. The two men were drawn toward their original proposal in the early eighties out of a mutual love of natural history, especially of Illinois's prairie heritage; Robertson loves the plants, as does Bouseman, who nonetheless sees them in a different light than his colleague. Researching insects in Africa in the early eighties, Bouseman noticed that crops grown there—some of them, like corn and wheat, also grown in the United States—did not suffer the same degree of insect damage as crops in Illinois, despite the fact that the African crops were not treated with insecticides. He saw that this was especially true where the crops were planted near savanna and prairie tallgrasses. He began to wonder what effect this might have in Illinois if farmers could turn some of their land over to prairie and develop a natural bio-system that would keep fields clean of economically damaging insects. Wasps, in general, are natural predators of a whole range of insects, including caterpillars, the immature stage of moths and butterflies. Many damaging insects do most of their dirty work while they are in the caterpillar stage.

"Many of the parasitic wasps require nectar as their energy source, and the forbs provide an abundance of nectar," he said. "If you provide the habitat for the wasps, they'll come in—I'm a firm believer in insects' great powers of dispersal. You could release 10 million insects at a site, on the other hand, and if the habitat is not suitable for them, they'll go elsewhere. There's a concern today about insecticides and health issues. We don't know the extent of the problem, really, but if the public perceives it as a problem, then you do have a problem. Midwestern farmers are notoriously practical people. You have to convince them thoroughly that something will work. If we can show them that prairie grown on set-aside acres can be a practical way to lessen insect problems, they'd grow it, I think."

The South Farm prairie, although a tiny ecosystem, is managed similarly to larger prairies in Illinois and other Heartland prairies in Missouri, Kansas, and Nebraska. Each spring either Robertson or Bouseman, or both, supervise a group of students who set fire to the small plot. Prairie scientists torch the plants they love because it is best for them; the prairie, which developed on a large scale in central North America from Indiana west to Nebraska, north to Saskatchewan and Alberta in Canada, and all the way south into Texas over 8,000 years ago during a hot, dry period known as the xerothermic period, was nurtured by fire. Fires eliminated the residue of stems and dead

leaves of prairie plants but most importantly prevented the encroachment of woody and shrubby plants in their domain. The trees and
shrubs were vulnerable to the fire because their viable parts close to
the soil surface were destroyed; prairie plants, however, especially the
grasses, have long taproots that can extend into the subsoil more than
ten feet beneath the surface. Because many of them are perennial
plants that are dormant during late autumn and winter, they survived
quite handily. The fires themselves over the centuries most often
resulted from extremely dry conditions—they were not triggered by
humans, but by natural occurrences. Yet there is evidence that Native
Americans set fires on purpose to propagate the prairie as habitat for
game or to protect other plants grown there.

John Bouseman's observations on fire and the prairie fall in line
with Washington University biologist Owen Sexton's "natural flukes"
theory. On a research trip to Bolivia and Brazil in the midsixties,
Bouseman had the rare privilege to watch the Indians there set fire to
the grasslands at the end of the growing season. He described the
tremendous wall of fire spreading throughout the grasslands as an
awesome, spectacular, humbling experience, similar in scale to watching tons of water flowing over Niagara Falls. Yet the Indians were not
setting the fire to protect the grasslands; instead, they burned the
grasses to make travel easier; the benefit to the grasslands was inciden-
tal to human intent. Similarly, the prairie plants with an accompanying diverse insect population found in healthy abundance along the
tracks of the Illinois Central Railroad near the towns of Farina and
Kinmundy, south of Champaign, thrive today, he believes, because of
fires started from the spewed cinders of steam locomotives and the
unwitting contribution of smokers tossing their cigarette butts out
the window along U.S. 37.

Say the word "prairie," and you somehow feel better. It comes from
the French, and it means meadow or grassy field for pasturing cattle.
Your first walk through a prairie, large or small, is an unforgettably
sensuous experience that you want repeated over and over again.
Americans, especially Heartland Americans, are used to seeing and
appreciating plants in ordered systems: long, straight rows of corn or
soybeans, uniform-colored stands of wheat and oats from their car

windows; lines of carrots, onions, and celery in their gardens, tomato plants in one corner, green peppers and broccoli in another; flower gardens are designed by color so that marigolds offset zinnias; bouquets at weddings are deliberately arranged for their aromatic as well as visual effect.

But a prairie doesn't exist in that orderly style. Instead, it is a crazy quilt of plants with no recognized pattern although it has a sort of fractured order—there is the repetitive occurrence of the tallgrasses serving as a brace for the congregation of wildflowers that pop up or lounge between the tall clumps of grass. But there is no way of knowing what the next flower around the bend will be, and thus there are delightfully shocking surprises with each step you take. Finding forbs hidden in the tallgrasses is like finding easter eggs on Resurrection morning itself. Walking along a path the scientists have kept open in the South Farm prairie, Robertson and Bouseman pointed out various kinds of sunflowers, asters, milkweeds, and yellow and purple coneflowers—for their characteristic cone-shaped flowering structures atop their stems—daisies, clovers, and the psychedelic blazing stars, their colors bursting in our faces. Big bluestem over six feet tall and the yellow flowers of prairie dock bobbed in the breeze.

We stopped and looked at the rattlesnake master and some sweet brown-eyed Susan and the ubiquitous compass plant, whose spreading leaves at the plant base are said always to lean toward the north ("I wouldn't set *my* compass by it," Bouseman said as we observed one tilting slightly to the west). Robertson bent the clumpy head of a rosinweed plant toward us, removed a head, split it open, and we whiffed the musky, pleasant aroma.

"There are twenty-three different prairie types in Illinois alone," Ken Robertson said. "What we have the beginnings of here is indicative of the Grand Prairie of central Illinois, but there are also several kinds of sand prairies found along the Mississippi, Kankakee, Illinois, and Green rivers in northwestern Illinois, dolomite and mesic, or wetlands, prairies as well. Of 102 counties, there were only nine that didn't have vast amounts of prairies. The funny thing is the earliest settlers from the eastern states didn't think the prairie was capable of being farmed—they couldn't see many trees in the region, and they figured if the soil won't support trees, it won't support crops. But what they couldn't see was the extent of the root system of these plants and the contribution of organic matter they gave to the soil. Big bluestem reaches more than seven feet under the soil, switchgrass as much as eleven feet. When parts of the roots die and decompose, they add organic matter to the soil. That's why prairie soils are so fertile."

The diversity of plants in a prairie is so great that more than one hundred different species can be found in areas of less than five acres. There were about thirty, with more coming in yearly, at the South Farm prairie.

Throughout the Heartland scientists and lay environmentalists have awakened to the beauties and joy of the prairie and the ecological importance of them. From a postage-stamp-sized re-creation such as the South Farm plot to hundreds of acres at Markham and the thousand-plus at Fermilab near Batavia to the near-pristine prairies in southwestern Missouri, where the prairie chicken, a relative of the grouse and an endemic species to the midwestern prairie, is making a comeback, new prairies are sprouting up and remnant prairies are being protected and increased. Bouseman mentioned a friend of his, Don Gardner, in northern Ford County, squarely in the middle of once-flourishing prairie country, who is restoring prairie in small doses on the family farm. He started with seed of remnant plants growing along fencerows on the farm and seed from other sources, and now has developed seed stock from which to plant new acres. In Lee County, outside Dixon, Illinois, Ronald Reagan's old hometown, an entomologist from Northeastern Illinois University is introducing insect species to the 2,000-acre Nachusa Grasslands Reserve, a prairie that, except for some cattle grazing in years past, is virgin; in nearby Amboy, my parents' hometown, a young Chicago industrialist has converted a duck-hunting club along the Green River into the Richardson Wildlife Foundation and is restoring prairie in 100-acre dollops. In Rock Hill, Missouri, just southwest of St. Louis, Steger Middle School has taken a vacant lot by the school and is planting prairie plants in it, an enduring science project for the students; at LaPetite Gemme Prairie and Friendly Prairie in southwestern Missouri,

Washington University biologist Dr. Wayne Nichols has isolated 500 different species of algae, all totally new to science, and has found they may make unique and heretofore unknown contributions to the prairie ecosystem. Bouseman and Robertson have been involved in a project to advise the Illinois Department of Transportation on seeding prairie plants in median strips along the interstates, spreading the prairie anew throughout Illinois. In Illinois, alone, there are more than sixty different prairies and re-created prairie reserves, mostly state owned but some in private hands, with more springing up each year.

Why?

"I think we got to a point where we realized how little we knew about our past and how little we had left of it," Robertson said. "With the aid of enough conservationists sounding the alarm, I think maybe people may have gotten scared to think that it truly would all be gone."

"It's a sort of nostalgia," Bouseman said. "I grew up in Black Hawk country in Savanna, Carroll County. Up there everything's named after Black Hawk. They even named one park in Rock Island County, Loud Thunder Park, after Black Hawk's son, who never gained any notoriety that I'm aware of. It's a funny thing, but I could guarantee you that in his time Black Hawk was the most hated and feared man in the area, yet long after he's gone everything's named after him. I think there is a sort of yearning out there to want a piece of something that is the way it was."

"Nostalgia," said Dr. Robert Betz, professor of biology at Northeastern Illinois University in Chicago, and one of the nation's best-known prairie restorationists. "A good part of the interest that people have in the prairie and nature is due to nostalgia. We live in a society in which almost everything we do is in a state of flux. Very little is permanent. We move from place to place, from one part of the country to another. Our friends are continually changing—here today, gone tomorrow. Nothing seems to be permanent.

"But here is the prairie, something that is relatively stable and unchanging, almost eternal, something we can anchor ourselves to. It's beautiful to look at with its myriads of colorful flowers and tall swaying grasses, and you can see the results of your work in a relatively short time when you are trying to restore it. A most satisfying experience is to discover new plant species that appear in the developing prairie three or four years *after* they were planted. It's also gratifying to tally the reinvasion of meadowlarks, savanna sparrows, shrikes, mink, gray foxes, bumblebees, butterflies, and a host of other prairie animals into the developing prairie."

We were standing on the fifteenth floor of the Robert Rathbun Wilson Building, a mammoth futuristic structure that is the focal point of the Fermilab, the high-energy physics research center operated by the U.S. Department of Energy outside of Batavia, Illinois. The laboratory is named after the famous University of Chicago physicist Dr. Enrico Fermi, one of the key developers of the atomic bomb. We were in the easternmost fringe of territory that the great war chief Black Hawk ranged 160 years ago. To the east, barely visible in the midsummer haze, the skyline of Chicago stood mistily solid. Beneath us was a 455-acre piece of land, entirely surrounded by a moat or cooling pond about twenty-five feet across. Buried a short distance from this moat is a ring four miles in circumference around which protons travel at speeds approaching the speed of light. At times they are shunted off to hit targets, releasing energy in the form of new particles, all in an effort to understand the conditions under which the universe was born. The waters in this circular pond help cool the magnets that run the accelerator.

There is an oak grove inside the ring; it and others on all sides of the Wilson Building are remnants of what settlers in the 1820s and 1830s called the Big Woods, an expansive tract of woods along the Fox River stretching from north of Elgin, Illinois, to just east of the Batavia area, extending, by some descriptions, all the way southwestward into Kendall and neighboring La Salle counties. In 1832, bands of roving Sac and Fox Indians, accompanied by some Potawatomis, loosely under the command of the Sac Indian chief Black Hawk, advanced all across northern and north-central Illinois along the Illinois, Fox, and Rock rivers, their territory until just a few years earlier. They terrorized settlers and massacred several groups as well, including a couple of families not far from the Big Woods southwest of here outside of Ottawa. Black Hawk and his followers, who, settlers worried, may have soon gotten reinforcements from sympathetic Winnebago and Potawatomi Indians, had been chastised for crossing the Mississippi River and planting corn in Rock Island County, near the present-day Quad Cities area. Black Hawk cherished this rich land that he considered his home. It was perfect for corn planting. Ignoring various treaties signed by other Sac and Fox chiefs that had ceded all of the Illinois territory to the Americans, he tried to move his tribe into Illinois to plant at least another crop. Then he would build a powerful alliance of Indian allies and drive the white settlers out of Illinois. His entry into the Prairie State sparked the war, which, not counting the Seminole siege in Florida, was the last major Indian conflict east of the Mississippi. It lasted a little longer than Operation Desert Storm, from April to August, ending with a slaughter of starving Sac and Fox warriors, old men, women, and children at the Battle of the Bad Axe River in southwestern Wisconsin. After rumors flew that Black Hawk and his warriors were advancing upon the Big Woods, many residents in the Big Woods vicinity—in 1991, a wellheeled enclave of suburbia—streamed into Chicago's Fort Dearborn, where they waited until it was certain Black Hawk no longer was an imminent threat.

Just twenty years ago, the land beneath us had been in corn, the property of Kane County farmers on the very fringe of the Chicago suburban spillover. In Black Hawk's time, it had been prairie.

Today, it is prairie once again, thanks to Robert Betz and his colleagues. During the past two decades, they have begun replacing one entrenched ecosystem with another one that hasn't been around for more than a century, a biological system not completely understood by ecological scientists. They are doing so in a seat-of-the-pants manner that, like Grant taking Vicksburg, has defied all conventional wisdom and logic.

Betz is a vigorous, medium-sized, muscular man, crowding seventy but looking fifty, a sparky individual, the kind that football coaches of his era liked to build an offense around. He sports a full beard and talks in an incessant, enthusiastic stream, punctuated by a hearty laugh when he makes a point or sees an epiphany in what he has said. Dr. Betz received part of his undergraduate training at Reed College in Portland, Oregon, another part at the University of Basel in Switzerland. He holds a doctorate in biochemistry from the Illinois Institute of Technology in Chicago, where he was well trained in mathematics and both the biological and physical sciences. He has a reading knowledge of a half dozen languages—including German, Spanish, and Romanian—which has enabled him to read ecological papers on such world grasslands as the Eurasian steppes, South American pampas, and others.

"The restoration and reconstruction of biological ecosystems is going to be a very big part of the ecological movement in coming years," he said as I followed his rapid strides toward an elevator that would take us to the main floor and then out we would go to the Fermilab prairie. "Then there will be money for the savannas, the wetlands, and the deserts, not only in this country but all around the world. They've wrecked almost everything. And how will we get it back?" I shrugged, stumped. "By *large-scale restorations*," he said slowly, then with a laugh.

That method of putting things back together again is at the core of the Betz legend, which is growing with each passing year. In 1971, he learned that the newly planned accelerator in Batavia would occupy nearly 7,000 acres of land, most of it untended. Betz had been pondering ways to reintroduce prairie into large tracts, because it is only in large prairie ecosystems that there can be sufficient populations and diversity of species to sustain catastrophic events that could exterminate some of the species. Moreover, large tracts would provide abundant seed to grow even more prairie.

At the time that he was probing the feasibility of large-scale prairie ecological restorations, there were two commonly held ideas concerning prairie. The first was that fire was harmful to the prairie plants. The second was that once a prairie had been destroyed it was "gone forever" and could not be reconstituted or restored. The work of Betz and his aides helped dispel both notions.

The attitude about fire and prairie was contrary to the accounts of the early French missionaries and explorers who commented on the Indians' burning of the prairies and numerous prairie fires started by lightning. It was also contradicted by the accounts of the early Illinois settlers who witnessed the invasion of trees and shrubs into prairies after the prairie fires ceased.

During the sixties and seventies, Betz and his colleague Dr. Herbert F. Lamp searched for old settler cemeteries with virgin prairie vegetation in them. Although these cemeteries were rich in species, many of them were degraded, sprouting weeds and woody vegetation, when they were first rediscovered. However, Betz and Lamp saw that when the cemetery plots were burned annually in the early spring, all of them responded to fire with increases of prairie species and a concomitant decrease of weeds and woody vegetation.

The development of the Curtis Prairie under the direction of Professor John T. Curtis at the University of Wisconsin Arboretum in Madison in the early thirties was the first demonstration that fire and prairie coexisted. Then, in the sixties, the restoration of the Schulenberg Prairie, carried out by Betz's friend and colleague Ray Schulenberg at the Morton Arboretum in Lisle, Illinois, further illustrated the sound relationship. While Betz notes that neither of these prairies is "virgin"—as they existed in presettlement times—there are indications that they are progressing in that direction.

"Both of these good-sized prairies, with their rich and beautiful array of prairie species, are some of the best examples of restored prairies anywhere on the North American continent," Betz told me.

But, although both of them were done over a relatively short time, they were labor-intensive and didn't really lend themselves to large-scale restorations, needed to preserve the prairies over the long haul. Betz reasoned that if large-scale prairies were to be reconstructed, it would be necessary to use modern agricultural machinery to do it. "In a way," as he has often said, "the tools that destroyed the virgin prairie would be the same tools that would put it back again."

In late summer 1974, Betz, his colleagues, and volunteers began the reconstruction of the Fermilab prairie on the 400-plus acres of old cultivated soil within the accelerator ring. The Fermilab grounds crew, some of them descendants of farmers who had plowed the Fermilab soils, plowed, disked, and prepared about ten acres of land for spring planting of the prairie seed. With that project underway, Betz and his prairie associates, plus nearly one hundred volunteers from all walks of life, collected seeds in the pitifully small remnant prairies scattered throughout the Chicago area. They cleaned about 400 pounds of seeds, placed them in large plastic bags soaked in water, and then stored them in a refrigerator. They kept the temperature above freezing and brought the seeds out in May to break the seed dormancy that an ordinary winter would have caused.

During the first week of June 1975, the seeds—representing seventy different species of native Illinois prairie plants—were planted with a Nisbet grain drill into the plowed and disked ten acres prepared in the fall of 1974 and spring of 1975. Betz and all the prairie participants— his colleagues, the grounds crew, the volunteers—waited hopefully.

"Within a month, the weeds came up and completely dominated the land," Betz recalled. "This was a terrible blow. I thought we'd lost the whole tract."

But underneath the annual and biennial weeds—the ragweed, pigweeds, foxtail grasses, bull and Canadian thistles, species characteristic of croplands—about eighteen of the seventy prairie species originally planted began to appear. Here and there tiny seedlings of big bluestem Indian grass, and switchgrass began to peek underneath the two- to three-feet-tall weed canopy. Here was a wild bergamot, over there a yellow coneflower beside a tall coreopsis. Like the legendary phoenix that arose from the ashes, the Fermilab prairie was arising anew from the century-old cultivated soil.

When the weeds died back in late summer and early fall, the young plants grabbed more sun and took on more vigor. They were no more than an inch or two tall, but their roots were more than double that, enabling them to grow fast in the spring competition with the Eurasian weeds. During the next spring, after overwintering, these twenty aggressive prairie species, or "prairie matrix," as Betz began calling them, took off, getting stronger than their competitors, the short-lived weeds that had to reestablish themselves almost every year from seed. Three years later, the prairie matrix plants were robust, six to eight feet tall with deep roots. There was enough growth to produce sufficient "fuel load," or dried prairie vegetation, to sustain a fire. In March of 1978, Betz and his group torched the prairie, burning such woody vegetation as brambles, cottonwoods, and green ash. At the same time, the prairie matrix plants were stimulated to produce abundant seed and they began the slow process of driving the weeds from the tract. The Betz "grand design" for prairie building had been established.

Over the years, he and his colleagues filled in the approximately 500 acres within the accelerator ring using the same general method with some twenty species of aggressive prairie matrix plants to drive out the weeds; in addition, they applied the grand design to 400 acres in various tracts outside the ring. Instead of planting ten-acre tracts, they now planted one hundred-acre or larger parcels with the prairie matrix. Heeding the advice of the farmers on the grounds crew staff, they abandoned use of the Nisbet drill to plant seed because it is slow and cumbersome and tends to place the prairie plants in rows, as agricultural planters do. Instead, they used a salt-spreading truck to spread the seed, then later an all-terrain commercial seed spreader. Today, they use a fertilizer buggy pulled by a tractor to sow the seed.

After the matrix is well established, within three or four years, he and his colleagues plant "second-wave" prairie plant seed by hand in selected areas called foci,—places that appear to be farther along into prairie succession than most of the other parts of the tract. Among these "second wavers" are purple and white prairie clovers (*Petalostemum*), white Indian quinine (*Parthenium*), purple coneflower (*Echinacea*), white culver's root (*Veronicastrum*), and yellow prairie betony (*Pedicularis*). When these matrix ("first-wave") and second-wave prairie plants increase their numbers sufficiently and there are noticeable changes in the physical and chemical properties of the soil, more fastidious third- and fourth-wave prairie plants, such as orange prairie lilies (*Lilium*) and cerulean blue prairie gentians (*Gentiana*) will be sowed in selected foci to take their place in the Fermilab prairie.

When the prairie matrix is well developed and most of the weedy vegetation has been eliminated from the tract, a front-end combine can be used in September to harvest the prairie seed to be used in future plantings. In general, Betz told me, one acre of prairie matrix is sufficient to plant ten acres of new land.

"When we burn in the spring, it changes the whole complexion of the field," Betz explained. We were inside the ring now, driving along a dirt road in his Ford Taurus. Walking through the prairie, Betz grew excited and his enthusiasm rubbed off on me. We waded through bluestem, switchgrass, and Indian grass nearly six feet tall and spotted wildflowers dispersed throughout the grass.

"As the prairie plants take the upper hand, they begin to run out the weeds. Exactly how it's done, we don't know. They might produce allelopathic chemicals or antibiotics that inhibit the weeds. It's possible that there is competition for water or the prairie plants might produce a dense shade that suppresses the weeds. That's for the ecologists to find out. My job is to build the prairie."

Of the seventy prairie species that were planted in the first plot in June 1975, fifty of them "went under," as Dr. Betz said. "From our experience it would appear that approximately twenty or so species of the two hundred found on virgin prairies are aggressive and capable of competing successfully against weeds. Now, in restoring three dozen or more old settler prairies in the sixties and seventies I observed that these twenty species were the same species that are the last to survive prairie degradation and the first ones to return when fires and other restoration procedures were initiated. It would appear that the first-wave species of the prairie matrix prepare the way for the second-wave species, and they in turn prepare the way for the third wave of more fastidious species. The reason for this may be due in part to changing the chemical and physical properties of the soil."

Betz's deduction has been confirmed by scientists from Argonne National Laboratory in Lemont, Illinois. They found that within ten years after introduction of prairie at Fermilab, the soil tilth has changed. Instead of soils with very little structure—as are found where crops are grown continuously—the Fermilab prairie soils contain more aggregations, making the soil crumbly, porous, and tending to "imbibe" water. Furthermore, the Fermilab prairie soil has an increased amount of organic-matter carbon, which has been lost from most cultivated Illinois soils.

"Aaahhh, look, see what I mean by second wavers?" Betz said, admiring purple blazing star (*Liatris*). "And look at this one here, rattle snake master (*Ernygium*). These are now becoming common throughout this tract."

He led me through a sea of grass, pulling apart switchgrass (*Panicum*) and bluestem (*Andropogon*) to reveal prairie phlox (*Phlox*), wild quinine, and then wading to his right toward some false sunflowers (*Heliopsis*) and prairie parsley (*Polytaenia*). "First I've ever seen here," he said. Then, laughing like a prospector who had found gold, he pointed. "Oh, look over there. That plant with the white flowers is *Pycanthemum virginianum*, the mountain mint. It has a very minty smell." He gave it to me, and I breathed in its delightful fragrance. He explained how he had developed such a foundation of knowledge about both prairie plants and their competitors.

"I told my friend and colleague Ray Schulenberg when we were first starting to work on prairies that we not only had to know the prairie plants and their requirements, but also the weedy species as well. The Bible says 'know thine enemy,' and if we are to properly manage and build prairies, we have to know the weeds and how to counteract them.

"You know, since I have never forgotten my experiences as a soldier in World War II, I sometimes think of the ecological struggle that occurs between the prairie plants and their weedy competitors in our planted tracts as a sort of battle. I often feel like a general having to lead his troops into battle. My colleagues and I lay down the matrix species and the ecological battle with the weeds begins. Listen closely to the breeze coming from the planted tract, and you can almost hear the screams and cries of the dying on both sides. In human conflicts, the outcome is often in doubt. But in the case of the ecological restoration of prairies, our army of prairie plants always wins. Through hundreds of thousands, even millions of years of evolution, they hold the ecological edge and are programmed to win these battles. There are many who believe that prairie plants are delicate and weak and need help in order to survive. On the contrary, when not stressed by human activities like trampling, overgrazing, plowing, and so forth, they are aggressive and unyielding."

We drove out of the ring, past tall oaks and ashes, several barns left over from the pre-Fermilab days, along newer seeded, green tracts, the prairie plants actively fighting their war with the weeds. Betz, it was apparent from our conversations, is adamant about saving prairie in his native state.

"Restoration of prairies is occurring in many areas of the Midwest," he said. "Part of the reason for this is that almost all of the presettlement prairies have been destroyed in this region. The land was too valuable to allow it to remain in prairie. It is postulated that no more than four or five square miles of prairie remain out of an estimated 40,000 square miles in the state of Illinois. That's only about one-tenth of one percent that has survived. The only way we can again have prairies—at least large ones with all the animals and plants that were originally here—is to build new ones from scratch."

Thirty years ago, he explained, when he first got "prairie fever," he looked at all the beautiful prairies in old settler cemeteries, along railroad rights-of-way, and in odd patches here and there, and became saddened that little or nothing was being done to save the remnants and to preserve them for future generations.

"I have always felt that it was immoral to destroy nature from which all of us have arisen," he said. "The prairie was being exterminated without even a whimper and without anyone caring. It is unfortunate that past generations thought so little of future generations that they left almost nothing for us. I felt, dare I say it in these times, a *moral* commitment to save it and give it to another generation. I have always maintained that the animals and plants of the prairie have as much right to live on this earth as we do, and it is immoral to exterminate them."

That Robert Betz gave up a promising research career in enzyme kinetics to devote his life to the study, restoration, and reconstruction of tallgrass prairie is an unusual story in itself. He was born in a working-class district of Chicago (Bridgeport), where the only natural vegetation was in small, weedy lots that locally were called prairies. He learned most of the weeds that grew in these "prairies" and those that sprouted up through the broken cracks of sidewalks and alleys. Because he had no plant keys or access to anyone who could tell him the names of these plants, he made up his own names for them. As long as he can remember, he has always been interested in science and would seek out adults who could enlighten him about science, history, and many other subjects. He was especially fascinated with the stories that his grandfather and great-uncle told of their boyhood on a pioneer farm carved out of the virgin Wisconsin forests, an area then still inhabited by Indians.

Betz pulled up to a great sward of prairie northwest of the Wilson building. To the east of the prairie a small patch of woods, remnant of the Big Woods, held its own against this battery of prairie, seeded in 1986. We walked into the tallgrass, a breeze kicking up and rustling through the green leaves. Mixing with the sounds of a young prairie—the calls of meadowlarks, dickcissels, and bluebirds in the strong, hot breeze—was the hum of traffic from Kirk Road, which links one subdivision after another interwoven into suburban cities. Betz told about a plan to build a savanna between the restored prairie and the woods along Indian Creek. This would first involve the building of a prairie; after it takes hold, young bur oaks grown from acorns would be scattered throughout this young prairie.

The oak savanna is a special plant community with its own ardent pack of supporters led, in the Chicago area, by Stephen Packard, of the Chicago branch of the Nature Conservancy, which helped sponsor Betz's prairie restoration at Fermilab during the first year of its development. For years a little-understood ecosystem, savannas in the Heartland have often been considered prairies with trees, or else an interface of prairie and woodland species. They are extremely rare, but, as Packard has demonstrated, restorable. He has also pointed out that the oak trees, by providing an alternating period of sun and shade, and thus a unique sort of photoperiod under which certain plants tend to adapt, were the major driving force of the savanna, the species that contributed to the development of an intriguing and enchanting understory that includes such rare plants as small sundrops (*Oenthora perennis*) and yellow pimpernel (*Taenidia integerrima*).

Packard, whom Betz admires and respects, has attracted a host of naturalists and conservationists to help in his renovation of oak savannas.

Betz looked out at the large piece of restored prairie that he and his broad cross-section of friends have built and, with satisfaction, smiled his warm, beaming, infectious smile. "If possible," he said, "I hope we'll be able to restore much of this land to prairies, savannas, and marshes and create a landscape as it was in the presettlement times, complete with the animals that were a part of this Illinois ecosystem. I also hope at some distant date when the work of Fermilab comes to an end, that either at the federal or state level, this land will be made into an Illinois prairie park for future generations to visit and enjoy. It would be nice if conservationists and naturalists who come after us will do that for those of us who helped build it."

I stood with Betz in the hot Illinois sun and, in addition to my gratitude for the work he has done, I couldn't help feeling a twinge of nostalgia. This, after all, was my part of the country. I had grown up in the Fox River valley and could remember when, before the great burst of suburban growth in the sixties, the prairies that Betz and company built and now tended were all in farms, the surrounding farms giving way piecemeal to the inexorable spread of suburbia from the east. I had fished the Fox River, hiked along its banks, played sports in all the little towns in the area. But those were my memories, and I was looking at something real in front of me—a prairie. I realized that in my life I had never really known the prairie. It had only been an abstraction, part of what was called a heritage. Thus, it was hard for me to think of the prairie with nostalgia—a feeling many of us reserve for things and times like old baseball teams, movies, and fashions, with which we have lived.

Yet, if it wasn't quite nostalgia the prairie stirred in me, I could feel something more than the July breeze moving through the swaying tallgrasses and forbs. There is a profusion of science involved in the work of Robert Betz and all of the Heartland conservationists who are preserving soil, habitat, plant and animal species, and ecosystems that have been threatened, some even ruined, by society's drive to better itself. But the science—to many people a cold, indifferent word—is put into effect by emotion. It comes down to a feeling. Many people of the baby-boomer generation as well as the Depression era in the Heartland have seen things they grew up with change drastically, disappear, or be destroyed in their lifetimes. We have all known the feeling of losing something forever. The prairie whispering in front of us said that it doesn't have to be that way.

AN INFORMAL
BIBLIOGRAPHY

There are many ways to explore the heart of the Heartland, Missouri and Illinois. You can choose from scores of hiking paths throughout state and federal parks, country roads, and city streets, all rich with history and local color. You can also learn about this part of the country through some careful reading. Much of history reveals a lot about nature and vice versa. Some of the following books I have come across over the years seemingly lean toward history, but there are many beautiful nuggets of observation of nature you can glean from them.

Take this choice description, written in the early 1940s, from Edgar Lee Masters's *The Sangamon*, one of the "Rivers of America" books published by Farrar and Rinehart: "Fifty years ago people marveled at the changes that had come to pass in the preceding fifty years, and wondered what the next fifty years would have to show. They should be here to see. They could not believe their eyes. Somehow wild animal life has greatly diminished in Illinois, much more so than it has in upper Connecticut, where deer and pheasant are plentiful enough, and roam at will by the stone fences and over the fields. In Illinois the prairie chicken, one of the most delectable of wild birds, has almost vanished, while it was once in abundant numbers over the state, on Sandridge, about Clary's Grove and New Salem Hill. There are still a few deer along the Sangamon River, but the wolf and the fox have almost disappeared. They have been exterminated as thieves. There are but few wild turkeys left in Illinois, and not enough quail in the northern part to make quail hunting attractive. Once the fields about New Salem Hill and over Menard County were full of quail. New Salem had wild turkey on feast days, and as an article of diet it outranks the domestic turkey." Masters's book was published in 1942, fifty years ago. More about it later.

In compiling this list of books and publications, I overlook many good sources. What is presented is given to provide a curious person a tantalizing glimpse of a rich, fulfilling part of the country.

HISTORY

I begin with this book primarily out of deference to the alphabet. Paul Angle's *Bloody Williamson*, Knopf, 1952, is one of the best histories of southern Illinois and the particularly wild times in the twenties when coal companies, unions, strikebreakers, the Ku Klux Klan, and some of the most outrageous, eccentric gangsters ever to inhabit the earth all clashed. Relying heavily on newspaper accounts, Angle, a Chicago newspaperman who also wrote a highly acclaimed biography of Abraham Lincoln, explores the dynamics that led to the bloody massacre of strikebreakers at Herrin as well as the rise and fall of Charlie Birger. Angle is especially strong on his history of coal and Illinois. The book is considered a classic. Similarly, in 1978 Donald Bain published *War in Illinois*, with Prentice-Hall, a book more novelistic in style about the feuds between the Sheltons and Charlie Birger. Included are photographs and drawings. The book captures the mayhem and insanity of the time and the wonderful blend of cultures that contribute to the intoxicating brew that is southern Illinois.

The Other Illinois by Baker Brownell, published by Duell, Sloan and Pearce, New York, 1958, is an excellent history of the region and its folklore, flora, and fauna, a bit poetically strained but very solid and illuminating.

Twilight of Empire by Allan W. Eckert is Book Six in the author's saga of the settlement of the American frontier. This installment is an excellently written narrative history of the Black Hawk War of 1832— mentioned often in this book. Eckert has a great feel for the natural beauties of the Illinois Country, and he leaves no stone unturned, no character or place name given short shrift in this exciting book that brought back to me the significance of that war in the part of northern Illinois where I grew up and the St. Louis area where I now live. Available in paperback from Bantam Books.

In *The Sangamon*, Edgar Lee Masters does with prose what he did with verse in *Spoon River Anthology* giving remarkably folksy sketches of the people in the Sangamon and Spoon River valleys and a loving description of the land. What is most interesting, perhaps, is the yarns he spins about the people, including John Armstrong, brother of the accused Duff Armstrong, and how they remembered Lincoln and the myths about him. Many Illinois families have Lincoln stories: ours, according to my father, goes that my great grandfather, Patrick Henry Morrissey, saw Lincoln speak in a field on a tree stump, which I will pass on to my children and they on to theirs. Such is the stuff of *The Sangamon*.

What book about Illinois does not owe something to Carl Sandburg's Lincoln biography? I first read the biography when I was in high school, and recently returned to the two-volume *Prairie Years* while writing this book. As a teenager, I marveled that I could recognize the places of which Sandburg wrote; that thrill of recognition endures, enriched by stories and descriptions of the places long forgotten.

Missouri, A Guide to the Show-Me State is part of the American Guide Series sponsored by the Writers' Program of the Works Projects Administration, Duell, Sloan and Pearce, 1941. Each state has a guide and history written by Depression-era writers. They are fascinating for their perspective of some fifty years back and they are revealing in the "quick-read" background they give about a region. They are excellently written and informative. Don't leave home without consulting them. Don't assume you know a state until you read them.

Similarly, *Illinois, a History of the Prairie State* by Robert P. Howard, William B. Eerdmans Publishing Company, 1972, is a thoroughly written, informative history of the state from its presettlement times to the modern era. Everything you need to know historically and culturally about Illinois can be found here—up till 1972. It's most valuable for the evocation of the Illinois Country's early years.

Missouri Heritage, by Lew Larkin, American Press, Inc., Columbia, Missouri, 1968, may qualify as my all-time favorite minihistory. It delves into trivia—if you don't mind a pun, "before trivia was cool." Larkin, a former *Kansas City Star* newspaperman, compiles many of the columns he wrote in the sixties that chronicled the state's history on a day-by-day basis. Did you know Iowa and Missouri almost went to war over honey? That the shot and cotton bales used by the United States in the Battle of New Orleans came from Herculaneum, Missouri and St. Louis? That George Washington Carver was born a slave in southwestern Missouri? One of the first battles of the Civil War took place in St. Louis, when Camp Jackson in St. Louis, a hotly contested prize since the attack on Fort Sumter in April, became the battle-ground of a split state militia seeking a foothold in the Gateway to the West. Finally, the camp was secured by Federal troops on May 10, but not before a battle that caused twenty-eight deaths and numerous injuries. The articles are masterpieces of brevity and drama, revealing history seldom reported in text books.

NATURE/PERSONAL ACCOUNTS

Farm, by Richard Rhodes, Simon and Schuster, 1989, available in paperback from Touchstone Books, is a year-long chronicle of the life of Missouri farmer Tom Bauer and his family. There are few books that approach the topic of modern-day farming with the depth and perception of this book. Rhodes's descriptions of how a combine works, how a soybean grows, how a young bull becomes a steer are precise, valuable, and remarkable. So, too, is his portrait of the Bauers, whom we all feel we know at the conclusion of the book.

What Rhodes does with farming and its people James Jackson does with Missouri's Meramec River in *Passages of a Stream: A Chronicle of the Meramec*, University of Missouri Press, 1984. This is a beautiful portrait of what a river does to the soul of one who loves it, and what those who are indifferent do to the soul of the river.

The Population Explosion, by Paul R. Ehrlich and Anne H. Ehrlich, Simon and Schuster, 1990, picks up where Paul Ehrlich's 1968 landmark book, *The Population Bomb*, left off. In 1968, the world's population was 3.5 billion; in 1990, it was 5.3 billion people, growing by 95 million a year, say the Ehrlichs. The authors look at the impact of the crowding of the planet on agriculture, the environment, public health, politics, and more.

Alfalfa happens to be one of my favorite plants. However, you wouldn't think a writer could base a whole book on it, but Verlyn Klinkenborg has in *Making Hay*, Vintage Books, 1987. The author reveals a people, a region, a culture, time, and technology as they revolve around one of the most environmentally friendly plants on earth.

What the River Knows, Fireside Books, Simon and Schuster, 1991, by Wayne Fields, a Washington University English professor, department chair, and writer of much merit, is ostensibly a book about a family vacation and fishing excursions, but it brims with a love and understanding of nature and shows how nature helps us examine and know ourselves. Fields's prose is cool and swift like another writer-fisherman many of us have read; his nature observations are keen and powerful, as are his insights into human nature.

Berger: Life in a Missouri River Town, University of Missouri Press, 1977, edited by Karen Torme Olson, is a photo-essay portrait of a little town in the Missouri River valley not far from Hermann and Gasconade. While events are a bit dated here, the photographs—all in black and white—are beautiful and expressive. The flavor of Missouri River towns is much the same today as then. Photographs are by University of Missouri School of Journalism faculty and students. There are some beauties in this volume.

The Naturalist's Path by Missouri author and illustrator Cathy Johnson, Walker and Company, 1991, is an eye-opening work. Cathy Johnson is one of our best nature writers *and* nature artists. The book is subtitled *Beginning the Study of Nature* and it is a primer for those of us who want to become reintroduced to the natural world around us in our backyards, neighborhood parks, fields, and streams. The pencil drawings are vivid, fine, and precise—they have a life of their own.

219

Some of Johnson's other books, including *The Nocturnal Naturalist*, Globe Pequot Press, 1989, and *On Becoming Lost: A Naturalist's Search for Meaning*, Gibbs Smith Publisher, 1990, provide further tips to enjoy nature here in the Heartland.

Robert Mohlenbrock, who appears in this book and is now probably embarking on his fortieth volume of nature and botanical writings, has given us many valuable books. His *Guide to the Vascular Flora of Illinois*, Southern Illinois University Press, 1985, revised edition, is an excellent description of the Illinois landscape and its plants. This is a great guidebook—with a helpful glossary in the back—that will reveal the Prairie State in a way you've never quite thought possible. *Where Have All the Wildflowers Gone?* published by Macmillan, 1983, is Mohlenbrock's classic region-by-region guide to threatened or endangered wildflowers. Take this book on vacation.

I N D E X